HEALTHY FOOD

BREAD MACHINE

*COOKBOOK FOR
BEGINNERS*

A FOOLPROOF GUIDE WITH 500 EASY-TO-
FOLLOW RECIPES TO MAKE DELICIOUS
HOMEMADE BREAD AND COOK FOR FUN
FOR YOUR FAMILY AND FRIENDS.

CAREN COOPER

The Table of
CONTENTS

Introduction

Bread making machine, otherwise known as a bread maker, is a home-based appliance that transforms uncooked ingredients into bread. It is made up of a saucepan for bread (or "tin"), with one or more built-in paddles at the bottom, present in the center of a small special-purpose oven. This little oven is usually operated via a control panel via a simple in-built computer utilizing the input settings. Some bread machines have diverse cycles for various forms of dough — together with white bread, whole grain, European-style (occasionally called "French"), and dough-only (for pizza dough and formed loaves baked in a traditional oven). Many also have a timer to enable the bread machine to work without the operator's attendance, and some high-end models allow the user to program a customized period.

To bake bread, ingredients are measured in a specified order into the bread pan (usually first liquids, with solid ingredients layered on top), and then the pan is put in the bread maker. The order of ingredients is important because contact with water triggers the instant yeast used in bread makers, so the yeast and water have to be kept separate until the program starts.

It takes the machine several hours to make a bread loaf. The products are rested first and brought to an optimal temperature. Stir with a paddle, and the ingredients are then shaped into flour. Use optimal temperature regulation, and the dough is then confirmed and then cooked.

When the bread has been baked, the bread maker removes the pan. Then leaving a slight indentation from the rod to which the paddle is connected. The finished loaf's shape is often regarded as unique. Many initial bread machines manufacture a vertically slanted towards, square, or cylindrical loaf that is significantly dissimilar from commercial bread; however, more recent units typically have a more conventional horizontal pan. Some bread machines use two paddles to form two lb. loaf in regular rectangle shape.
Bread machine recipes are often much smaller than regular bread recipes. Sometimes standardized based on the machine's pan capacity, most popular in the US market is 1.5 lb. /700 g units. Most recipes are written for that capacity; however, two lb. /900 g units are not uncommon. There are prepared bread mixes, specially made for bread makers, containing pre-measured ingredients and flour and yeast, flavorings, and sometimes dough conditioners.

Bread makers are also fitted with a timer for testing when bread-making starts. For example, this allows them to be loaded at night but only begin baking in the morning to produce a freshly baked bread for breakfast. They may also be set only for making dough, for example, for making pizza. Apart from bread, some can also be set to make other things like jam, pasta dough, and Japanese rice cake. Some of the new developments in the facility of the machine includes automatically adding nut. It also contains fruit from a tray during the kneading process. Bread makers typically take between three and four hours to bake a loaf. However, recent "quick bake" modes have become standard additions, many of which can produce a loaf in less than an hour.

Chapter 1.
How to Bake Using a Bread Machine

Home bread makers are designed in such a way that any housewife can use it without much difficulty. However, for the stove to serve for a long time, and the bread always turns out to be high, lush, and tasty, specific rules must be followed.

You need to install the bread maker away from batteries, stoves, and sunlight since all temperature factors affect the oven's heating.

Before each new cooking, make sure that no crumbs are stuck on the blades and that the edge is on the shaft until it stops.

When laying the components, you must strictly follow the instructions: for example, if you want to start with liquids, then first pour in water, milk, or other liquid product. The flour is run to cover the liquid layer entirely, and then different dry ingredients are poured. Salt, sugar, hard butter (butter) is placed in the grooves made in the stacked layers to not come into contact with each other. Then, in the middle of the dry components layer, depression is caused, and yeast is poured into it (the depression should not reach the liquid coating).
A container with food is placed in the oven (usually there are special fasteners), the lid is closed, and the oven is plugged into a power outlet. Choose a program, the finished product's size, and the crust (if provided in the model). Press the "Start" or "Start" button. After that, the kneading process begins. If the oven has a timer, then you can set the time for preparing the bread for a specific time.

During kneading, the dough is checked by periodically opening the lid. To make good bread, the dough should be slightly sticky to the touch. If the dough is too soft and moist, add a little flour; if it turns out to be very dense, add liquid.
It is essential to assess the state of the dough during the lifting process. The dough may rise too high on hot days, and then it falls out of the mold and falls on the heating coils.
To not change the baking program, the dough can be punctured in several places to fall off. Or, cancel the originally specified program and set the mode, which in many models is called "Baking only."

All additives fall asleep after the stove signal about the end of the kneading, also, by a timer indicating that the kneading process is completed. If the stove has an automatic addition mode, then all components are poured into a special compartment at the beginning of cooking, as we have already mentioned earlier.
At the end of the cycle, the bread maker beeps. It either turns off itself in automatic mode, or you should press the "Stop" button. After that, the lid is opened, gloves are put on. The bread is then taken out (it is not recommended to lean close to the open stove and also rely on it).

Then turn the mold over the board, take out the bread, put it on the wire rack so that it cools down gradually. They then turn off the stove from the network and let it cool down (it is not recommended to start preparing a new portion of bread without waiting for the furnace to cool down).
It is recommended to use freshly baked bread for food within two to three days. It must be remembered that products containing eggs stale faster. Bread containing honey and butter retains its freshness and elasticity longer.

Chapter 2.
How to Use a Bread Machine

Meet Your New Bread Machine

Hot golden crescents, freshly baked breakfast cakes, aromatic tea cakes and delicious cakes to accompany your morning coffee All of these can be cooked with a bread machine in minutes and with a little effort on your part. Also, these delicious and healthy baked goods can be made with the simplest and most common ingredients. The only special thing you need to add is your love and creativity!

As for the boring and routine tasks, such as baking, mixing, stirring, the bread machine will take care of them leaving you the best and most enjoyable, that is, the choice of the recipe and the choice of ingredients. Isn't this a great way to enjoy the unique aroma and flavor of exactly the type of baked goods you need?

Even if you're not good at using modern appliances, put your worries behind you, because bread machines have simple, easy-to-use controls. They are fun and easy to use! Besides making fresh bread, they can also make and knead any type of dough, bake dough out of the box, and even make dough jam. When you get to know this handy device, it will truly become an essential and exceptional aid in your kitchen.

It's so simple
Insert the baking sheet into the machine.
Attach the dough blades.
Add ingredients as shown in your machine manual.
Close the lid.
Turn on the machine.
Select the required function.

What Else Can It Do?

Different bread machines may differ in their design, capacity, number of accessories, and programs available. When choosing your bread machine, think of your own preferences and needs: What will you do with the machine? Do you need any particular programs and additional modes, or is the basic functionality enough?
Bread machines can knead the dough, let it rest, bake a crunchy baguette, make sweet cupcakes or unleavened bread, and much more.

Main Ingredients
The ingredients needed for bread making are very simple: flour, yeast, salt, and liquid. There are other ingredients that add flavor, texture, and nutrition to your bread, such as sugar, fats, and eggs. The basic ingredients include:

Flour is the foundation of bread. The protein and gluten in flour forms a network that traps the carbon dioxide and alcohol produced by the yeast. Flour also provides simple sugar to feed the yeast and it provides flavor, depending on the type of flour used in the recipe.

Yeast is a living organism that increases when the right amount of moisture, food, and heat are applied. Rapidly multiplying yeast gives off carbon dioxide and ethyl alcohol. When yeast is allowed to go through its life cycle completely, the finished bread is more flavorful. The best yeast for bread

machines is bread machine yeast or active dry yeast, depending on your bread machine model.

Salt strengthens gluten and slows the rise of the bread by retarding the action of the yeast. A slower rise allows the flavors of the bread to develop better, and it will be less likely the bread will rise too much.

Liquid activates the yeast and dissolves the other ingredients. The most commonly used liquid is water, but ingredients such as milk can also be substituted. Bread made with water will have a crisper crust, but milk produces rich, tender bread that offers more nutrition and browns easier.

Oils and fats add flavor, create a tender texture, and help brown the crust. Bread made with fat stays fresh longer because moisture loss in the bread is slowed. This component can also inhibit gluten formation, so the bread does not rise as high.

Sugar is the source of food for the yeast. It also adds sweetness, tenderness, and color to the crust. Too much sugar can inhibit gluten growth or cause the dough to rise too much and collapse. Other sweeteners can replace sugar, such as honey, molasses, maple syrup, brown sugar, and corn syrup.

Eggs add protein, flavor, color, and a tender crust. Eggs contain an emulsifier, lecithin, which helps create a consistent texture, and a leavening agent, which helps the bread rise well.

Chapter 3.
What are the Most Common Ingredients

Bread making consists of a few very basic ingredients flour, liquids, yeast, butter, etc. Knowing the role of these ingredients helps you to understand the baking process. Moreover, the order in which you add ingredients is crucial when making bread in your bread machine. Do not commit the cardinal sin of bread making by adding the ingredients randomly to the bread pan.
The following sections highlight the correct order to put ingredients in the bread pan to bake perfect loaves of bread.

Water/Milk

All of the other basic bread ingredients, including flour, salt, and yeast, need a liquid medium to do their respective tasks. Water is the most common liquid ingredient; milk, buttermilk, cream, and juice are some common substitutes.
The liquid is usually the first ingredient to be added to the bread pan. This is very important as it maintains the ideal texture of your bread. The liquid should not be cold; ensure that it is lukewarm (between 80 and 90°F) whenever possible.

Butter/Oil

Butter, oil, or fat is usually added after the liquid. This is what gives bread crust its attractive brown color and crispy texture. Do not use cold butter that has just been taken out of the refrigerator. You can either microwave it for a few seconds or keep it at room temperature until it gets soft.

Sugar/honey (if using)

Sweet ingredients such as honey, corn syrup, maple syrup, and sugar are usually added after the butter as they mix easily with water and butter. However, the sweetener can be added before the butter as well. Sugar, honey, etc. serve as a feeding medium for yeast, so fermentation is stronger with the addition of sweet ingredients.

Eggs (if using)

Eggs need to be at room temperature before they are added to the bread pan. If the eggs are taken from the refrigerator, keep them outside at room temperature until they are no longer cold. They keep the crust tender and add protein and flavor to the bread.

Chilled Ingredients

If you are using any other ingredient that is kept chilled, such as cheese, milk, buttermilk or cream, keep it outside at room temperature until it is no longer cold, or microwave it for a few seconds to warm it up.

Salt

Use table salt or non-iodized salt for better results. Salt that is high in iodine can hamper the activity of the yeast and create problems with fermentation. Furthermore, salt itself is a yeast inhibitor and should not be touching yeast directly; that is why salt and yeast are never added together or one after another.

Spices (if using)

Spices such as cinnamon, nutmeg, and ginger are often used to add flavor to the bread. They may be added before or after the flour.

Flour

Flour is the primary ingredient for any bread recipe. It contains gluten (except for the gluten-free flours) and protein, and when the yeast produces alcohol and carbon dioxide, the gluten and protein trap the alcohol and carbon dioxide to initiate the bread-making process.

There are many different types of flours used for preparing different types of bread. Bread machine flour or white bread flour is the most common type as it is suitable for most bread recipes. It's so versatile because it contains an ideal proportion of protein for bread baking.

Usually, flour is stored at room temperature, but if you keep your flour in your fridge, allow it to warm up before using it.

Seeds (if using)

If a recipe calls for adding seeds such as sunflower seeds or caraway seeds, these should be added after the flour. However, when two different flours are being used, it is best to add the seeds in between the flours for a better mix.

Yeast

Yeast is the ingredient responsible for initiating the vital bread-making process of fermentation. Yeast needs the right amount of heat, moisture and liquid to grow and multiply. When yeast multiplies, it releases alcohol and carbon dioxide.

You can use active dry yeast or bread machine yeast (both will be available in local grocery stores). Cool, dry places are ideal to store yeast packs.
Yeast is added to the bread pan last, after the flour and other dry ingredients. (For certain types of bread, like fruit and nut bread, yeast is technically not the last ingredient, as the fruits or nuts are added later by the machine. However, yeast is the last ingredient to be added before starting the bread machine.)

Chapter 4.
Tips and tricks in Order to have a Better Final

Product and to Save Money and Time

When you are using a bread machine for the first time, it's common to have some concerns. However, they are quite easy to fix. The following are some useful tips and quick-and-easy fixes for the most common problems encountered while baking bread in a bread machine.

Dough Check

You can check the progress of the dough while the bread machine is mixing the ingredients. Take a quick check after 5 minutes of kneading. An ideal dough with the right amount of dry and wet ingredients makes one smooth ball and feels slightly tacky. You can open the lid to evaluate the dough. Do not worry about interfering with the kneading process by opening the lid; the bread structure won't be affected even if you poke it to get a feel for the dough.

If the dough feels too wet/moist or does not form into a ball shape, you can add 1 tablespoon of flour at a time and check again after a few minutes. If you feel that the dough is too dry, or it has formed two or three small balls, you can add 1 teaspoon of water at a time and check again after a few minutes.

Fruit/Nut Bread

When making fruit or nut bread, it is very important to add fruits or nuts at the right time. Not all bread machines come with a nut/fruit dispenser or hopper. If yours doesn't have one, don't worry; the machine will signal you with a beep series when it's time to add the fruits or nuts.

Citrus Ingredients

Citrus ingredients such as lemon zest, orange zest, orange juice, lemon juice, and pineapple juice can create issues with yeast fermentation if added in excess. Do not add more than the quantity specified in a recipe. The same goes for alcohol and cinnamon.

Salt Adjustment

When making small loaves (around 1 pound), sometimes the loaf rises more or less than expected. In many such instances, the issue is with the quantity of salt added. To avoid problems, try using less salt or cutting back on the quantity specified in the recipe. Using sea salt or coarse salt can also help prevent problems with small loaves.

Bread Collapse
The amount of yeast is very important for proper rising. The most common reason for bread collapse during the baking process is adding too much or too little yeast. Do not add more yeast than specified in the recipe. Also, check the expiration date on the yeast pack; freshly packed yeast provides the best results. Other reasons for bread collapse are using cold water and adding excess salt.

Failure to Rise

Many factors can contribute to the failure of dough to rise completely. Insufficient gluten content, miscalculated ingredients, excess salt, excess sugar, and using cold ingredients are the most common reasons. Always warm any chilled ingredients or place them at room temperature for a while before adding them to the bread pan. However, if you are warming any ingredients in your oven, make sure not to over-heat them. They need to be lukewarm, at between 80 and 90°F, and not too hot. Also make sure that the yeast does not come in direct contact with the salt, as this creates problems with rising (that is why yeast is added last).

Texture Troubles

•   If your bread has a coarse texture, try adding more salt and reducing the amount of liquid.
•   If your bread looks small and feels dense, try using flour with higher protein content. Bread flour has a sufficient amount of protein, but slightly denser loaves are common when you use heavier flours such as rye flour and whole wheat flour. Use additional ingredients such as fruits, nuts, and vegetables in their specified quantities. Adding too much of such ingredients will make your loaf too heavy, small, and dense.

•   Moist or gummy loaves are less common, but it can happen if you have added too much liquid or used too much sugar. Too much liquid can also result in a doughy center.

•   If your bread has an unbrowned top, try adding more sugar. This can also happen if your bread machine has a glass top.

•   If your loaf has a mushroom top, it is probably due to too much yeast or water. Try reducing the amount of water and/or yeast.

•   Sometimes a baked loaf has some flour on one side. When you bake the next time, try to remove any visible flour during the kneading cycle with a rubber spatula.

•   If your loaf has an overly dark crust, try using the Medium crust setting next time. This also happens if you've added too much sugar and when you fail to take out the bread pan after the end of the baking process. It is always advisable to remove the bread pan right after the process is complete.

•   If your loaf has a sunken top, it is probably because of using too much liquid or overly hot ingredients. This is also common during humid or warm weather.

Excess Rise

Many times, a loaf rises more than expected; the most common reasons are too much yeast, too little salt, and using cold water. But also make sure that the capacity of your bread pan is sufficient for the size of loaf you have selected; trying to make a large loaf in a small bread pan will obviously lead to such trouble.

Paddles

After the bread machine completes its baking process the paddles may remain inside the bread loaf. Allow the freshly made bread to cool down and then place it on a cutting board and gently take out the paddles.

Spraying the paddles with a cooking spray before you add the ingredients to the bread pan will make it easier to clean them after the bread is baked.
Cleaning
After you take the baked loaf from the bread pan, do not immerse the pan in water. Rather, fill it with warm soapy water.

Breakfast Bread

NUTRITION Calories: 234 , Fat: 23g , Carb: 1g , Protein: 7g

INGREDIENTS

- ½ tsp. Xanthan gum
- ½ tsp. salt
- 2 Tbsp. coconut oil
- ½ cup butter, melted
- 1 tsp. baking powder
- 2 cups of almond flour
- Seven eggs

DIRECTION

- Preheat the oven to 355F.
- Beat eggs in a bowl on high for 2 minutes.
- Add coconut oil and butter to the eggs and continue to beat.
- Line a pan with baking paper and then pour the beaten eggs.
- Pour in the rest of the ingredients and mix until it becomes thick.
- Bake until a toothpick comes out dry. It takes 40 to 45 minutes.

PREPARATION	COOKING TIME	SERVINGS
15	40 mints	16 slice

Peanut Butter and Jelly Bread

NUTRITION Calories: 153 Cal Carbohydrates: 20 g Fat: 9g, Cholesterol: 0mg Protein: 4g Fiber: 2g Sugar: 11g Sodium: 244mg Potassium: 120mg

INGREDIENTS

- 1 1/2 tablespoons vegetable oil
- 1 cup of water
- ½ cup blackberry jelly
- ½ cup peanut butter
- One teaspoon salt
- One tablespoon white sugar
- 2 cups of bread flour
- 1 cup whole-wheat flour
- 1 1/2 teaspoons active dry yeast

DIRECTION

- Put everything in your bread machine pan.
- Select the basic setting.
- Press the start button.
- Take out the pan when done and set aside for 10 minutes.

PREPARATION	COOKING TIME		SERVINGS
2 HOURS	1 mins	10 mins	1 loaf

Low-Carb Bagel

NUTRITION Calories: 134 Fat: 6.8g Carb: 4.2g Protein: 12.1g

INGREDIENTS

- 1 cup protein powder, unflavored
- 1/3 cup coconut flour
- 1 tsp. baking powder
- ½ tsp. sea salt
- ¼ cup ground flaxseed
- 1/3 cup sour cream
- 12 eggs
- Seasoning topping:
- 1 tsp. dried parsley
- 1 tsp. dried oregano
- 1 tsp. Dried minced onion
- ½ tsp. Garlic powder
- ½ tsp. Dried basil
- ½ tsp. sea salt

DIRECTION

- Preheat the oven to 350F.
- In a mixer, blend sour cream and eggs until well combined.
- Whisk together the flaxseed, salt, baking powder, protein powder, and coconut flour in a bowl.
- Mix the dry ingredients until it becomes wet ingredients. Make sure it is well blended.
- Whisk the topping seasoning together in a small bowl. Set aside.
- Grease 2 donut pans that can contain six donuts each.
- Sprinkle pan with about 1 tsp. topping seasoning and evenly pour batter into each.
- Sprinkle the top of each bagel evenly with the rest of the seasoning mixture.
- Bake in the oven for 25 minutes, or until golden brown.

PREPARATION	COOKING TIME	SERVINGS
15	25 mins	12

Puri Bread

NUTRITION Calories: 106 Fat: 3g Carb: 6g Protein: 3g

INGREDIENTS

- 1 cup almond flour, sifted
- ½ cup of warm water
- 2 Tbsp. clarified butter
- 1 cup olive oil for frying
- Salt to taste

DIRECTION

- Salt the water and add the flour.
- Make some holes in the center of the dough and pour warm clarified butter.
- Knead the dough and let stand for 15 minutes, covered.
- Shape into six balls.
- Flatten the balls into six thin rounds using a rolling pin.
- Heat enough oil to cover a round frying pan completely.
- Place a puri in it when hot.
- Fry for 20 seconds on each side.
- Place on a paper towel.
- Repeat with the rest of the puri and serve.

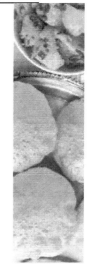

PREPARATION	COOKING	SERVINGS
10	5 mins	6

Hot Dog Buns

NUTRITION Calories: 104   Fat: 8g   Carb: 1g   Protein: 4g

PREPARATION	COOKING TIME	SERVINGS
10	50 mins	10

DIRECTION

- Preheat the oven to 350F
- In a bowl, put all dry ingredients and mix well.
- Add boiling water, lemon juice, and egg whites into the dry mixture and whisk until combined.
- Mould the dough into ten portions and roll into buns.
- Transfer into the preheated oven and cook for 40 to 50 minutes on the lower oven rack.
- Check for doneness and remove it.
- Top with desired toppings and hot dogs.
- Serve.

INGREDIENTS

- One ¼ cups almond flour
- 5 tbsp. psyllium husk powder
- 1 tsp. sea salt
- 2 tsp. baking powder
- One ¼ cups boiling water
- 2 tsp. lemon juice
- Three egg whites

Healthy Low Carb Bread

NUTRITION Calories: 229 Fat: 25.5g Carb: 6.5g   Protein: 8.5g

PREPARATION	COOKING TIME	SERVINGS
15	35 mints	8

DIRECTION

- Preheat the oven to 350F.
- Grease a loaf pan with 1 to 2 tsp. Melted coconut oil and place it in the freezer to harden.
- Add eggs into a bowl and mix for 2 minutes with a hand mixer.
- Add coconut oil into the eggs and mix.
- Add dry ingredients to a second bowl and whisk until mixed.
- Put the dry ingredients into the egg mixture and mix on low speed with a hand mixer until dough is formed and the mixture is incorporated.
- Add the dough into the prepared loaf pan, transfer into the preheated oven, and bake for 35 minutes.
- Take out the bread pan from the oven.
- Cool, slice, and serve.

INGREDIENTS

- 2/3 cup coconut flour
- 2/3 cup coconut oil (softened not melted)
- Nine eggs
- 2 tsp. Cream of tartar
- ¾ tsp. xanthan gum
- 1 tsp. Baking soda
- ¼ tsp. salt

Spicy Bread

NUTRITION Calories: 240 Fat: 20g

PREPARATION	COOKING TIME	SERVINGS
10	40 mins	6

INGREDIENTS

- ½ cup coconut flour
- Six eggs
- Three large jalapenos, sliced
- 4 ounces' turkey bacon, sliced
- ½ cup ghee
- ¼ tsp. baking soda
- ¼ tsp. salt
- ¼ cup of water

DIRECTION

- Preheat the oven to 400F.
- Cut bacon and jalapenos on a baking tray and roast for 10 minutes.
- Flip and bake for five more minutes.
- Remove seeds from the jalapenos.
- Place jalapenos and bacon slices in a food processor and blend until smooth.
- In a bowl, add ghee, eggs, and ¼-cup water. Mix well.
- Then add some coconut flour, baking soda, and salt. Stir to mix.
- Add bacon and jalapeno mix.
- Grease the loaf pan with ghee.
- Pour batter into the loaf pan.
- Bake for 40 minutes.
- Enjoy.

Fluffy Paleo Bread

NUTRITION Calories: 149 Cal Fat: 12.9 g Carbohydrates: 4.4 g

PREPARATION	COOKING TIME	SERVINGS
10	40 mins	15

DIRECTION

- Ur, sed milles ut laborpor autem facepra ne serum arumet aut reperae con exceped que ea esero qui acerem aspella borror a ipsanda eratiore est, consequam arcim am quamenis samet quo offictem.

-
- Ita della quis que pernamet, que poriam fuga. Et vene pos et volum eum est quatur sed quis as aceatus ciendae rorrumentur autenih iliati dit occullestis veliciis eosam.
- Erionemquam lam simpor alita alibusciat.
- Sediam, sam doluptatus nonserunt. Asiniasped ea vero-vita pratem intiae nos aturemposam.

INGREDIENTS

- Restiberorio
- Pudavenemis
- Vollorpori
- Cusaper
- Natempelit
- Pratiremnecea
- Optatque
- Ditatur
- Omnihilit
- Fugiatur

English muffin Bread

NUTRITION Carbs: 13 g   Fat: 1 g   Protein: 2 g   Calories: 62

INGREDIENTS

- 1 teaspoon vinegar
- 1/4 to 1/3 cup water
- 1 cup lukewarm milk
- 2 Tablespoon butter or 2 Tablespoon vegetable oil
- 1½ teaspoon salt
- 1½ teaspoon sugar
- ½ teaspoon baking powder
- 3½ cups unbleached all-purpose flour
- 2 1/4 teaspoon instant yeast

DIRECTION

- Add each ingredient to the bread machine in the order and at the temperature recommended by your bread machine manufacturer.
- Close the lid, select the basic bread, low crust setting on your bread machine, and press start.
- When the bread machine has finished baking, remove the bread and put it on a cooling rack.

PREPARATION	COOKING TIME		SERVINGS
15	3	40 *mints*	*14*

Cranberry Orange Breakfast Bread

NUTRITION Carbs: 29 g   Fat: 2 g   Protein: 9 g   Calories: 56

INGREDIENTS

- 1 1/8 cup orange juice
- 2 Tablespoon vegetable oil
- 2 Tablespoon honey
- 3 cups bread flour
- 1 Tablespoon dry milk powder
- ½ teaspoon ground cinnamon
- ½ teaspoon ground allspice
- 1 teaspoon salt
- 1 (.25 ounce) package active dry yeast
- 1 Tablespoon grated orange zest
- 1 cup sweetened dried cranberries
- 1/3 cup chopped walnuts

DIRECTION

- Add each ingredient to the bread machine in the order and at the temperature recommended by your bread machine manufacturer.
- Close the lid, select the basic bread, low crust setting on your bread machine, and press start.
- Add the cranberries and chopped walnuts 5 to 10 minutes before last kneading cycle ends.
- When the bread machine has finished baking, remove the bread and put it on a cooling rack.

PREPARATION	COOKING TIME		SERVINGS
15 MINTS	3 *hour*	10 *mints*	*14*

Buttermilk Honey Bread

NUTRITION Carbs: 19 g   Fat: 1 g   Protein: 2 g   Calories: 92

INGREDIENTS

- ½ cup water
- ¾ cup buttermilk
- ¼ cup honey
- 3 Tablespoon butter, softened and cut into pieces
- 3 cups bread flour
- 1½ teaspoon salt
- 2¼ teaspoon yeast (or 1 package)

DIRECTION

- Add each ingredient to the bread machine in the order and at the temperature recommended by your bread machine manufacturer.
- Close the lid, select the basic bread, medium crust setting on your bread machine and press start.
- When the bread machine has finished baking, remove the bread and put it on a cooling rack.

PREPARATION	COOKING	SERVINGS
5 MINTS	3 45 *hour*	14

Whole Wheat Breakfast Bread

NUTRITION Carbs: 11 g   Fat: 3 g   Protein: 1 g   Calories: 60

INGREDIENTS

- 3 cups white whole wheat flour
- ½ teaspoon salt
- 1 cup water
- ½ cup coconut oil, liquified
- 4 Tablespoon honey
- 2½ teaspoon active dry yeast

DIRECTION

- Add each ingredient to the bread machine in the order and at the temperature recommended by your bread machine manufacturer.
- Close the lid, select the basic bread, medium crust setting on your bread machine and press start.
- When the bread machine has finished baking, remove the bread and put it on a cooling rack.

PREPARATION	COOKING	SERVINGS
5 MINTS	3 45 *hour mints*	14

Cinnamon-Raisin Bread

NUTRITION Carbs: 38 g   Fat: 2 g   Protein: 4 g   Calories: 180

INGREDIENTS

- 1 cup water
- 2 Tablespoon butter, softened
- 3 cups Gold Medal Better for Bread flour
- 3 Tablespoon sugar
- 1½ teaspoon salt
- 1 teaspoon ground cinnamon
- 2½ teaspoon bread machine yeast
- ¾ cup raisins

DIRECTION

- Add each ingredient except the raisins to the bread machine in the order and at the temperature recommended by your bread machine manufacturer.
- Close the lid, select the sweet or basic bread, medium crust setting on your bread machine and press start.
- Add raisins 10 minutes before the last kneading cycle ends.
- When the bread machine has finished baking, remove the bread and put it on a cooling rack.

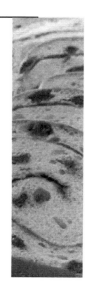

PREPARATION	COOKING TIME	SERVINGS
5	3 *hour*	14

Butter Bread Rolls

NUTRITION Carbs: 38 g   Fat: 2 g   Protein: 4 g   Calories: 18

INGREDIENTS

- 1 cup warm milk
- 1/2 cup butter or 1/2 cup margarine, softened
- 1/4 cup sugar
- 2 eggs
- 1 1/2 teaspoons salt
- 4 cups bread flour
- 2 1/4 teaspoons active dry yeast

DIRECTION

- In bread machine pan, put all ingredients in order suggested by manufacturer.
- Select dough setting.
- When cycle is completed, turn dough onto a lightly floured surface.
- Divide dough into 24 portions.
- Shape dough into balls.
- Place in a greased 13 inch by 9-inch baking pan.
- Cover and let rise in a warm place for 30-45 minutes.
- Bake at 350 degrees for 13-16 minutes or until golden brown.

PREPARATION	COOKING TIME	SERVINGS
5 MINTS	45 *mins*	24 rolls

Cranberry & Golden Raisin Bread

NUTRITION *Carbs: 33 g   Fat: 3 g   Protein: 4 g   Calories: 175*

INGREDIENTS

- 1 1/3 cups water
- 4 Tablespoon sliced butter
- 3 cups flour
- 1 cup old fashioned oatmeal
- 1/3 cup brown sugar
- 1 teaspoon salt
- 4 Tablespoon dried cranberries
- 4 Tablespoon golden raisins
- 2 teaspoon bread machine yeast

DIRECTION

- Add each ingredient except cranberries and golden raisins to the bread machine one by one, according to the manufacturer's instructions.
- Close the lid, select the sweet or basic bread, medium crust setting on your bread machine and press start.
- Add the cranberries and golden raisins 5 to 10 minutes before the last kneading cycle ends.
- When the bread machine has finished baking, remove the bread and put it on a cooling rack.

PREPARATION	COOKING TIME	SERVINGS
5	3 *hours*	14

Chapter 6.
Whole-Wheat Bread

33

Whole Wheat Bread

NUTRITION Calories: 160 Carbs: 30.1g Fat: 3,1g Protein: 5g

INGREDIENTS

- Lukewarm water
- Olive oil
- Whole wheat flour sifted
- Salt
- Soft brown sugar
- Dried milk powder, skimmed
- Fast-acting, easy-blend dried yeast

DIRECTION

- Add the water and olive oil to your machine, followed by half of the flour.
- Now apply the salt, sugar, dried milk powder, and remaining flour.
- Make a little well or dip at the top of the flour. Then carefully place the yeast into it, making sure it doesn't come into contact with any liquid.
- Set the wholemeal or whole-wheat setting according to your machine's manual, and alter the crust setting to your particular liking.
- Once baked, carefully remove the bowl from the machine and remove the loaf, placing it on a wire rack to cool. I prefer not to add any toppings to this particular loaf, but you can, of course, experiment and add whatever you want.
- Once cool, remove the paddle; and, for the very best results, slice with a serrated bread knife. Enjoy!

PREPARATION	COOKING TIME	SERVINGS
9	4 *hours*	*12 slices*

Honey Whole-Wheat Bread

NUTRITION Calories: 101 Carbs: 19g Fat: 2g Protein: 4g

INGREDIENTS

- Water at 90°F-100°F (320C-370C)
- Honey
- Melted butter, at room temperature
- Salt
- Whole-wheat flour
- Active dry yeast

DIRECTION

- Place the ingredients in your bread machine follow the order of your manufacturer's suggestion.
- Choose the Whole Wheat program, light or medium crust, and press START.
- Once baked, let the loaf cool for 10 minutes.
- Gently wiggle the bucket to remove the loaf. Then transfer it onto a rack to cool.
- Enjoy!

PREPARATION	COOKING TIME	SERVINGS
10 MINTS	3 *hours* 40 *mints*	*8 slices*

Whole Wheat Peanut Butter and Jelly Bread

NUTRITION Calories: 230 Carbs: 39g Fat: 6g Protein: 9g

INGREDIENTS

- Water at 90°F-100°F (320C-370C)
- Smooth peanut butter
- Strawberry jelly (or any preferable jelly)
- Vital wheat gluten
- Salt
- Baking soda
- Active dry yeast
- Baking powder
- Light brown sugar
- Whole wheat flour

DIRECTION

- As you prep the bread machine pan, add the following in this particular order: water, jelly, salt, peanut butter, brown sugar, baking powder, baking soda, gluten, whole wheat flour, and yeast.
- Choose 1 ½ Pound Loaf, Medium Crust, Wheat cycle, and then START the machine.
- Once baked, place it on a rack to cool and then serve.
- Enjoy!

PREPARATION	COOKING TIME	SERVINGS
10	3 *hours*	*12 slices*

Bread Machine Ezekiel Bread

NUTRITION Calories: 192 Carbs: 31g Fat: 5g Protein: 6g

INGREDIENTS

- Whole wheat flour
- Bread flour
- Spelled flour
- Honey
- Millet
- Olive oil
- Wheat germ
- Dry kidney beans
- Barley
- Dry lentils
- Bread machine yeast
- Dry black beans
- Water at 90°F (320C)
- Salt

DIRECTION

- Soak all beans and grains in separate bowls overnight.
- Boil the black beans, dry kidney beans for about 1 hour, and then add lentils, millet, and barley. Next, boil for 15 minutes more.
- Assemble boiled ingredients in a food processor and mix until mashed.
- Spread water into the bread machine pan, add 2 tbsp. of olive oil and honey, and then add the flour, wheat germ. In one corner, add salt in another one yeast and START the Dough cycle.
- When the bread machine beeps, add the mash to the dough and press the Whole Wheat cycle. Enjoy!

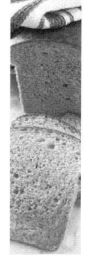

PREPARATION	COOKING	SERVINGS
10 MINTS	3 *hours*	*12 slices*

Honey-Oat-Wheat Bread

NUTRITION Calories: 281 Carbs: 45g Fat: 9g Protein: 6g

INGREDIENTS

- *Active dry yeast*
- *Sugar*
- *Water at 1100F (450C)*
- *All-purpose flour*
- *Whole wheat flour*
- *Rolled oats*
- *Powdered milk*
- *Salt*
- *Honey*
- *Vegetable oil*
- *Butter softened*
- *Cooking spray*

DIRECTION

- Place the following into the pan of a bread machine: yeast, sugar, and water. Let the yeast dissolve and foam for approximately 10 minutes. In the meantime, in a bowl, combine the all-purpose flour, powdered milk, whole wheat flour, salt, and rolled oats. Pour the butter, honey, and vegetable oil into the yeast mixture. Then add the flour mixture on top.
- Choose the Dough cycle and then push the START button. Let the bread machine fully finish the process, which spans approximately 1 ½ hour. Place the dough into a 9x5-inch loaf pan that's coated with cooking spray. Leave the bread to rise in a warm place for 1 hour.
- Preheat the oven.
- Bake for approximately 35 minutes in the warmed oven until the top turns golden brown.
- Enjoy!

PREPARATION	COOKING TIME		SERVINGS
10	3	45 *mins*	*16 slices*

Butter Up Bread

NUTRITION Calories: 231 Carbs: 36g Fat: 6g Protein: 8g

INGREDIENTS

- *Bread flour*
- *Margarine, melted*
- *Buttermilk at 1100F (450C)*
- *Sugar*
- *Active dry yeast*
- *Egg, at room temperature*
- *Salt*

DIRECTION

- Prepare the bread machine pan by adding buttermilk, melted margarine, salt, sugar, flour, and yeast in the order specified by your manufacturer.
- Select Basic/White Setting and press START.
- Once baked, transfer onto wire racks to cool before slicing.
- Enjoy!

PREPARATION	COOKING TIME		SERVINGS
10 MINTS	3 *hours*	00 *mints*	*12 slices*

Butter Honey Wheat Bread

NUTRITION Calories: 170 Carbs: 27g Fat: 6g Protein: 3g

INGREDIENTS

- *Buttermilk*
- *Butter, melted*
- *Honey*
- *Bread flour*
- *Whole wheat flour*
- *Salt*
- *Baking soda*
- *Active dry yeast*

DIRECTION

- Put all ingredients into the bread machine, by way of recommended by the manufacturer.
- In my case, liquids always go first.
- Run the bread machine for a loaf (1½ lbs.) on the Whole Wheat setting.
- Once the baking process is done, transfer the baked bread to a wire rack and cool before slicing.
- Enjoy!

PREPARATION	COOKING TIME	SERVINGS
15	3 45 mints	*12 slices*

Buttermilk Wheat Bread

NUTRITION Calories: 141 Carbs: 26g Fat: 2.5g Protein: 5g

INGREDIENTS

- *Buttermilk, at room temperature*
- *White sugar*
- *Olive oil*
- *Salt*
- *Baking soda*
- *Unbleached white flour*
- *Whole wheat flour*
- *Active dry yeast*

DIRECTION

- In the bread machine pan, measure all ingredients in the order the manufacturer recommends.
- Set the machine to the Basic White Bread setting and press START.
- After a few minutes, add more buttermilk if the ingredients don't form a ball. If it's too loose, apply a handful of flour.
- One baked, let the bread cool on a wire rack before slicing.
- Enjoy!

PREPARATION	COOKING	SERVINGS
8 MINTS	4 30 hour mints	*16 slices*

Cracked Fit and Fat Bread

NUTRITION Calories: 65 Carbs: 12.4g Fat: 1g Protein: 2g

INGREDIENTS

- *Water*
- *Butter softened*
- *Brown sugar*
- *Salt*
- *Bread flour*
- *Whole wheat flour*
- *Cracked wheat*
- *Active dry yeast*

DIRECTION

- In the bread machine pan, measure all components according to the manufacturer's suggested order.
- Choose Basic/White cycle, medium crust, and 2lbs weight of loaf, and then press START.
- Once baked, allow the bread to cool on a wire rack before slicing.
- Enjoy!

PREPARATION	COOKING TIME	SERVINGS
5	3 25 *mints*	*16 slices*

Crunchy Honey Wheat Bread

NUTRITION Calories: 199 Carbs: 37g Fat: 4.2g Protein: 6.2g

INGREDIENTS

- *Warm water at 1100F (450C)*
- *Vegetable oil*
- *Honey*
- *Salt*
- *Bread flour*
- *Whole wheat flour*
- *Granola*
- *Active dry yeast*

DIRECTION

- Place the ingredients into the bread machine following the order recommended by the manufacturer.
- Choose the Whole Wheat setting or the Dough cycle on the machine. Press the START button.
- Once the machine has finished the whole cycle of baking the bread in the oven, form the dough and add it into a loaf pan that's greased. Let it rise in volume in a warm place until it becomes double its size. Insert into the preheated 350°F (175°C) oven and bake for 35-45 minutes.
- Enjoy!

PREPARATION	COOKING TIME	SERVINGS
7 MINTS	3 30 *hour mints*	*12 slices*

Easy Home Base Wheat Bread

NUTRITION Calories: 180 Carbs: 33g Fat: 2g Protein: 7g

INGREDIENTS

- Whole wheat flour
- Bread flour
- Butter softened
- Warm water at 900F (320C)
- Warm milk at 900F (320C)
- Active dry yeast
- Egg, at room temperature
- Salt
- Honey

DIRECTION

- Add the ingredients into the pan of the bread machine following the order suggested by the manufacturer.
- Use the Whole Wheat cycle. choose the crust color, weight, and START the machine.
- Check how the dough is kneading after five minutes pass because you may need to add either one tbsp. of water or one tbsp. of flour-based on consistency.
- When the bread is complete, cool it on a wire rack before slicing.
- Enjoy!

PREPARATION	COOKING TIME	SERVINGS
10	3 50 *mints*	*12 slices*

Whole Wheat Yogurt Bread

NUTRITION Calories: 158 Carbs: 20g Fat: 5g Protein: 6g

INGREDIENTS

- Ground nutmeg (optional)
- Water
- Butter, melted
- Plain yogurt
- Dry milk
- Honey
- Active dry yeast
- Whole wheat flour
- Bread flour
- Ground cinnamon
- Salt

DIRECTION

- Begin by pouring ingredients into the bread pan in the instruction your manufacturer endorses. In my case, liquids always go first.
- So, I begin with water, yogurt, butter, honey, sieve flour, dry milk, add salt, ground cinnamon, and yeast in different corners of the pan.
- Select the Whole grain setting, light or medium crust, and press START.
- When ready, allow it to cool and then serve.
- Enjoy!

PREPARATION	COOKING TIME	SERVINGS
10 MINTS	3 40 *hour mints*	*12 slices*

Chapter 7.
Classic Bread

Almond Flour Bread

NUTRITION Calories: 110 Carbohydrates: 2.4g Protein: 4g Fat: 10g

INGREDIENTS

- *Four egg whites*
- *Two egg yolks*
- *2 cups almond flour*
- *1/4 cup butter, melted*
- *2 tbsp. psyllium husk powder*
- *1 1/2 tbsp. baking powder*
- *1/2 tsp. xanthan gum*
- *Salt*
- *1/2 cup + 2 tbsp. warm water*
- *2 1/4 tsp. yeast*

DIRECTION

- Make use of a small mixing bowl to combine the dry ingredients except for the yeast.
- In the bread machine pan, add all the wet ingredients.
- Add all of your dry ingredients from the lower mixing bowl to the bread machine pan. Top with the yeast.
- Set the bread machine to the basic bread setting.
- When the bread is completed, remove the bread machine pan from the bread machine.
- Let cool a little before moving to a cooling rack.
- The bread can be stored for up to 4 days on the counter and three months in the freezer.

PREPARATION	COOKING TIME	SERVINGS
10 MINTS	10 *mints*	*10*

Coconut Flour Bread

NUTRITION Calories: 174 Carbohydrates: 4g Protein: 7g Fat: 15g

INGREDIENTS

- Six eggs
- 1/2 cup coconut flour
- 2 tbsp. psyllium husk
- 1/4 cup olive oil
- 1 1/2 tsp. salt
- 1 tbsp. xanthan gum
- 1 tbsp. baking powder
- 2 1/4 tsp. yeast

DIRECTION

- Use a small mixing bowl to combine dry ingredients except for the yeast.
- In the bread machine pan, add all the wet ingredients.
- Add all of your dry ingredients from the small mixing bowl to the bread machine pan. Top with the yeast.
- Set the bread machine to the basic bread setting.
- When the bread is done, eradicate the bread machine pan from the bread machine.
- Let cool slightly before transferring to a cooling rack.
- The bread can be stockpiled for up to 4 days on the counter and three months in the freezer.

PREPARATION	COOKING TIME	SERVINGS
10	15 *mints*	12

Cloud Savory Bread Loaf

NUTRITION Calories: 90 Carbohydrates: 2g Protein: 6g Fat: 7g

INGREDIENTS

- Six egg whites
- Six egg yolks
- 1/2 cup whey protein powder, unflavored
- 1/2 tsp. cream of tartar
- 6 oz. sour cream
- 1/2 tsp. baking powder
- 1/4 tsp. garlic powder
- 1/4 tsp. onion powder
- 1/4 tsp. salt

DIRECTION

- Beat the egg whites, including the cream of tartar, till you have stiff peaks forming. Set aside.
- Combine all other ingredients into another bowl and mix.
- Fold the mixtures together, a little at a time.
- Pour mixture into your bread machine pan.
- Set the bread machine to quick bread.
- When the bread is finished, remove the bread machine pan from the bread machine.
- Let cool slightly before transferring to a cooling bracket.
- The bread may be kept for up to 3 days on the counter.

PREPARATION	COOKING	SERVINGS
10 MINTS	15 *mints*	10

Sandwich Buns

NUTRITION Calories: 99   Fat: 6g   Carb: 10g   Protein: 5.3g

INGREDIENTS

- Four eggs
- 2 ½ oz. almond flour
- 1 Tbsp. coconut flour
- 1 oz. psyllium
- 1 ½ cups eggplant, finely grated, juices drained
- 3 Tbsp. sesame seeds
- 1 ½ tsp. baking powder
- Salt to taste

DIRECTION

- Whisk eggs until foamy, and then add grated eggplant.
- In a separate bowl, mix all dry ingredients.
- Add them to the egg mixture. Mix well.
- Line a baking sheet with parchment paper, then shape the buns with your hands.
- Bake at 374F for 20 to 25 minutes.

PREPARATION	COOKING TIME	SERVINGS
10	25 mints	8

French Bread

NUTRITION Calories: 121   Fiber: 1.1 g   Fat: 1.9 g   Carbs: 2.9g   Protein: 3.9 g.

INGREDIENTS

- 1 1/3 cups warm water
- 1 ½ tablespoon olive oil
- 1 ½ teaspoons salt
- Two tablespoons sugar
- 4 cups all-purpose flour; or bread flour
- Two teaspoons yeast

DIRECTION

- Put the warm water in your bread machine first.
- Next, put in the olive oil, then the salt, and finally the sugar. Make sure to follow that exact order. Then put in the flour. Make sure to cover the liquid ingredients.
- In the center of the flour, make a small indentation. Make sure the indentation doesn't go down far enough to touch the liquid. Put the yeast in the indentation.
- Set the bread machine to the French Bread Cycle.
- After 5 minutes of kneading, check on the dough. If the dough is stiff and dry, add ½ - 1 tablespoon of water until the dough becomes a softball.
- If the dough is too damp, add one tablespoon of flour until the right consistency is reached. Allow the bread cool for about 10 minutes, then cut it.

PREPARATION	COOKING TIME	SERVINGS
2 30 mins	30 mints	14

Hazelnut Honey Bread

NUTRITION Carbohydrates 5 g Fats 2.8 g Protein 3.6 g Calories 113

INGREDIENTS

- ½ CUP LUKEWARM MILK
- TWO TEASPOONS BUTTER, MELTED AND COOLED
- TWO TEASPOONS LIQUID HONEY
- 2/3 TEASPOONS SALT
- 1/3 CUP COOKED WILD RICE, COOLED
- 1/3 CUP WHOLE GRAIN FLOUR
- 2/3 TEASPOONS CARAWAY SEEDS
- 1 CUP ALMOND FLOUR, SIFTED
- ONE TEASPOON ACTIVE DRY YEAST
- 1/3 CUP HAZELNUTS, CHOPPED

DIRECTION

- Prepare all of the ingredients for your bread and measuring means (a cup, a spoon, kitchen scales).
- Carefully measure the Ingredients into the pan, except the nuts and seeds.
- Place all of the ingredients into the bread bucket in the right order.
- Then follow the manual for your bread machine.
- Close the cover.
- Select the program of your bread machine to basic and choose the crust color to medium.
- Press starts.
- After the signal, add the nuts and seeds into the dough.
- Wait until the program completes.
- When done, take the bucket out and let it cool for 5-10 minutes.
- Shake the loaf from the pan and let cool for 30 minutes on a cooling rack.
- Slice, serve and enjoy the taste of fragrant homemade bread.

PREPARATION	COOKING TIME	SERVINGS
3 hours	30 mins	10

Simple Egg Bread

NUTRITION

INGREDIENTS

- 4 cups almond flour
- 1 cup milk
- Two eggs
- One teaspoon yeast
- 1 ½ teaspoons salt
- Two ¼ tablespoons sugar
- 1 ½ tablespoons butter

DIRECTION

- Lay the products in the bread pan according to the instructions for your device. In the beginning, liquid, therefore, we pour warm milk, and we will add salt.
- Then increase the eggs (pre-loosen with a fork) and melted butter, which must be cooled to a warm state.
- Now add the sifted almond flour.
- Top the yeast - dry active ones since they do not need pre-activation with liquid.
- In the end, mix the yeast with sugar.
- Select the basic program (on mine, it is 1 of 12). The time will automatically be set for 3 hours. When the batch begins, this is the most crucial moment. Kneading on this program lasts precisely 10 minutes, from which a ball of all products is produced.
- Ideally, it is formed after the first 4-5 minutes of kneading, then, you can help the bread maker. First, scrape off the flour from the walls, which the blade sometimes does not entirely grasp and thus interferes with the dough. Second, you need to look carefully, as different flours from different manufacturers have different degrees of humidity, so that it may take a little more - about 2-3 tablespoons. It is when you see that the dough cannot condense and gather in a ball.
- It is rarely rare, but sometimes there is not enough liquid, and the dough turns into lumps. If so, add a little more water and thereby help the bread maker knead the dough.
- After exactly 3 hours, you will hear the signal, but much sooner, your home will be filled with the fantastic aroma of homemade bread. Turn off the appliance, open the lid, and take out the bowl of bread. Handsome!
- Take out the hot egg bread and remove the paddle if it does not stay in the bowl but is at the loaf's bottom. Cool the loaves on a grate. In general, it is always advised to cool the bread on its side.
- This bread is quite tall - 12 cm.
- Only when the loaf completely cools you can cut the egg bread!
- Help yourself!

PREPARATION	COOKING	SERVINGS
3 HOURS	30 mins	8

White Bread

NUTRITION Carbohydrates 3 g   Fats 5.6 g   Protein 9.6 g   Calories 319

INGREDIENTS

- 1 cup of lukewarm water (110 degrees F/45 degrees C)
- Three tablespoons of white sugar
- 1 1/2 teaspoons of salt
- Three tablespoons of vegetable oil
- 3 cups of bread flour
- 2 1/4 teaspoons of active dry yeast

DIRECTION

- Put water, sugar, salt, oil, bread flour, and yeast into the bread machine.
- Bake on setting White Bread. Before slicing, let it cool on wire racks.

PREPARATION	COOKING TIME	SERVINGS
5	3 5 *mints*	8

Ciabatta Bread

NUTRITION Carbohydrates 3 g   Fats 5.6 g   Protein 9.6 g   Calories 319

INGREDIENTS

- 1 1/2 cup water
- 1 1/2 teaspoon salt
- One teaspoon white sugar
- One tablespoon olive oil
- 3 1/4 cup bread flour
- 1 1/2 teaspoon bread machine yeast

DIRECTION

- Mix all ingredients in your stand mixer but for olive oil. Mix with dough hook at low speed. Mix for 10 minutes. Scrape down the sides if necessary.
- Add the olive oil and whisk for another 5 minutes.
- The dough will be pretty sticky and wet; this is what you want, so you can avoid the desire to add more flour.
- Put the dough on a kindly floured surface, cover it with a large bowl or oily plastic wrap then leave it for 15 minutes.
- Dust Baking sheets with light flour, or cover them with parchment paper.
- Divide the dough into two parts using a serrated knife and shape each piece into a 3×14-inch oval.
- Place the loaves on prepared sheets and dust with flour.
- Cover the dough loaves and leave it to rise for about 45 minutes at a draft-free spot.
- Preheat oven to 425 F.
- Spritz loaves with water.
- In the oven, put loaves, placed on the middle rack.
- Bake, for approximately 25 to 35 mins, until its color is golden brown.
- Serve, and have fun.

PREPARATION	COOKING TIME	SERVINGS
15	30-35 *mints*	8

Zojirushi Bread Machine Light Sourdough Bread

NUTRITION Carbohydrates 3 g Fats 5.6 g Protein 9.6 g Calories 319

INGREDIENTS

- Sourdough starter:
- 1 1/2 cups of water
- 2 cups (256 grams) of bread flour
- 2 tsp. of active dry yeast
- Bread Ingredients:
- 3 tbsp. of apple cider vinegar
- 2 tbsp. of lemon juice
- 3 cups of bread flour
- 1 tsp. of fine sea salt
- 2 tsp. of active dry yeast

DIRECTION

- Put the kneading blades in the Zojirushi Home Bakery Supreme bread machine; Place the pan of bread into the machine.
- Add the bread flour and leaven in the bowl.
- Set a "sourdough starter" course and press Start. It will take around 2 hours to complete.
- The starting point is all bubbly.
- For the bread:
- Hit cancel to clear once the sourdough starter ends and beeps.
- Add in the specified ingredients, with yeast placed on top of the flour.
- Close the cover and set a "basic" sequence.
- When the bread is baked (just 4 hours), pop out and knock out onto a cooling rack.
- When cooled, the bread can be cut and frozen for long time storage.

PREPARATION	COOKING TIME	SERVINGS
5	25 mints	8

Softest Soft Bread with Air Pockets Using Bread Machine

NUTRITION Carbohydrates 3 g Fats 5.6 g Protein 9.6 g Calories 319

INGREDIENTS

- 1 cup of lukewarm (105 to 115 degrees F/40 to 45 degrees C)
- Four teaspoons of honey
- Two teaspoons of active dry yeast
- 2 cups of all-purpose flour
- Four teaspoons of olive oil
- 1/2 teaspoon of salt

DIRECTION

- Put warm water into the bread machine pan and sprinkle honey in warm water until honey is dissolved. Add yeast to the mixture and let it sit for about 10 minutes before yeast begins to foam. In the manufacturer's suggested order, add flour, olive oil, and salt to the bread pan.
- If the machine has that choice, select a soft setting; otherwise, set a standard-setting, and start the machine. Let the bread cool before slicing.

PREPARATION	COOKING	SERVINGS
15 MINTS	3 20 hour mints	8

Bread Machine Basic Bread - Easy as Can Be

NUTRITION Carbohydrates 3 g Fats 5.6 g Protein 9.6 g Calories 319

INGREDIENTS

- 1 cup (227 g) lukewarm water
- 1/3 cup (74 g) lukewarm milk
- Three tablespoons (43 g) butter
- 3 3/4 cups (447 g) Unbleached All-Purpose Flour
- Three tablespoons (35 g) of sugar
- 1 1/2 teaspoons salt
- 1 1/2 teaspoons of active dry yeast or instant yeast

DIRECTION

- Load all the ingredients into your machine according to the manufacturer's prescribed order.
- Program the simple white bread machine, and then press start.
- Remove the pan from the oven when a loaf is finished. Shake the pan gently after about 5 minutes to dislodge the loaf, then turn it onto a rack to cool down.
- Store well-wrapped, four days at the shelf, or freeze for up to 3 months.

PREPARATION	COOKING TIME	SERVINGS
5	2 20 mints	1 loaf

Bread Machine Olive Oil Bread

NUTRITION Carbohydrates 3 g Fats 5.6 g Protein 9.6 g Calories 319

INGREDIENTS

- 1 cup of hot water
- 2 cups of white sugar
- 1.25 ounce of bread machine yeast
- 1/4 cup of olive oil
- 2 1/2 cups of bread flour
- 1/2 cup of whole wheat flour
- 1/2 tbsp. of salt

DIRECTION

- Place the water, sugar, and leaven in the bread machine bowl. Let sit for 10 minutes — melt the yeast, and foam it.
- Apply the oil, flour, and salt to the pot. Do not combine.
- Set the bread machine to the configuration of white bread, and start the machine. (This takes about three hours to bake.)
- Gobble up!

PREPARATION	COOKING TIME	SERVINGS
15 MINTS	3 00 hour mints	8

Homemade White Bread Less Dense

NUTRITION Carbohydrates 3 g Fats 5.6 g Protein 9.6 g Calories 319

INGREDIENTS

- 1 cup and three tablespoons of water
- Two tablespoons of vegetable oil
- 1 1/2 teaspoons of salt
- Two teaspoons of sugar
- 3 cups of white bread flour
- Two teaspoons of active dry yeast

DIRECTION

- In the bread-pan, add water and oil. Stir in water, and add sugar. Add flour to a pan.
- Create a slight indentation on top of the flour and make sure that the ingredients do not contact the flour. To the indentation, apply the yeast.
- Keep leaven off the water.
- Put the pan in the bread machine and press to snap it down. Secure the cover.
- Choose the settings of 1.5 lb. loaf, basic bread, and medium crust (3 hrs. 15 minutes)
- When the bread is baked, remove the bread pan using oven mitts. Turning over the bread pan and shaking it to release the loaf. Let the loaf reach room temperature on a wire rack for about 30 minutes.

PREPARATION	COOKING TIME	SERVINGS
10	3 15 *mints*	8

Bread Machine Sandwich Bread

NUTRITION Carbohydrates 3 g Fats 5.6 g Protein 9.6 g Calories 319

INGREDIENTS

- 1 cup of heated water (45 degrees C)
- Two tablespoons of white sugar
- 2 1/4 teaspoon yeast
- 1/4 cup of olive oil
- 3 cups of bread flour
- 1 1/2 teaspoon salt

DIRECTION

- Put the water, sugar, and yeast altogether in the bread machine pan.
- Dissolve the yeast, then foam for 10 minutes.
- Add the yeast to sugar, flour, and salt.
- Select Basic configuration, and then press start. The entire cycle takes 3 hours to complete.

PREPARATION	COOKING	SERVINGS
5 MINTS	25 *mints*	8

Bread Machine Peasant Bread

NUTRITION Carbohydrates 3 g   Fats 5.6 g   Protein 9.6 g   Calories 319

INGREDIENTS

- Two tablespoons of yeast
- 2 cups of white bread flour
- 1 1/2 tablespoon of sugar
- One tablespoon of salt
- 7/8 cup of water
- Topping of olive oil poppy seeds, sesame seeds, or cornmeal

DIRECTION

- Mix yeast, flour, sugar, salt, and water in the bread machine in the manufacturer's suggested order.
- Pick a normal setting of the bread and the light crust.
- Upon completing the baking process, let the bread cool for 5 minutes and then remove it from the oven. Keep the bread on a cooling rack and brush lightly with olive oil on top of the loaf,
- And sprinkle with poppy seeds, sesame seeds, or cornmeal. Before slicing or storing, let cool completely.
- Place at room temperature in an enclosed container, or freeze.

PREPARATION	COOKING TIME	SERVINGS
20-25	25 *mints*	*1 loaf*

Bread Machine Country White Bread

NUTRITION Carbohydrates 3 g   Fats 5.6 g   Protein 9.6 g   Calories 319

INGREDIENTS

- 1 1/2 cups of water, lukewarm
- 2 1/2 cups of all-purpose flour
- 1 cup of bread flour
- 1/4 teaspoon of baking soda
- 2 1/2 teaspoons of a bread machine or instant yeast
- One tablespoon plus one teaspoon of olive oil
- 1 1/2 teaspoon of sugar
- One teaspoon of salt

DIRECTION

- In the sequence suggested by your bread machine company, add all the ingredients to your bread machine pan.
- Use the medium crust and the quick or moderate setting; press start.
- Turn the bread out to cool onto a shelf.
- Cut, and have fun!

PREPARATION	COOKING TIME	SERVINGS
10 MINTS	2 *hour* 00 *mints*	8 / 1 loaf

Best-Ever Wheat Sandwich Bread

NUTRITION Carbohydrates 3 g Fats 5.6 g   Protein 9.6 g Calories 319

INGREDIENTS

- 1-1/3 cups plus two tbsp. of light buttermilk
- Two tbsp. of dry milk
- Three tbsp. of local honey
- Two tbsp. of extra virgin olive oil
- 1-3/4 tbsp. of white whole wheat flour
- 2-1/4 cups of bread flour
- 2 tsp. of bread machine yeast

DIRECTION

- Put all the ingredients into the bread machine in the given sequence.
- When you use the delay timer and don't make the bread right away, putting the yeast in a little well in the flour is especially important because it doesn't come into contact with any of the liquid below.
- The process according to instructions from the manufacturer.

PREPARATION	COOKING TIME	SERVINGS
2 HOUR	1 hour	6

Chapter 8.
Spice and Herb Bread

Herb Bread

NUTRITION Calories: 65 Cal Fat: 0 g Carbohydrates:13 g Protein: 2 g

INGREDIENTS

- 3/4 to 7/8 cup milk
- 1 tablespoon Sugar
- 1 teaspoon Salt
- tablespoon Butter or margarine
- 1/3 cup chopped onion
- cups bread flour
- 1/2 teaspoon Dried dill
- 1/2 teaspoon Dried basil
- 1/2 teaspoon Dried rosemary
- 11/2 teaspoon Active dry yeast

DIRECTION

- Place all the Ingredients in the bread pan. Select medium crus then the rapid bake cycle. Press starts.
- After 5-10 minutes, observe the dough as it kneads, if you hear straining sounds in your machine or if the dough appears stiff and dry, add 1 tablespoon Liquid at a time until the dough becomes smooth, pliable, soft, and slightly tacky to the touch.
- Remove the bread from the pan after baking. Place on rack and allow to cool for 1 hour before slicing.

PREPARATION	COOKING TIME	SERVINGS
80	50 mints	1 loaf

Rosemary Bread

NUTRITION Calories: 142 Cal Fat: 3 g Carbohydrates:25 g Protein: 4 g Fiber: 1 g

INGREDIENTS

- ¾ cup + 1 tablespoon water at 80 degrees F
- 1⅔ tablespoons melted butter, cooled
- teaspoons sugar
- 1 teaspoon salt
- 1 tablespoon fresh rosemary, chopped
- cups white bread flour
- 1⅓ teaspoons instant yeast

DIRECTION

- Add all of the ingredients to your bread machine, carefully following the instructions of the manufacturer.
- Set the program of your bread machine to Basic/White Bread and set crust type to Medium.
- Press START.
- Wait until the cycle completes.
- Once the loaf is ready, take the bucket out and let the loaf cool for 5 minutes.
- Gently shake the bucket to remove the loaf.
- Transfer to a cooling rack, slice, and serve.

PREPARATION	COOKING TIME	SERVINGS
2 hour 10 mints	50 mins	1 loaf

Original Italian Herb Bread

NUTRITION Calories: 386 Cal Fat: 7 g Carbohydrates:71 g Protein: 10 g Fiber: 1 g

INGREDIENTS

- 1 cup water at 80 degrees F
- ½ cup olive brine
- 1½ tablespoons butter
- tablespoons sugar
- teaspoons salt
- 5⅓ cups flour
- teaspoons bread machine yeast
- 20 olives, black/green
- 1½ teaspoons Italian herbs

DIRECTION

- Cut olives into slices.
- Add all of the ingredients to your bread machine (except olives), carefully following the instructions of the manufacturer.
- Set the program of your bread machine to French bread and set crust type to Medium.
- Press START.
- Once the maker beeps, add olives.
- Wait until the cycle completes.
- Once the loaf is ready, take the bucket out and let the loaf cool for 5 minutes.
- Gently shake the bucket to remove the loaf.
- Transfer to a cooling rack, slice, and serve.

PREPARATION	COOKING TIME	SERVINGS
2 40	50 *mints*	2 loaves

Lovely Aromatic Lavender Bread

NUTRITION Calories: 144 Cal Fat: 2 g Carbohydrates:27 g Protein: 4 g Fiber: 1 g

INGREDIENTS

- ¾ cup milk at 80 degrees F
- 1 tablespoon melted butter, cooled
- 1 tablespoon sugar
- ¾ teaspoon salt
- 1 teaspoon fresh lavender flower, chopped
- ¼ teaspoon lemon zest
- ¼ teaspoon fresh thyme, chopped
- cups white bread flour
- ¾ teaspoon instant yeast

DIRECTION

- Add all of the ingredients to your bread machine
- Set the program of your bread machine to Basic/White Bread and set crust type to Medium.
- Press START.
- Wait until the cycle completes.
- Once the loaf is ready, take the bucket out and let the loaf cool for 5 minutes.
- Gently shake the bucket to remove the loaf.
- Transfer to a cooling rack, slice, and serve.

PREPARATION	COOKING	SERVINGS
2 10 *hour mints*	50 *mins*	1 loaf

Oregano Mozza-Cheese Bread

NUTRITION Calories: 209 Cal Fat: 2.1 g Carbohydrates:40 g Protein: 7.7 g Fiber: 1 g

INGREDIENTS

- 1 cup (milk + egg) mixture
- ½ cup mozzarella cheese
- 2¼ cups flour
- ¾ cup whole grain flour
- tablespoons sugar
- 1 teaspoon salt
- teaspoons oregano
- 1½ teaspoons dry yeast

DIRECTION

- Add all of the ingredients to your bread machine
- Set the program of your bread machine to Basic/White Bread and set crust type to Dark.
- Press START.
- Wait until the cycle completes.
- Once the loaf is ready, take the bucket out and let the loaf cool for 5 minutes.
- Gently shake the bucket to remove the loaf.
- Transfer to a cooling rack, slice, and serve.

PREPARATION	COOKING TIME	SERVINGS
2 10 *hour*	50	*2 loaves*

Garlic Bread

NUTRITION Calories: 175 calories; Total Carbohydrate: 29.7 g Cholesterol: 1 mg Total Fat: 3.7 g Protein: 5.2 g Sodium: 332 mg

INGREDIENTS

- 1 3/8 cups water
- tablespoons olive oil
- 1 teaspoon minced garlic
- cups bread flour
- tablespoons white sugar
- teaspoons salt
- 1/4 cup grated Parmesan cheese
- 1 teaspoon dried basil
- 1 teaspoon garlic powder
- tablespoons chopped fresh chives
- 1 teaspoon coarsely ground black pepper
- 1/2 teaspoons bread machine yeast

DIRECTION

- Follow the order of putting the ingredients into the pan of the bread machine recommended by the manufacturer.
- Choose the Basic or the White Bread cycle on the machine and press the Start button.

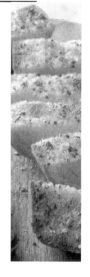

PREPARATION	COOKING TIME	SERVINGS
2 30 *hour*	40 *mints*	*I loaf*

Cumin Bread

NUTRITION Calories: 368 calories; Total Carbohydrate: 67.1 g Cholesterol: 0 mg Total Fat: 6.5 g Protein: 9.5 g

INGREDIENTS

- 1/3 cups bread machine flour, sifted
- 1½ teaspoon kosher salt
- 1½ Tablespoon sugar
- 1 Tablespoon bread machine yeast
- 1¾ cups lukewarm water
- Tablespoon black cumin
- Tablespoon sunflower oil

DIRECTION

- Place all the dry and liquid ingredients in the pan and follow the instructions for your bread machine.
- Set the baking program to BASIC and the crust type to MEDIUM.
- If the dough is too dense or too wet, adjust the amount of flour and liquid in the recipe.
- When the program has ended, take the pan out of the bread machine and let cool for 5 minutes.
- Shake the loaf out of the pan. If necessary, use a spatula.
- Wrap the bread with a kitchen towel and set it aside for an hour. Otherwise, you can cool it on a wire rack.

PREPARATION	COOKING TIME	SERVINGS
3 30	15 mints	8

Saffron Tomato Bread

NUTRITION

INGREDIENTS

- 1 teaspoon bread machine yeast
- 2½ cups wheat bread machine flour
- 1 Tablespoon panifarin
- 1½ teaspoon kosher salt
- 1½ Tablespoon white sugar
- Tablespoon extra-virgin olive oil
- Tablespoon tomatoes, dried and chopped
- 1 Tablespoon tomato paste
- ½ cup firm cheese (cubes)
- ½ cup feta cheese
- 1 pinch saffron
- 1½ cups serum

DIRECTION

- Five minutes before cooking, pour in dried tomatoes and 1 tablespoon of olive oil. Add the tomato paste and mix.
- Place all the dry and liquid ingredients, except additives, in the pan and follow the instructions for your bread machine.
- Pay particular attention to measuring the ingredients. Use a measuring cup, measuring spoon, and kitchen scales to do so.
- Set the baking program to BASIC and the crust type to MEDIUM.
- Add the additives after the beep or place them in the dispenser of the bread machine.
- Shake the loaf out of the pan. If necessary, use a spatula.
- Wrap the bread with a kitchen towel and set it aside for an hour. Otherwise, you can cool it on a wire rack.

PREPARATION	COOKING	SERVINGS
3 30	15 mints	10

Cracked Black Pepper Bread

NUTRITION Calories: 141 calories; Total Carbohydrate: 27 g Total Fat: 2g Protein: 4 g Sodium: 215 mg Fiber:

INGREDIENTS

- ¾ cup water, at 80°F to 90°F
- 1 tablespoon melted butter, cooled
- 1 tablespoon sugar
- ¾ teaspoon salt
- tablespoons skim milk powder
- 1 tablespoon minced chives
- ½ teaspoon garlic powder
- ½ teaspoon cracked black pepper
- cups white bread flour
- ¾ teaspoon bread machine or instant yeast

DIRECTION

- Place the ingredients in your bread machine as recommended by the manufacturer.
- Program the machine for Basic/ White bread, select light or medium crust, and press Start.
- When the loaf is done, remove the bucket from the machine.
- Let the loaf cool for 5 minutes.
- Gently shake the bucket to remove the loaf, and turn it out onto a rack to cool.

PREPARATION	COOKING TIME	SERVINGS
3 30	15 mints	8

Spicy Cajun Bread

NUTRITION Calories: 141 calories; Total Carbohydrate: 27 g Total Fat: 2g Protein: 4 g Sodium: 215

INGREDIENTS

- ¾ cup water, at 80°F to 90°F
- 1 tablespoon melted butter, cooled
- teaspoons tomato paste
- 1 tablespoon sugar
- 1 teaspoon salt
- tablespoons skim milk powder
- ½ tablespoon Cajun seasoning
- ⅛ teaspoon onion powder
- cups white bread flour
- 1 teaspoon bread machine or instant yeast

DIRECTION

- Place the ingredients in your bread machine as recommended by the manufacturer.
- Program the machine for Basic/ White bread, select light or medium crust, and press Start.
- When the loaf is done, remove the bucket from the machine.
- Let the loaf cool for 5 minutes.
- Gently shake the bucket to remove the loaf, and turn it out onto a rack to cool.

PREPARATION	COOKING TIME	SERVINGS
2 HOURS	15 mints	8

Anise Lemon Bread

NUTRITION Calories: 158 calories; Total Carbohydrate: 27 g Total Fat: 5g Protein: 4 g Sodium: 131

INGREDIENTS

- ⅔ Cup water, at 80°F to 90°F
- 1 egg, at room temperature
- 2⅔ tablespoons butter, melted and cooled
- 2⅔ tablespoons honey
- ¼ Teaspoon salt
- ⅔ Teaspoon anise seed
- ⅔ Teaspoon lemon zest
- cups white bread flour
- 1½ teaspoons bread machine or instant yeast

DIRECTION

- Place the ingredients in your bread machine as recommended by the manufacturer.
- Program the machine for Basic/White bread, select light or medium crust, and press Start.
- When the loaf is done, remove the bucket from the machine.
- Let the loaf cool for 5 minutes.
- Gently shake the bucket to remove the loaf, and turn it out onto a rack to cool.

PREPARATION	COOKING TIME	SERVINGS
2 HOURS	15 mins	8

Cardamon Bread

NUTRITION Calories: 149 calories; Total Carbohydrate: 29 g Total Fat: 2g Protein: 5 g Sodium: 211

INGREDIENTS

- ½ cup milk, at 80°F to 90°F
- 1 egg, at room temperature
- 1 teaspoon melted butter, cooled
- teaspoons honey
- ⅔ Teaspoon salt
- ⅔ Teaspoon ground cardamom
- cups white bread flour
- ¾ teaspoon bread machine or instant yeast

DIRECTION

- Place the ingredients in your bread machine as recommended by the manufacturer.
- Program the machine for Basic/White bread, select light or medium crust, and press Start.
- When the loaf is done, remove the bucket from the machine.
- Let the loaf cool for 5 minutes.
- Gently shake the bucket to remove the loaf, and turn it out onto a rack to cool.

PREPARATION	COOKING	SERVINGS
2 HOURS	15 mins	8

Chapter 9.

Garlic and Herb Flatbread Sourdough

NUTRITION Calories: 89 Cal Fat: 3.7 g Protein: 1.8 g

INGREDIENTS

- Dough
- 1 cup sourdough starter, fed or unfed
- 3/4 cup warm water
- teaspoons instant yeast
- cups all-purpose flour
- 1 1/2 teaspoons salt
- tablespoons olive oil
- Topping
- 1/2 teaspoon dried thyme
- 1/2 teaspoon dried oregano
- 1/2 teaspoon dried marjoram
- 1 teaspoon garlic powder
- 1/4 teaspoon onion powder
- 1/4 teaspoon salt
- 1/4 teaspoon pepper
- 3 tablespoons olive oil

DIRECTION

- Combine all the dough ingredients in the bowl of a stand mixer, and knead until smooth. Place in a lightly greased bowl and let rise for at least one hour. Punch down, then let rise again for at least one hour.
- To prepare the topping, mix all ingredients except the olive oil in a small bowl.
- Lightly grease a 9x13 baking pan or standard baking sheet, and pat and roll the dough into a long rectangle in the pan. Brush the olive oil over the dough, and sprinkle the herb and seasoning mixture over top. Cover and let rise for 15-20 minutes.
- Preheat oven to 425F and bake for 25-30 minutes.

PREPARATION	COOKING TIME	SERVINGS
1 HOURS	25-30 mints	12

Dinner Rolls

NUTRITION Calories: 128 Cal Fat: 2.4 g Protein: 3.2 g Sugar: 1.1 g

INGREDIENTS

- 1 cup sourdough starter
- 1 1/2 cups warm water
- 1 tablespoon yeast
- 1 tablespoon salt
- tablespoons sugar
- 2 tablespoons olive oil
- cups all-purpose flour
- 2 tablespoons butter, melted

DIRECTION

- In a large bowl, mix the sourdough starter, water, yeast, salt, sugar, and oil. Add the flour, stirring until the mixture forms a dough. If needed, add more flour. Place the dough in a greased bowl, and let it rise until doubled in size, about 2 hours.
- Remove the dough from the bowl, and divide it into 2-3 inch sized pieces. Place the buns into a greased 9x13 pan, and let them rise, covered, for about an hour.
- Preheat oven to 350F, and bake the rolls for 15 minutes. Remove from the oven, brush with the melted butter, and bake for an additional 5-10 minutes.

PREPARATION	COOKING TIME	SERVINGS
3 HOURS	25-30 mints	24 rolls

Sourdough Boule

NUTRITION Calories: 243 Cal Fat: 0.7 g Protein: 6.9 g

INGREDIENTS

- 275g Warm Water
- 500g sourdough starter
- 550g all-purpose flour
- 20g Salt

DIRECTION

- Combine the flour, warm water, and starter, and let sit, covered for at least 30 minutes.
- After letting it sit, stir in the salt, and turn the dough out onto a floured surface. It will be quite sticky, but that's okay. Flatten the dough slightly (it's best to "slap" it onto the counter), then fold it in half a few times.
- Cover the dough and let it rise. Repeat the slap and fold a few more times. Now cover the dough and let it rise for 2-4 hours.
- When the dough at least doubles in size, gently pull it so the top of the dough is taught. Repeat several times. Let it rise for 2-4 hours once more.
- Preheat to oven to 475F, and either place a baking stone or a cast iron pan in the oven to preheat. Place the risen dough on the stone or pot, and score the top in several spots. Bake for 20 minutes, then lower the heat to 425F, and bake for 25-35 minutes more. The boule will be golden brown.

PREPARATION	COOKING	SERVINGS
4 HOURS	25-30 mins	12

Herbed Baguette

NUTRITION Calories: 197 Cal Fat: 0.6 g Protein: 5.8 g

INGREDIENTS

- 1 1/4 cups warm water
- cups sourdough starter, either fed or unfed
- to 5 cups all-purpose flour
- 2 1/2 teaspoons salt
- 2 teaspoons sugar
- 1 tablespoon instant yeast
- 1 tablespoon fresh oregano, chopped
- 1 teaspoon fresh rosemary, chopped
- 1 tablespoon fresh basil, chopped
- Any other desired herbs

DIRECTION

- In the bowl of a stand mixer, combine all ingredients, knead with a dough hook (or use your hands) until smooth dough forms -- about 7 to 10 minutes, if needed, add more flour.
- Place the dough in an oiled bowl, cover, and allow to rise for about 2 hours.
- Punch down the dough, and divide it into 3 pieces. Shape each piece of dough into a baguette -- about 16 inches long. You can do this by rolling the dough into a log, folding it, rolling it into a log, then folding it and rolling it again.
- Place the rolled baguette dough onto lined baking sheets, and cover. Let rise for one hour.
- Preheat oven to 425F, and bake for 20-25 minutes

PREPARATION	COOKING TIME	SERVINGS
45 MINTS	25-30 *mints*	*12*

Pumpernickel Bread

NUTRITION Calories: 97 Cal Fat: 1 g Carbohydrates: 19 g Protein: 3 g

INGREDIENTS

- 1 1/8 cups warm water
- 1 ½ tablespoons vegetable oil
- 1/3 cup molasses
- tablespoons cocoa
- 1 tablespoon caraway seed (optional)
- 1 ½ teaspoon salt
- 1 ½ cups of bread flour
- 1 cup of rye flour
- 1 cup whole wheat flour
- 1 ½ tablespoons of vital wheat gluten (optional)
- 2 ½ teaspoon of bread machine yeast

DIRECTION

- ADD ALL INGREDIENTS TO BREAD MACHINE PAN.
- CHOOSE BASIC BREAD CYCLE.
- TAKE BREAD OUT TO COOL AND ENJOY!

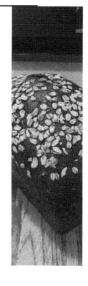

PREPARATION	COOKING TIME	SERVINGS
2 HOURS 10 MINTS	50 MINTS	*1 loaf*

Sauerkraut Rye

NUTRITION *Calories: 74 Cal Fat: 2 g Carbohydrates:12 g Protein: 2 g Fiber: 1 g*

INGREDIENTS

- 1 cup sauerkraut, rinsed and drained
- ¾ cup warm water
- 1½ tablespoons molasses
- 1½ tablespoons butter
- 1½ tablespoons brown sugar
- 1 teaspoon caraway seeds
- 1½ teaspoons salt
- 1 cup rye flour
- cups bread flour
- 1½ teaspoons active dry yeast

DIRECTION

- Add all of the ingredients to your bread machine.
- Set the program of your bread machine to Basic/White Bread and set crust type to Medium
- Press START
- Wait until the cycle completes
- Once the loaf is ready, take the bucket out and let the loaf cool for 5 minutes
- Gently shake the bucket to remove the loaf
- Transfer to a cooling rack, slice and serve

PREPARATION	COOKING TIME	SERVINGS
2 HOUR 20 MINTS	50 *mins*	*1 loaf*

Crusty Sourdough Bread

NUTRITION *Calories: 165 calories; Total Carbohydrate: 37 g Total Fat: 0 g Protein: 5 g Sodium: 300 mg Fiber:*

INGREDIENTS

- 1/2 cup water
- cups bread flour
- tablespoons sugar
- 1 ½ teaspoon salt
- 1 teaspoon bread machine or quick active dry yeast

DIRECTION

- Measure 1 cup of starter and remaining bread ingredients, add to bread machine pan.
- Choose basic/white bread cycle with medium or light crust color.

PREPARATION	COOKING	SERVINGS
15 MINTS	3 00 *hour mints*	*1 loaf*

Honey Sourdough Bread

NUTRITION Calories: 175 calories; Total Carbohydrate: 33 g Total Fat: 0.3 g Protein: 5.6 g Sodium: 121 mg Fiber: 1.9 g

INGREDIENTS

- 2/3 cup sourdough starter
- 1/2 cup water
- 1 tablespoon vegetable oil
- tablespoons honey
- 1/2 teaspoon salt
- 1/2 cup high protein wheat flour
- cups bread flour
- 1 teaspoon active dry yeast

DIRECTION

- Measure 1 cup of starter and remaining bread ingredients, add to bread machine pan.
- Choose basic/white bread cycle with medium or light crust color.

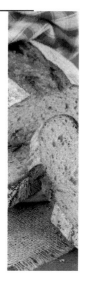

PREPARATION	COOKING TIME	SERVINGS
15 MINTS	3 HOURS	1 loaf

Olive and Garlic Sourdough Bread

NUTRITION Calories: 150 calories; Total Carbohydrate: 26.5 g Total Fat: 0.5 g Protein: 3.4 g Sodium: 267 mg Fiber: 1.1 g

INGREDIENTS

- cups sourdough starter
- cups flour
- tablespoons olive oil
- tablespoons sugar
- 2 teaspoon salt
- 1⁄2 cup chopped black olives
- cloves chopped garlic

DIRECTION

- Add starter and bread ingredients to bread machine pan.
- Choose dough cycle.
- Conventional Oven:
- Preheat oven to 350 degrees.
- When cycle is complete, if dough is sticky add more flour.
- Shape dough onto baking sheet or put into loaf pan
- Bake for 35- 45 minutes until golden.
- Cool before slicing.

PREPARATION	COOKING TIME		SERVINGS
15 MINTS	3	00	1 loaf
	hour	mints	

Chapter 10.
Sweet Bread

Brownie Bread

NUTRITION *Calories: 70 Cal Fat: 3 g Carbohydrates:10 g Protein   : 1 g*

INGREDIENTS

- 1 egg
- 1 egg yolk
- 1 teaspoon Salt
- 1/2 cup boiling water
- 1/2 cup cocoa powder, un-sweetened
- 1/2 cup warm water
- 1/2 teaspoon Active dry yeast
- tablespoon Vegetable oil
- teaspoon White sugar
- 2/3 cup white sugar
- cups bread flour

DIRECTION

- Put the cocoa powder in a small bow. Pour boiling water and dissolve the cocoa powder.
- Put the warm water, yeast and the 2 teaspoon White sugar in another bowl. Dissolve yeast and sugar. Let stand for about 10 minutes, or until the mix is creamy.
- Place the cocoa mix, the yeast mix, the flour, the 2/3 cup white sugar, the salt, the vegetable, and the egg in the bread pan. Select basic bread cycle. Press start.

PREPARATION	COOKING	SERVINGS
1 HOUR 15 MINTS	50 MINTS	1 loaf

Black Forest Bread

NUTRITION Calories: 240 Cal Fat : 4 g Carbohydrates: 29 g Protein : 22 g

PREPARATION
2 HOUR 15 MINTS

COOKING TIME
50 MINTS

SERVINGS
1 loaf

INGREDIENTS

- 1 1/8 cups Warm water
- 1/3 cup Molasses
- 1 1/2 tablespoons Canola oil
- 1 1/2 cups Bread flour
- 1 cup Rye flour
- 1 cup Whole wheat flour
- 1 1/2 teaspoons Salt
- tablespoons Cocoa powder
- 1 1/2 tablespoons Caraway seeds
- teaspoons Active dry yeast

DIRECTION

- Place all ingredients into your bread maker according to manufacture.
- Select type to a light crust.
- Press start.
- Remembering to check while starting to knead.
- If mixture is too dry add tablespoon warm water at a time.
- If mixture is too wet add flour again a little at a time.
- Mixture should go into a ball form, and just soft and slightly sticky to the finger touch. This goes for all types of bread when kneading.

Sweet Almond Anise Bread

NUTRITION Calories: 87 Cal Fat: 4 g Carbohydrates: 7 g Protein : 3 g Fiber: 1 g

PREPARATION
2 hour 20 mints

COOKING TIME
50 mints

SERVINGS
1 loaf

DIRECTION

- Add all of the ingredients to your bread machine, carefully following the instructions of the manufacturer
- Set the program of your bread machine to Basic/White Bread and set crust type to Medium
- Press START
- Wait until the cycle completes
- Once the loaf is ready, take the bucket out and let the loaf cool for 5 minutes
- Gently shake the bucket to remove the loaf
- Transfer to a cooling rack, slice and serve
- Enjoy!

INGREDIENTS

- 3/4 cup water
- 1/4 cup butter
- 1/4 cup sugar
- 1/2 teaspoon salt
- cups bread flour
- 1 teaspoon anise seed
- teaspoons active dry yeast
- 1/2 cup almonds, chopped

Chocolate Ginger and Hazelnut Bread

NUTRITION *Calories: 273 calories; Total Carbohydrate: 43 g Total Fat: 11 g Protein: 7 g*

PREPARATION
2 HOURS   50 MINTS

COOKING TIME
45
mints

SERVINGS
2 loaves

DIRECTION

- Put all the ingredients, except the hazelnuts, in the pan in this order: water, butter, coconut, candied ginger, brown sugar, milk, salt, flour, and yeast.
- Secure the pan in the machine and close the lid. Put the toasted hazelnuts in the fruit and nut dispenser.
- Turn the machine on. Select the basic setting and your desired color of the crust and press start.
- Once done, carefully transfer the baked bread to a wire rack until cooled.

INGREDIENTS

- 1/2 cup chopped hazelnuts
- teaspoon bread machine yeast
- 1/2 cups bread flour
- 1 teaspoon salt
- 1 1/2 tablespoon dry skim milk powder
- tablespoon light brown sugar
- tablespoon candied ginger, chopped
- 1/3 cup unsweetened coconut
- 1 1/2 tablespoon unsalted butter, cubed
- 1 cup, plus 2 tablespoon water, with a temperature of 80 to 90 degrees F (26 to 32 degrees C)

White Chocolate Bread

NUTRITION *Calories: 277 calories; Total Carbohydrate: 39 g Cholesterol: 30 mg Total Fat: 10.5 g Protein: 6.6 g Sodium: 253 mg*

PREPARATION
3 HOURS

COOKING TIME
15
mints

SERVINGS
16 slices

DIRECTION

- Put all the ingredients together, except for the white chocolate chips, into the bread machine pan following the order suggested by the manufacturer. Choose the cycle on the machine and press the Start button to run the machine. Put in the white chocolate chips at the machine's signal if the machine used has a Fruit setting on it or you may put the white chocolate chips about 5 minutes before the kneading cycle ends.

INGREDIENTS

- 1/4 cup warm water
- 1 cup warm milk
- 1 egg
- 1/4 cup butter, softened
- cups bread flour
- tablespoons brown sugar
- tablespoons white sugar
- 1 teaspoon salt
- 1 teaspoon ground cinnamon
- 1 (.25 oz.) package active dry yeast
- 1 cup white chocolate chips

Cinnamon Raisin Bread

NUTRITION Calories: 141 calories;, Total Carbohydrate: 26 g, Cholesterol: 00 mg, Total Fat: 2 g, Protein: 3.5 g ,Sodium: 329 mg, Fiber: 1 g

PREPARATION	COOKING TIME	SERVINGS
5 MINT	3 HOUR	*1 loaf*

DIRECTION

- Add all the ingredients into pan except raisins.
- Choose sweet bread setting.
- When the machine beeps, add in raisins.

INGREDIENTS

- 1 cup water
- tablespoons margarine
- cups flour
- tablespoons sugar
- 1 1/2 teaspoons salt
- 1 teaspoon cinnamon
- 1/2 teaspoons yeast
- 3/4 cup raisins

Chocolate Chip Bread

NUTRITION Calories: 184 calories;, Total Carbohydrate: 30.6 g, Cholesterol: 14 mg, Total Fat: 5.2 g, Protein: 3.5 g, Sodium: 189 mg, Fiber: 1.3 g

PREPARATION	COOKING TIME	SERVINGS
10 MINTS	2 hour 50 mints	*1 loaf*

DIRECTION

- Add all the ingredients into pan except chocolate chips.
- Choose mix bread
- When the machine beeps, add in chips

INGREDIENTS

- 1/4 cup water
- 1 cup milk
- 1 egg
- cups bread flour
- tablespoons brown sugar
- tablespoons white sugar
- 1 teaspoon salt
- 1 teaspoon ground cinnamon
- 1 1/2 teaspoon active dry yeast
- tablespoons margarine, softened
- 3/4 cup semisweet chocolate chips

Peanut Butter Bread

NUTRITION *Calories: 82 calories;, Total Carbohydrate: 13 g, Cholesterol: 13 mg ,Total Fat: 2.2 g,Protein: 2.5 g,Sodium: 280 mg, Fiber: 1 g*

PREPARATION
10 MINTS

COOKING TIME
3
hour

SERVINGS
1 loaf

INGREDIENTS

- 1 1/4 Cups water
- 1/2 cup Peanut butter - creamy or chunky
- 1 ½ cups whole wheat flour
- tablespoons Gluten flour
- 1 ½ cups bread flour
- 1/4 cup Brown sugar
- 1/2 teaspoon Salt -
- ¼ teaspoons Active dry yeast

DIRECTION

- Add all the ingredients into pan.
- Choose whole wheat bread setting, large loaf.

Hot Buttered Rum Bread

NUTRITION *Calories: 170 calories;, Total Carbohydrate: 31 g, Cholesterol: 25 mg, Total Fat: 2.0 g, Protein: 4 g, Sodium: 270 mg, Fiber: 1 g*

PREPARATION
10 MINTS

COOKING TIME
3
hour
40
mints

SERVINGS
1 loaf

DIRECTION

- Break egg into 1 cup, and add water to fil out measuring cup
- Place egg mixture and bread ingredients into pan.
- Choose basic bread setting and medium/light crust color.
- While bread bakes, combine topping ingredients in small bowl, and brush on top of bread when there is 40 – 50 minutes remaining of the cook time.

INGREDIENTS

- 1 egg
- 1 tablespoon rum extract
- tablespoons butter, softened
- cups bread flour
- tablespoons packed brown sugar
- 1 ¼ teaspoon salt
- 1/2 teaspoon ground cinnamon
- 1/4 teaspoon ground nutmeg
- 1/4 teaspoon ground cardamom
- 1 teaspoon bread machine or quick active dry yeast
- Topping:
- 1 egg yolk, beaten
- 1 ½ teaspoon finely chopped pecans
- 1 ½ teaspoon packed brown sugar

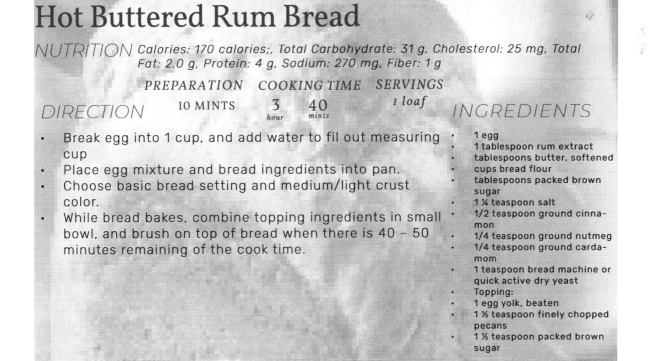

Buttery Sweet Bread

NUTRITION Calories: 130 calories;, Total Carbohydrate: 17 g, Total Fat: 5 g, Protein: 3 g

PREPARATION	COOKING TIME		SERVINGS
10 MINT	3 Hour	40 mins	1 Loaf

DIRECTION

- 1 Put ingredients into bread machine pan.

INGREDIENTS

- 1-Pound Loaf
- 1/3 Cup Milk
- 1/4 Cup Water
- 1 Large Egg
- Tablespoons Butter Or Margarine, Cut Up
- 3/4 Teaspoon Salt
- 2-1/4 Cups Bread Flour
- Tablespoons Sugar
- 1-1/2 Teaspoons Fleischmann's Bread Machine Yeast
- 1-1/2-Pound Loaf
- 1/2 Cup Milk
- 1/3 Cup Water
- 1 Large Egg
- 1/4 Cup Butter Or Margarine, Cut Up
- 1 Teaspoon Salt
- 3-1/3 Cups Bread Flour
- 1/4 Cup Sugar
- Teaspoons Fleischmann's Bread

Sweet Pineapples Bread

NUTRITION Calories: 144 calories;, Total Carbohydrate: 18 g, Total Fat: 9 g, Protein: 6 g

PREPARATION	COOKING TIME	SERVINGS
2 HOUR	40 mins	5

DIRECTION

- Place the raisins into the warm water and leave for 20 minutes.
- In a bowl, combine the sifted wheat flour, baking powder, brown sugar and vanilla.
- Add the raisins and pineapples and mix well.
- Whisk the eggs with the sugar until they have a smooth and creamy consistency.
- Combine the eggs mixture with the flour and dried fruits mixture.
- Pour the dough into the bread machine, close the lid and turn the bread machine on the basic/white bread program.
- Bake the bread until the medium crust and after the bread is ready take it out and leave for 1 hour covered with the towel and only then you can slice the bread.

INGREDIENTS

- oz. dried pineapples
- oz. raisins
- oz. wheat flour
- eggs
- teaspoon baking powder
- oz. brown sugar
- oz. sugar
- Vanilla

Almond and Chocolate Chip Bread

NUTRITION Calories: 130 calories;, Total Carbohydrate: 18 g, Total Fat: 7 g, Protein: 1 g, Protein: 3 g

PREPARATION	COOKING TIME	SERVINGS
15 MINT	3 Hour 40 mins	1 loaf

INGREDIENTS

- 1 cup plus 2 tablespoons water
- tablespoons butter or margarine, softened
- ½ teaspoon vanilla
- cups Gold Medal™ Better for Bread™ flour
- ¾ cup semisweet choc-olate chips
- tablespoons sugar
- 1 tablespoon dry milk
- ¾ teaspoon salt
- 1 ½ teaspoons bread machine or quick active dry yeast
- 1/3 cup sliced almonds

DIRECTION

- Measure and put all ingredients except almonds in bread machine pan. Add almonds at the Nut signal or 5 - 10 minutes before kneading cycle ends.
- Select White cycle. Use Light crust color.
- Take out baked bread from pan.

Sweet Coconut Bread

NUTRITION Calories: 164 calories;, Total Carbohydrate: 12 g, Total Fat: 8 g, Protein: 7 g

PREPARATION	COOKING TIME	SERVINGS
2 HOUR	40 mins	6

DIRECTION

- Whisk the eggs until they have a smooth and creamy consistency.
- Combine the coconut butter with the brown sugar and vanilla and mix well, adding the eggs.
- Combine the sifted wheat flour with the baking powder and eggs mixture and mix well until they have a smooth consistency.
- Combine the dough with the shredded coconut and wal-nuts and then mix well.
- Pour the dough into the bread machine, close the lid and turn the bread machine on the basic/white bread program.
- Bake the bread until the medium crust and after the bread is ready take it out and leave for 1 hour covered with the towel and only then you can slice the bread.

INGREDIENTS

- oz. shredded coconut
- oz. walnuts, ground
- oz. wheat flour
- oz. coconut butter
- eggs
- teaspoon baking pow-der
- oz. brown sugar
- Vanilla

Sweet Lemon Bread

NUTRITION Calories: 69 calories;, Total Carbohydrate: 6 g, Total Fat: 4 g, Protein: 3 g

PREPARATION	COOKING TIME	SERVINGS
3 HOUR	40 *mins*	6

DIRECTION

- Add the yeast and sugar into the warm water and melt them mixing in a bowl until smooth consistency.
- After 20 minutes combine the yeast mixture with the olive oil and sifted wheat flour.
- Combine the lemon zest with the dough, using a dough mixer, spiral mixer or food processor.
- Spoon the dough into the bread machine and lubricate the surface of the dough with the water or the egg yolk.
- Now close the lid and turn the bread machine on the basic/white bread program.
- After the bread is ready take it out and leave for 1 hour covered with the towel and then you can eat the bread.

INGREDIENTS

- oz. lemon zest, minced
- oz. of warm water (110-120 °F)
- 25 oz. wheat flour
- teaspoon instant yeast
- tablespoon olive oil
- oz. sugar

Chocolate Sour Cream Bread

NUTRITION Calories: 347, Total Fat: 16g, Saturated Fat: 9g, Carbohydrates: 48g, Fiber: 2g, Sodium: 249mg,, Protein: 6g

PREPARATION	COOKING TIME	SERVINGS
25 MINT	10 *mins*	12 slices

DIRECTION

- In a small bowl, stick together the sour cream, eggs, sugar, butter, and yogurt until just combined.
- Transfer the wet ingredients to the bread machine bucket, and then add the flour, cocoa powder, baking powder, salt, and chocolate chips.
- Program the machine for Quick/Rapid bread, and press Start.
- When the loaf is done, stick a knife into it, and if it comes out clean, the loaf is done.
- If the loaf needs a few more minutes, check the control panel for a Bake Only button and extend the time by 10 minutes.
- When the loaf is done, remove the bucket from the machine.
- Let the loaf cool for 5 minutes.
- Gently rock the can to remove the loaf and place it out onto a rack to cool.

INGREDIENTS

- 1 cup sour cream
- Two eggs, at room temperature
- 1 cup of sugar
- 1/2 cup (1 stick) butter, at room temperature
- 1/4 cup plain Greek yogurt
- 13/4 cups all-purpose flour
- 1/2 cup unsweetened cocoa powder
- 1/2 teaspoon baking powder
- 1/2 teaspoon salt
- 1 cup milk chocolate chips

Chocolate Chip Peanut Butter Banana Bread

NUTRITION Calories: 297, Total Fat: 14g, Saturated Fat: 7g, Carbohydrates: 40g, Fiber: 1g, Sodium: 255mg, Protein: 4g

PREPARATION
25 MINT

COOKING TIME
10
mins

SERVINGS
12 to16 slices

DIRECTION

- Stir together the bananas, eggs, butter, milk, and vanilla in the bread machine bucket and set it aside.
- In a medium bowl, toss together the flour, sugar, baking powder, baking soda, salt, peanut butter chips, and chocolate chips.
- Add the dry ingredients to the bucket.
- Program the machine for Quick/Rapid bread, and press Start.
- When the cake is made, stick a knife into it, and if it arises out clean, the loaf is done.
- If the loaf needs a few more minutes, look at the management panel for a Bake Only button, and extend the time by 10 minutes.
- When the loaf is done, remove the bucket from the machine.
- Let the loaf cool for 5 minutes.
- Gently rock the can to remove the bread and turn it out onto a rack to cool.

INGREDIENTS

- Two bananas, mashed
- Two eggs, at room temperature
- 1/2 cup melted butter, cooled
- Two tablespoons milk, at room temperature
- One teaspoon pure vanilla extract
- cups all-purpose flour
- 1/2 cup sugar
- 11/4 teaspoons baking powder
- 1/2 teaspoon baking soda
- 1/2 teaspoon salt
- 1/2 cup peanut butter chips
- 1/2 cup semisweet chocolate chips

Nectarine Cobbler Bread

NUTRITION Calories: 218, Total Fat: 9g, Saturated Fat: 5g, Carbohydrates: 32g, Fiber: 1g, Sodium: 270mg, Protein: 3g

PREPARATION
10 MINT

COOKING TIME
5
mins

SERVINGS
12 to16 slices

DIRECTION

- Place the butter, eggs, sugar, milk, vanilla, and nectarines in your bread machine.
- Program the machine for Quick/Rapid bread and press Start.
- While the wet ingredients are mixing, stir together the flour, baking soda, salt, nutmeg, and baking powder in a small bowl.
- After the first fast mixing is done and the machine signals, add the dry ingredients.
- When the loaf is done, remove the bucket from the machine.
- Let the loaf cool for 5 minutes.
- Gently shake the bucket to remove the loaf, then turn it out onto a rack to cool.

INGREDIENTS

- 1/2 cup (1 stick) butter, at room temperature
- Two eggs, at room temperature
- 1 cup of sugar
- 1/4 cup milk, at room temperature
- One teaspoon pure vanilla extract
- 1 cup diced nectarines
- 1 3/4 cups all-purpose flour
- One teaspoon baking soda
- 1/2 teaspoon salt
- 1/2 teaspoon ground nutmeg
- 1/4 teaspoon baking

Sour Cream Maple Bread

NUTRITION Calories: 149, Total Fat: 4g, Saturated Fat: 3g, Carbohydrates: 24g, Fiber: 1g, Sodium: 168mg, Protein: 4g

PREPARATION 5 MINT

COOKING TIME 10 mins

SERVINGS 8 slices

INGREDIENTS

- Six tablespoons water, at 80°F to 90°F
- Six tablespoons sour cream, at room temperature
- 1 1/2 tablespoons butter, at room temperature
- ¾ tablespoon maple syrup
- ½ teaspoon salt
- 1 3/4 cups white bread flour
- 1 1/6 teaspoons bread machine yeast

DIRECTION

- Place the ingredients in your bread machine as recommended by the manufacturer.
- Program the machine for Basic/White bread
- Select light or medium crust, and then press Start.
- When the loaf is done, remove the bucket from the machine.
- Let the loaf cool for 5 minutes.
- Gently shake the pan to get the loaf and turn it out onto a rack to cool.

Apple Butter Bread

NUTRITION Calories: 178, Total Fat: 3g, Saturated Fat: 2g, Carbohydrates: 34g, Fiber: 1g, Sodium: 220mg, Protein: 4g

PREPARATION 5 MINT

COOKING TIME 25 mins

SERVINGS 8 slices

DIRECTION

- Place the ingredients in your bread machine as recommended by the manufacturer.
- Program the system for Basic, choose light or medium crust, and press Start.
- When the loaf is done, remove the bucket from the machine.
- Let the loaf cool for 5 minutes.
- Gently shake the bucket to remove the loaf and put it out onto a rack to cool.
- Ingredient tip: Apple butter is simple to make in a slow cooker with very little fuss or mess. Making your own ensures you know what ingredients go into this tasty spread.

INGREDIENTS

- 2/3 cup milk
- 1/3 cup apple butter, at room temperature
- Four teaspoons melted butter, cooled
- Two teaspoons honey
- 2/3 teaspoon salt
- 2/3 cup whole-wheat flour
- 1 1/2 cups white bread flour
- One teaspoon instant yeast

Barmbrack Bread

NUTRITION Calories: 175, Total Fat: 2g, Saturated Fat: 1g, Carbohydrates: 35g, Fiber: 1g, Sodium: 313mg. Protein: 5g

PREPARATION
10 MINT

COOKING TIME
25
mins

SERVINGS
8 slices

INGREDIENTS

- 2/3 cup water
- One tablespoon melted butter cooled
- Two tablespoons sugar
- Two tablespoons skim milk powder
- One teaspoon salt
- One teaspoon dried lemon zest
- 1/4 teaspoon ground allspice
- 1/8 teaspoon ground nutmeg
- cups of white bread flour
- 1 1/2 teaspoons bread machine or active dry yeast
- 1/2 cup dried currants

DIRECTION

- Place the ingredients, except the currants, in your bread machine as recommended by the manufacturer.
- Program the system for Basic, select light or medium crust, and press Start.
- Add the currants when your machine signals or when the second kneading cycle starts.
- When the loaf is done, remove the bucket from the machine.
- Let the loaf cool for 5 minutes.
- Gently wobble the bucket to get the loaf and turn it out onto a rack to cool.

Crusty Honey Bread

NUTRITION Calories: 119, Total Fat: 1g, Saturated Fat: 1g, Carbohydrates: 24g, Fiber: 1g, Sodium: 155mg, Protein: 3g

PREPARATION
5 MINT

COOKING TIME
25
mins

SERVINGS
8 slices

DIRECTION

- Place the ingredients in your bread machine as recommended by the manufacturer.
- Program the vehicle for Basic/White bread, select light or medium crust, and press Start.
- When the loaf is done, remove the bucket from the machine.
- Let the loaf cool for 5 minutes.
- Gently shake the bucket to remove the bread and turn it out onto a rack to cool.
- Variation tip: Try adding semisweet chocolate chips and butterscotch chips for an unexpected twist on this simple bread. The resulting product will be gilded with the sweetness that gives the plain version a significant face-lift.

INGREDIENTS

- 2/3 cup water
- One tablespoon honey
- 3/4 tablespoon melted butter, cooled
- 1/2 teaspoon salt
- 1 3/4 cups white bread flour
- One teaspoon instant yeast

Honey Granola Bread

NUTRITION Calories,151 Total Fat: 5g, Saturated Fat: 2g, Carbohydrates: 33g, Fiber: 2g, Sodium: 218mg ,Protein: 6g

PREPARATION	COOKING TIME	SERVINGS
5 MINT	25 mins	8 slices

DIRECTION

- Place the ingredients in your bread machine as recommended by the manufacturer.
- Program the system for Basic/White bread, select light or medium crust, and press Start.
- When the loaf is done, remove the bucket from the machine.
- Let the loaf cool for 5 minutes.
- Gently shake the bucket to remove the loaf and place it out onto a rack to cool.
- Ingredient tip: Choose granola with no dried fruit because you will be crushing it for this recipe. Dried fruit would create a lumpy mess in the dough, which would wreck the finished loaf texture.

INGREDIENTS

- 3/4 cups milk
- Two tablespoons honey
- One tablespoon butter, melted and cooled
- 3/4 teaspoons salt
- 1/2 cup whole-wheat flour
- 1/2 cup prepared granola, crushed
- 11/4 cups white bread flour
- One teaspoon instant yeast

Apple Cider Bread

NUTRITION Calories: 164, Total Fat: 3g, Saturated Fat: 1g, Carbohydrates: 31g, Fiber: 1g, Sodium: 70mg, Protein: 4g

PREPARATION	COOKING TIME	SERVINGS
5 MINT	25 mins	8 slices

DIRECTION

1. Place the ingredients, except the apple, in your bread machine as recommended by the manufacturer.
2. Program the machine for Basic/White bread, select light or medium crust, and press Start.
3. Add the apple when the machine signals or 5 minutes before the last kneading cycle is complete.
4. When the loaf is done, remove the bucket from the machine.
5. Let the loaf cool for 5 minutes.
6. Gently shake the bucket to remove the loaf and turn it out onto a rack to cool.
7. Ingredient tip: Look for apple cider sweetened and spiced well, so your bread rises nicely.

INGREDIENTS

- 1/4 cup milk
- Two tablespoons apple cider, at room temperature
- Two tablespoons sugar
- Four teaspoons melted butter, cooled
- One tablespoon honey
- 1/4 teaspoon salt
- cups white bread flour
- 3/4 teaspoons bread machine or instant yeast
- 2/3 apple, peeled, cored, and finely diced

Black Bread

NUTRITION Calories: 123, Total Fat: 2g, Saturated Fat: 0g, Carbohydrates: 23g, Fiber: 3g, Sodium: 150mg, Protein: 4g

PREPARATION
5 MINT

COOKING TIME
25 mins

SERVINGS
8 slices

INGREDIENTS

- 1/2 cup water
- 1/4 cup brewed coffee, at 80°F to 90°F
- One tablespoon balsamic vinegar
- One tablespoon olive oil
- One tablespoon dark molasses
- 1/2 tablespoon light brown sugar
- 1/2 teaspoon salt
- One teaspoon caraway seed
- Two tablespoons unsweetened cocoa powder
- 1/2 cup dark rye flour
- 11/4 cups white bread flour
- One teaspoon instant yeast

DIRECTION

- Place the ingredients in your bread machine as recommended by the manufacturer.
- Program the machine for Whole-Wheat/Whole-Grain bread, select light or medium crust, and press Start.
- When the loaf is done, remove the bucket from the machine.
- Let the loaf cool for 5 minutes.
- Gently shake the bucket to pick the loaf and turn it out onto a rack to cool.

Chapter II.
Cheese Bread

Parmesan Tomato Basil Bread

NUTRITION Calories 183, Carbs 20.3g, Fat 6.8g, Protein 7.9g

PREPARATION	COOKING TIME	SERVINGS
5 MINT	2 *hour*	10

INGREDIENTS

- Sun-dried tomatoes – ¼ cup, chopped
- Yeast – 2 tsp.
- Bread flour – 2 cups.
- Parmesan cheese – 1/3 cup, grated
- Dried basil – 2 tsp.
- Sugar – 1 tsp.
- Olive oil – 2 tbsp.
- Milk – ¼ cup.
- Water – ½ cup.
- Salt – 1 tsp.

DIRECTION

- Add all ingredients except for sun-dried tomatoes into the bread machine pan.
- Select the basic setting, then select medium crust and press start.
- Add sun-dried tomatoes just before the final kneading cycle.
- Once the loaf is done, remove the loaf pan from the machine.
- Allow it to cool for 10 minutes
- Slice and serve.

Delicious Italian Cheese Bread Menu

NUTRITION Calories 163, Carbs 31.1g, Fat 1.8g, Protein 5.3g

PREPARATION	COOKING TIME	SERVINGS
5 MINT	2 *hour*	10

DIRECTION

- First, add all ingredients to the bread machine pan.
- Select a basic setting, then select a light/medium crust and start.
- Once the loaf is done, remove the loaf pan from the machine.
- Allow it to cool for 10 minutes.
- Slice and serve.

INGREDIENTS

- Active dry yeast – 2 tsp.
- Brown sugar – 2 tbsp.
- Parmesan cheese – 2 tbsp., grated
- Ground black pepper – 1 tsp.
- Italian seasoning – 2 tsp.
- Pepper jack cheese – 1/2 cup., shredded
- Bread flour – 3 cups.
- Warm water – 1 ¼ cups
- Salt – 1 ½ tsp.

Cheese Buttermilk Bread

NUTRITION Calories 182, Carbs 30g, Fat 3.4g, Protein 6.8g

PREPARATION	COOKING TIME	SERVINGS
5 MINT	2 *hour*	10

DIRECTION

- Place all ingredients into the bread machine pan based on the bread machine manufacturer instructions.
- Select basic bread setting, then select light/medium crust and start.
- Once the loaf is done, remove the loaf pan from the machine.
- Allow it to cool for 10 minutes.
- Slice and serve.

INGREDIENTS

- Buttermilk – 1 1/8 cups
- Active dry yeast – 1 ½ tsp.
- Cheddar cheese – ¾ cup., shredded
- Sugar – 1 ½ tsp.
- Bread flour – 3 cups.
- Buttermilk – 1 1/8 cups.
- Salt – 1 1/2 tsp.

Beer Cheese Bread

NUTRITION Calories 245, Carbs 32.1g, Fat 7.8g, Protein 9.2g

PREPARATION	COOKING TIME	SERVINGS
5 MINT	2 *hour*	10

DIRECTION

- Place the ingredients into the pan of the bread machine.
- Select the basic setting, then select a light crust and start.
- Once the loaf is done, remove the loaf pan from the machine.
- Allow it to cool for 10 minutes.
- Slice and serve.

INGREDIENTS

- Monterey Jack cheese – 4 oz., shredded
- American cheese – 4 oz., shredded
- Beer – 10 oz.
- Butter – 1 tbsp.
- Sugar – 1 tbsp.
- Bread flour – 3 cups.
- Active dry yeast – 1 packet
- Salt – 1 ½ tsp.

Moist Cheddar Cheese Bread

NUTRITION Calories 337, Carbs 32.8g, Fat 17.7g, Protein 11.8g

PREPARATION	COOKING TIME	SERVINGS
5 MINT	3 hour 45 mins	10

DIRECTION

- Add milk and butter into the bread pan.
- Add remaining ingredients except for yeast to the bread pan.
- Make a narrow hole into the flour with your finger and add yeast to the punch.
- Make sure yeast will not be mixed with any liquids.
- Select the basic setting, then select a light crust and start.
- Once the loaf is done, remove the loaf pan from the machine.
- Allow it to cool for 10 minutes.
- Slice and serve.

INGREDIENTS

- Milk – 1 cup
- Butter – ½ cup, melted
- All-purpose flour – 3 cups
- Cheddar cheese – 2 cups, shredded
- Garlic powder – ½ tsp.
- Kosher salt – 2 tsp.
- Sugar – 1 tbsp.
- Active dry yeast – 1 ¼ oz.

Gluten-Free Cheesy Bread

NUTRITION Calories 317, Carbs 43.6g, Fat 11g, Protein 10.6g

PREPARATION	COOKING TIME	SERVINGS
5 MINT	4 hour	10

DIRECTION

- In a bowl, mix eggs, water, and oil and pour it into the bread machine pan.
- In a large bowl, mix the other ingredients and pour over wet ingredient mixture into the bread pan.
- Select the whole wheat setting, then select light/medium crust and start.
- Once the loaf is done, remove the loaf pan from the machine.
- Allow it to cool for 10 minutes.
- Slice and serve.

INGREDIENTS

- Eggs – 3
- Olive oil – 2 tbsp.
- Water – 1 ½ cups.
- Active dry yeast – 2 ¼ tsp.
- White rice flour – 2 cups.
- Brown rice flour – 1 cup.
- Milk powder – ¼ cup.
- Sugar – 2 tbsp.
- Poppy seeds – 1 tbsp.
- Xanthan gum – 3 ½ tsp.
- Cheddar cheese – 1 ½ cups.. shredded
- Salt – 1 tsp.

Cheese Pepperoni Bread

NUTRITION *Calories 176, Carbs 34.5g, Fat 1.5g, Protein 5.7g*

PREPARATION 5 MINT

COOKING TIME 2 *hour*

SERVINGS 10

DIRECTION

- Add all ingredients except for pepperoni into the bread machine pan.
- Select basic setting, then selects medium crust and press start.
- Add pepperoni just before the final kneading cycle.
- Once the loaf is done, remove the loaf pan from the machine.
- Allow it to cool for 10 minutes.
- Slice and serve.

INGREDIENTS

- Pepperoni – 2/3 cup, diced
- Active dry yeast – 1 ½ tsp.
- Bread flour – 3 ¼ cups.
- Dried oregano – 1 ½ tsp.
- Garlic salt – 1 ½ tsp.
- Sugar – 2 tbsp.
- Mozzarella cheese – 1/3 cup., shredded
- Warm water – 1 cup+2 tbsp.

Garlic Parmesan Bread

NUTRITION *Calories 335, Carbs 37.7g, Fat 15.4g, Protein 9.7g*

PREPARATION 5 MINT

COOKING TIME 3 *hour* 45 *mins*

SERVINGS 10

DIRECTION

- Add water, oil, butter, and garlic into the bread pan.
- Add remaining ingredients except for yeast to the bread pan.
- Make a small hole in the flour with your finger and add yeast to the spot.
- Make sure yeast will not be mixed with any liquids.
- Select the basic setting, then selects a light crust and start.
- Once the loaf is done, remove the loaf pan from the machine.
- Allow it to cool for 10 minutes.
- Slice and serve.

INGREDIENTS

- Active dry yeast – ¼ oz.
- Sugar– 3 tbsp.
- Kosher salt – 2 tsp.
- Dried oregano – 1 tsp.
- Dried basil – 1 tsp.
- Garlic powder – ½ tsp.
- Parmesan cheese – ½ cup grated
- All-purpose flour – 3 ½ cups
- Garlic – 1 tbsp., minced
- Butter – ¼ cup, melted
- Olive oil – 1/3 cup
- Water – 1 1/3 cups

Cheese Jalapeno Bread

NUTRITION Calories 174, Carbs 31.1g, Fat 3.1g ,Protein 5.1g

PREPARATION	COOKING TIME	SERVINGS
5 MINT	2 *hour*	10

DIRECTION

- Begin by adding all fixings to the bread machine pan according to the bread machine manufacturer instructions.
- Select basic bread setting, then select light/medium crust and start.
- Once the loaf is done, remove the loaf pan from the machine.
- Allow it to cool for 10 minutes.
- Slice and serve.

INGREDIENTS

- Monterey jack cheese – ¼ cup shredded
- Active dry yeast – 2 tsp.
- Butter – 1 ½ tbsp.
- Sugar – 1 ½ tbsp.
- Milk – 3 tbsp.
- Flour – 3 cups.
- Water – 1 cup.
- Jalapeno pepper – 1, minced
- Salt – 1 ½ tsp.

Cheddar Cheese Basil Bread

NUTRITION Calories 174, Carbs 31.1g, Fat 3.1g, Protein 5.1g

PREPARATION	COOKING TIME	SERVINGS
10 MINT	25 *mins*	8

DIRECTION

- Preparing the Ingredients. Place the ingredients in your Zojirushi bread machine.
- Select the Bake cycle. Program the machine for Regular Basic, choose light or medium crust, and then press Start.
- If the loaf is done, remove the bucket from the machine.
- Let the loaf cool for 5 minutes.
- Softly shake the canister to remove the loaf and put it out onto a rack to cool.

INGREDIENTS

- 1 cup milk
- One tablespoon melted butter cooled
- One tablespoon sugar
- One teaspoon dried basil
- ¾ cup (3 ounces) shredded sharp Cheddar cheese
- ¾ teaspoon salt
- cups white bread flour
- 1½ teaspoons active dry yeast

Italian Herb Cheese Bread

NUTRITION Calories 247, Carbs 32.3g, Fat 9.4g, Protein 8g

PREPARATION	COOKING TIME	SERVINGS
5 MINT	3 hour	10

DIRECTION

- Add milk into the bread pan.
- Add remaining ingredients except for yeast to the bread pan.
- Make a small hole into the flour with your finger and add yeast to the spot.
- Make sure yeast will not be mixed with any liquids.
- Select a basic setting, then selects a light crust and start.
- Once the loaf is done, remove the loaf pan from the machine.
- Allow it to cool for 10 minutes.
- Slice and serve.

INGREDIENTS

- Yeast – 1 ½ tsp.
- Italian herb seasoning – 1 tbsp.
- Brown sugar – 2 tbsp.
- Cheddar cheese – 1 cup., shredded
- Bread flour – 3 cups.
- Butter – 4 tbsp.
- Warm milk – 1 ¼ cups.
- Salt – 2 tsp.

Herb and Parmesan Cheese Loaf

NUTRITION Calories 174, Carbs 31.1g, Fat 3.1g, Protein 5.1g

PREPARATION	COOKING TIME	SERVINGS
10 MINT	25 mins	8

DIRECTION

- Preparing the Ingredients. Place all fixings in the bread pan in the liquid-cheese and herb-dry-yeast layering.
- Put the pan in the Zojirushi bread machine.
- Select the Bake cycle. Choose Regular Basic Setting.
- Press start and wait until the loaf is cooked.
- The machine will start the keep warm mode after the bread is complete.
- Just allow it to stay in that mode for about 10 minutes before unplugging.
- Remove the pan and wait for it to cool down for about 10 minutes.

INGREDIENTS

- cups + 2 tbsp. all-purpose flour
- 1 cup of water
- tbsp. oil
- tbsp. sugar
- tbsp. milk
- 1 tbsp. instant yeast
- 1 tsp. garlic powder
- tbsp. parmesan cheese
- 1 tbsp. fresh basil
- 1 tbsp. fresh oregano
- 1 tbsp. fresh chives or rosemary

Olive Cheese Bread

NUTRITION Calories 174, Carbs 31.1g, Fat 3.1g, Protein 5.1g

PREPARATION	COOKING TIME	SERVINGS
10 MINT	25 mins	8

DIRECTION

- Preparing the Ingredients. Place the ingredients in your Zojirushi bread machine, tossing the flour with the cheese first.
- Program the machine for Regular Basic, choose light or medium crust, and press Start.
- Next, when the loaf is done, you may remove the bucket from the machine.
- Let the loaf cool for 5 minutes.
- Mildly shake the pot to eliminate the loaf and turn it out onto a rack to cool.

INGREDIENTS

- 1 cup milk
- 1½ tablespoons melted butter, cooled
- One teaspoon minced garlic
- 1½ tablespoons sugar
- One teaspoon salt
- cups white bread flour
- ¾ cup (3 ounces) shredded Swiss cheese
- One teaspoon bread machine or instant yeast
- 1/3 cup chopped black olives

Blue Cheese Onion Bread

NUTRITION Calories 174, Carbs 31.1g, Fat 3.1g, Protein 5.1g

PREPARATION	COOKING TIME	SERVINGS
10 MINT	25 mins	8

DIRECTION

- Preparing the Ingredients. Place the ingredients in your Zojirushi bread machine.
- Program the machine for Regular Basic, select light or medium crust, and press Start.
- Remove the bucket from the machine.
- Let the loaf cool for 5 minutes.
- Gently shake the container to remove the loaf and turn it out onto a rack to cool.

INGREDIENTS

- 1¼ cup water, at 80°F to 90°F
- One egg, at room temperature
- One tablespoon melted butter cooled
- ¼ cup powdered skim milk
- One tablespoon sugar
- ¾ teaspoon salt
- ½ cup (2 ounces) crumbled blue cheese
- One tablespoon dried onion flake
- 3 cups white bread flour
- ¼ cup instant mashed potato flakes
- One teaspoon bread machine or active dry yeast

Beer and Cheese Bread

NUTRITION *Calories 174, Carbs 31.1g, Fat 3.1g, Protein 5.1g*

PREPARATION	COOKING TIME	SERVINGS
10 MINT	25 mins	8

DIRECTION

- Place all elements, except cheeses, in the bread pan in the liquid-dry-yeast layering.
- Put the pan in the Zojirushi bread machine.
- Select the Bake cycle. Choose Regular Basic Setting. Press Start.
- When the kneading process is about to end, add the cheese.
- Wait until the loaf is cooked.
- The machine will start the keep warm mode after the bread is complete.
- Do not forget to let it stay in that mode for about 10 minutes before unplugging.
- Lastly, remove the pan and let it cool down for about 10 minutes.

INGREDIENTS

- 3 cups bread or all-purpose flour
- 1 tbsp. instant yeast
- 1 tsp. salt
- 1 tbsp. sugar
- 1 1/2 cup beer at room temperature
- 1/2 cup shredded Monterey cheese
- 1/2 cup shredded Edam cheese

Cheese Loaf

NUTRITION *Calories 174, Carbs 31.1g, Fat 3.1g, Protein 5.1g*

PREPARATION	COOKING TIME	SERVINGS
10 MINT	25 mins	8

DIRECTION

- Begin through placing all ingredients in the bread pan in the liquid-dry-yeast layering.
- Put the pan in the Zojirushi bread machine.
- Select the Bake cycle. Choose Regular Basic Setting and light crust.
- Press start and wait until the loaf is cooked.
- The machine will start the keep warm mode after the bread is complete.
- For about 10 minutes, let the bread stay for 10 minutes in that mode before unplugging.
- You may now want to remove the pan and let it cool down for about 10 minutes.

INGREDIENTS

- 1/4 cups flour
- tsp. instant yeast
- 1 3/4 cups water
- tbsp. sugar
- 1 1/2 cup shredded cheddar cheese
- tbsp. parmesan cheese
- 1 tsp. mustard
- 1 tsp. paprika
- tbsp. minced white onion
- 1/3 cup butter

Double Cheese Bread

NUTRITION Calories 174, Carbs 31.1g, Fat 3.1g, Protein 5.1g

PREPARATION
10 MINT

COOKING TIME
25
mins

SERVINGS
8

DIRECTION

- Preparing the Ingredients. Place the ingredients in your Zojirushi bread machine.
- Program the machine for Regular Basic, select light or medium crust, and press Start.
- Now, if the loaf is done, remove the bucket from the machine.
- Let the loaf cool for 5 minutes.
- Moderately shake the bucket to transfer the loaf
- The last step is by putting it out onto a rack to cool.

INGREDIENTS

- 1¼ cups milk
- One tablespoon butter, melted and cooled
- Two tablespoons sugar
- One teaspoon salt
- ½ teaspoon freshly ground black pepper
- Pinch cayenne pepper
- 1½ cups (6 ounces) shredded aged sharp Cheddar cheese
- ½ cup (2 ounces) shredded or grated Parmesan cheese
- cups white bread flour
- 1¼ teaspoons bread machine or instant yeast

Spinach and Feta Whole Wheat Bread

NUTRITION Calories 174, Carbs 31.1g, Fat 3.1g, Protein 5.1g

PREPARATION
10 MINT

COOKING TIME
25
mins

SERVINGS
8

DIRECTION

- Preparing the Ingredients. Place all ingredients, except spinach, butter, and feta, in the bread pan in the liquid-dry-yeast layering.
- Put the pan in the Zojirushi bread machine.
- Select the Bake cycle. Choose Regular Whole Wheat. Press start.
- When the dough has gathered, manually add the feta and spinach.
- Resume and wait until the loaf are cooked. Once cooked, brush with butter.
- The machine will start the keep warm mode after the bread is complete.
- Make it stay in that mode for about 10 minutes before unplugging.
- Remove the pan and just cool it down for about 10 minutes.

INGREDIENTS

- 2/3 cups whole wheat flour
- 1 1/2 tsp. instant yeast
- 1/4 cup unsalted butter, melted
- 1 cup lukewarm water
- tbsp. sugar
- 1/2 tsp. salt
- 3/4 cups blanched and chopped spinach, fresh
- 1/2 tsp. pepper
- 1/2 tsp. paprika
- 1/3 cup feta cheese, mashed

Three Cheese Bread

NUTRITION Calories 174, Carbs 31.1g, Fat 3.1g, Protein 5.1g

PREPARATION	COOKING TIME	SERVINGS
10 MINT	25 mins	8

INGREDIENTS

- cups bread or all-purpose flour
- 1 1/4 cup warm milk
- tbsp. oil
- tbsp. sugar
- 1 tsp. instant yeast or one packet
- 1 cup cheddar cheese
- 1/2 cup parmesan cheese
- 1/2 cup mozzarella cheese

DIRECTION

- Preparing the Ingredients. Place all ingredients in the bread pan with the liquid-dry-yeast layering.
- Put the pan in the Zojirushi bread machine.
- Select the Bake cycle. Choose Regular Basic Setting.
- Press start and wait until the loaf is cooked.
- The machine will start the keep warm mode after the bread is complete.
- Let it stay in that mode for approximately 10 minutes before unplugging.
- Remove the pan and wait for it to cool down for about 10 minutes.

Mozzarella and Salami Bread

NUTRITION Calories 174, Carbs 31.1g, Fat 3.1g, Protein 5.1g

PREPARATION	COOKING TIME	SERVINGS
10 MINT	25 mins	8

INGREDIENTS

- 1 cup water plus two tablespoons, at 80°F to 90°F
- ½ cup (2 ounces) shredded mozzarella cheese
- Two tablespoons sugar
- One teaspoon salt
- One teaspoon dried basil
- ¼ teaspoon garlic powder
- 3¼ cups white bread flour
- 1½ teaspoons bread machine or instant yeast
- ¾ cup finely diced hot

DIRECTION

- Preparing the Ingredients. Place the ingredients, except the salami, in your Zojirushi bread machine.
- Program the machine for Regular Basic, select light or medium crust, and press Start.
- Add the salami when your machine signals or 5 minutes before the second kneading cycle is finished.
- You need to remove the bucket from the machine.
- Next is by letting the loaf cool for 5 minutes.
- Gently shake the bucket to eliminate the loaf and turn it out onto a rack to cool.

Cheese Swirl Loaf

NUTRITION Calories 174, Carbs 31.1g, Fat 3.1g, Protein 5.1g

PREPARATION
10 MINT

COOKING TIME
25
mins

SERVINGS
8

INGREDIENTS

- cups all-purpose flour
- 1 1/4 cup lukewarm milk
- tbsp. sugar
- 1 tsp. salt
- 1 1/2 tsp. instant yeast
- tbsp. melted butter
- Four slices of Monterey cheese
- 1/2 cup mozzarella cheese
- 1/2 cup edam or any quick melting cheese
- 1/2 tsp. paprika

DIRECTION

- Preparing the Ingredients. Place all ingredients, except cheeses, in the bread pan in the liquid-dry-yeast layering.
- Put the pan in the Zojirushi bread machine.
- Select the Bake cycle. Choose Regular Basic Setting. Press start.
- Place all the cheese in a microwavable bowl. Melt in the microwave for 30 seconds. Cool, but make sure to keep soft.
- After 10 minutes into the kneading process, pause the machine. Take out half of the dough. Roll it flat on the work surface.
- Spread the cheese on the flat dough, then roll it thinly. Return to the bread pan carefully.
- Resume and wait until the loaf are cooked.
- The machine will start the keep warm mode after the bread is complete.
- Let it stay in that mode for about 10 minutes before unplugging.
- To end by removing the pan and let it cool down for about 10 minutes.

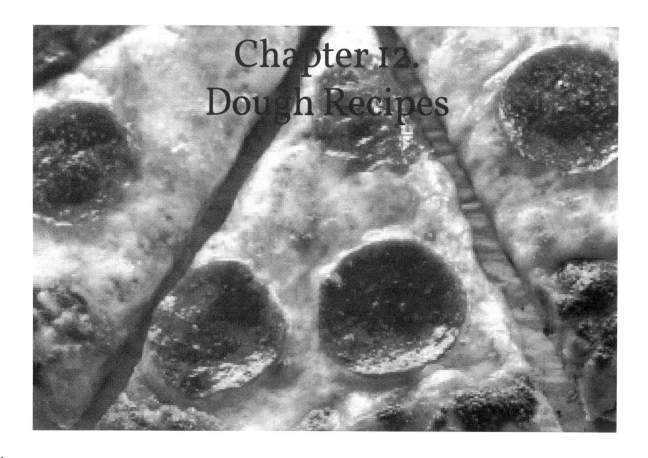

Chapter 12.
Dough Recipes

Chili Cheese Bacon Bread

NUTRITION Calories 174, Carbs 31.1g, Fat 3.1g, Protein 5.1g

PREPARATION	COOKING TIME	SERVINGS
10 MINT	25 mins	8

DIRECTION

- Preparing the Ingredients. Place the ingredients in your Zojirushi bread machine.
- Select the Bake cycle. Program the machine for Regular Basic, select light or medium crust, and press Start.
- Remove the bucket from the machine.
- Let the loaf cool for 5 minutes.
- Gently swing the can to remove the loaf and put it out onto a rack to cool.

INGREDIENTS

- ½ cup milk
- 1½ teaspoons melted butter, cooled
- 1½ tablespoons honey
- 1½ teaspoons salt
- ½ cup chopped and drained green chiles
- ½ cup (2 ounces) grated Cheddar cheese
- ½ cup chopped cooked bacon
- cups white bread flour
- Two teaspoons bread machine or instant yeast

Cheddar Biscuits

NUTRITION Calories: 125 , Fat: 7g , Carb: 10g , Protein: 5g

PREPARATION	COOKING TIME	SERVINGS
10 MINT	25 mins	12

DIRECTION

- Preheat the oven to 350F. Grease a baking sheet.
- Mix together the butter, eggs, milk, salt, baking soda, garlic powder, cheese, and herbs until well blended.
- Add the coconut flour to the batter and mix until well blended. Let the batter sit then mix again.
- Spoon about 2 tbsp. batter for each biscuit onto the greased baking sheet.
- Bake for 25 minutes.
- Serve warm.

INGREDIENTS

- eggs
- ¼ cup unsalted butter, melted
- 1 ¼ cups, coconut milk
- ¼ tsp. salt
- ¼ tsp. baking soda
- ¼ tsp. garlic powder
- ½ cup finely shredded sharp cheddar cheese
- 1 Tbsp. fresh herb
- 2/3 cup coconut flour

Savory Waffles

NUTRITION Calories: 183 , Fat: 13g , Carb: 4g , Protein: 12g

PREPARATION	COOKING TIME	SERVINGS
10 MINT	25 mins	4

DIRECTION

- Preheat the waffle iron to medium heat.
- Mix all the ingredients using a bowl. Let the batter sit and mix once more.
- Scoop ½ cup to 1-cup batter (depending on the size of the waffle iron) and pour onto the iron. Cook according to the manufacturer's directions.
- Serve warm.

INGREDIENTS

- eggs
- 1 tsp. olive oil
- ½ cup sliced scallions
- ¾ cup grated pepper Jack cheese
- ¼ tsp. baking soda
- Pinch salt
- Tbsp. coconut flour

Snicker doodles

NUTRITION Calories: 86 , Fat: 7g , Carb: 3g , Protein: 3g

PREPARATION	COOKING TIME	SERVINGS
10 MINT	10 mins	20

DIRECTION

- Preheat the oven to 350F.
- Whisk the almond flour, coconut flour, salt and baking soda together using a bowl.
- In another bowl, cream the butter, sweetener, milk and vanilla.
- Put the flour mixture to the butter mixture and blend well.
- Line baking sheets with parchment paper.
- Blend the ground cinnamon and low-carb granulated sweetener together in a bowl. With your hands, roll a tbsp. of dough into a ball.
- Reel the dough ball in the cinnamon mixture to fully coat.
- Put the dough balls on the cookie sheet, spread about an inch apart, and flatten with the underside of a jar.
- Bake for 8 to 10 minutes.
- Cool and serve.

INGREDIENTS

- cups almond flour
- Tbsp. coconut flour
- ¼ tsp. baking soda
- ¼ tsp. salt
- Tbsp. unsalted butter, melted
- 1/3 cup low-carb sweetener
- ¼ cup coconut milk
- 1 Tbsp. vanilla extract
- Tbsp. ground cinnamon
- Tbsp. low-carb granulated sweetener

Chocolate Chip Scones

NUTRITION *Calories: 213 , Fat: 18g , Carb: 10g , Protein: 8g*

PREPARATION 10 MINT

COOKING TIME 10 *mins*

SERVINGS 8

INGREDIENTS

- cups almond flour
- 1 tsp. baking soda
- ¼ tsp. sea salt
- 1 egg
- Tbsp. low-carb sweetener
- Tbsp. milk, cream or yogurt
- ½ cup sugar-free chocolate chips

DIRECTION

- Preheat the oven to 350F.
- Using a bowl, add almond flour, baking soda, and salt and blend.
- Then add the egg, sweetener, milk, and chocolate chips. Blend well.
- Tap the dough into a ball and place it on parchment paper.
- Roll the dough with a rolling pin into a large circle. Slice it into 8 triangular pieces.
- Place the scones and parchment paper on a baking sheet and separate the scones about 1 inch or so apart.
- For 7 to 10 minutes, bake until lightly browned.
- Cool and serve.

No Corn Cornbread

NUTRITION *Calories: 65 , Fat: 6g , Carb: 2g , Protein: 2g*

PREPARATION 10 MINT

COOKING TIME 20 *mins*

SERVINGS 8

DIRECTION

- Preheat the oven to 325F. Line a baking pan.
- Combine dry ingredients in a bowl.
- Put all the dry ingredients to the wet ones and blend well.
- Dispense the batter into the baking pan and bake for 20 minutes.
- Cool, slice, and serve.

INGREDIENTS

- ½ cup almond flour
- ¼ cup coconut flour
- ¼ tsp. salt
- ¼ tsp. baking soda
- eggs
- ¼ cup unsalted butter
- Tbsp. low-carb sweetener
- ½ cup coconut milk

Garlic Cheese Bread Loaf

NUTRITION Calories: 299 , Fat: 27g , Carb: 4g , Protein: 11g

PREPARATION
10 MINT

COOKING TIME
45
mins

SERVINGS
10

DIRECTION

- 1 Preheat the oven to 355F.
- 2 Line a baking pan with parchment paper.
- 3 In a food blender, pulse the eggs until smooth. Then combine the butter and pulse for 1 minute more.
- 4 Blend the almond flour and baking powder for 90 seconds or until thickens.
- 5 Finally, combine the garlic, oregano, parsley, and cheese until mixed.
- 6 Pour into the prepared and bake in the oven for 45 minutes.
- 7 Cool, slice, and serve.

INGREDIENTS

- 1 Tbsp. parsley, chopped
- ½ cup butter, unsalted and softened
- Tbsp. garlic powder
- large eggs
- ½ tsp. oregano seasoning
- 1 tsp. baking powder
- cups almond flour
- ½ tsp. xanthan gum
- 1 cup cheddar cheese, shredded
- ½ tsp. salt

Chocolate Zucchini Bread

NUTRITION Calories: 149 , Fat: 8g , Carb: 7g , Protein: 3g

PREPARATION
10 MINT

COOKING TIME
20
mins

SERVINGS
10

DIRECTION

- Preheat the oven to 350F.
- Grease the baking pan and line the entire pan with parchment paper.
- In a food processor, blend the eggs, zucchini, oil, sweetener, and vanilla.
- Add the flour, cocoa, baking soda, and salt to the zucchini mixture and stir until mixed. For a few seconds, let the batter sit.
- Mix in the chocolate chips, then dispense the batter into the prepared pan.
- Bake for 45 to 50 minutes.
- Cool, slice, and serve

INGREDIENTS

- cups grated zucchini, excess moisture removed
- eggs
- Tbsp. olive oil
- 1/3 cup low-carb sweetener
- 1 tsp. vanilla extract
- 1/3 cup coconut flour
- ¼ cup unsweetened cocoa powder
- ½ tsp. baking soda
- ½ tsp. salt
- 1/3 cup sugar-free chocolate chips

Iranian Flat Bread (Sangak)

NUTRITION Calories: 26 , Fat: 1g , Carb: 3.5g , Protein: 0.7g

PREPARATION	COOKING TIME	SERVINGS
3 HOUR	15 mins	6

INGREDIENTS

- cups almond flour
- ½ cups warm water
- 1 Tbsp. instant yeast
- tsp. sesame seeds
- Salt to taste

DIRECTION

- Add 1 tbsp. yeast to ½ cup warm water using a bowl and allow to stand for 5 minutes.
- Add salt add 1 cup of water. Let stand for 10 minutes longer.
- Put one cup of flour at a time, and then add the remaining water.
- Knead the dough and then shape into a ball and let stand for 3 hours covered.
- Preheat the oven to 480F.
- By means of a rolling pin, roll out the dough, and divide into 6 balls.
- Roll each ball into ½ inch thick rounds.
- Place a parchment paper on the baking sheet and place the rolled rounds on it.
- With a finger, make a small hole in the middle and add 2 tsp sesame seeds in each hole.
- Bake for 3 to 4 minutes, then flip over and bake for 2 minutes more.
- Serve.

Cauliflower Breadticks

NUTRITION Calories: 165 , Fat: 10g , Carb: 5g , Protein: 13g

PREPARATION	COOKING TIME	SERVINGS
10 MINT	35 mins	8

DIRECTION

- Preheat the oven to 350F. Grease a baking sheet.
- Beat the eggs until mixed well.
- Combine riced cauliflower, mozzarella cheese, Italian seasoning, pepper, garlic, and salt and blend on low speed in a food processor. Combine with eggs.
- Pour the dough into the prepared cookie sheet and pat the dough down to ¼ thick across the pan.
- Bake for 30 minutes and dust the breadticks with the parmesan cheese.
- Put the breadticks on the broil setting for 2 to 3 minutes, so the cheese melts.
- Slice and serve.

INGREDIENTS

- cups riced cauliflower
- 1 cup mozzarella, shredded
- 1 tsp. Italian seasoning
- eggs
- ½ tsp. ground pepper
- 1 tsp. salt
- ½ tsp. granulated garlic
- ¼ cup Parmesan cheese as a topping

Cheddar Crackers

NUTRITION *Calories: 200 , Fat: 18g , Carb: 4g , Protein: 7g*

PREPARATION
10 MINT

COOKING TIME
55
mins

SERVINGS
8

INGREDIENTS

- Tbsp. unsalted butter, softened slightly
- 1 egg white
- ¼ tsp. salt
- 1 cup plus 2 Tbsp. almond flour
- 1 tsp. minced fresh thyme
- 1 cup shredded sharp white cheddar cheese

DIRECTION

- Preheat the oven to 300F.
- Using a bowl, beat together the butter, egg white, and salt.
- Stir in the almond flour, and thyme and then the cheddar until mixed.
- Move the dough out between two pieces of parchment paper to a rectangle.
- Peel off the top parchment paper and place the dough with the bottom parchment paper on a sheet pan.
- Cut the dough into crackers with a pizza cutter.
- Bake until golden, about 45 to 55 minutes, rotating the tray once halfway through.
- Cool and serve.

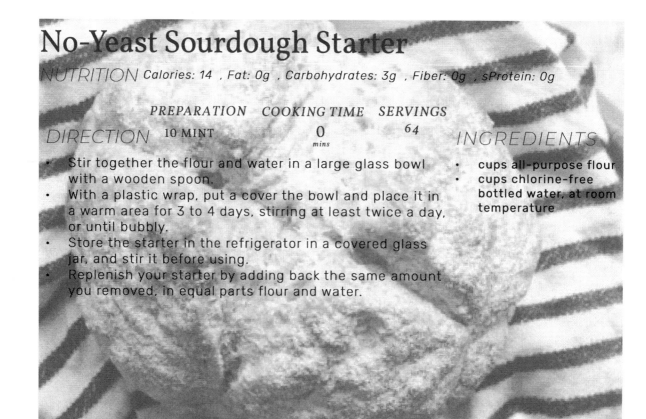

No-Yeast Sourdough Starter

NUTRITION *Calories: 14 , Fat: 0g , Carbohydrates: 3g , Fiber: 0g , sProtein: 0g*

PREPARATION
10 MINT

COOKING TIME
0
mins

SERVINGS
64

INGREDIENTS

- cups all-purpose flour
- cups chlorine-free bottled water, at room temperature

DIRECTION

- Stir together the flour and water in a large glass bowl with a wooden spoon.
- With a plastic wrap, put a cover the bowl and place it in a warm area for 3 to 4 days, stirring at least twice a day, or until bubbly.
- Store the starter in the refrigerator in a covered glass jar, and stir it before using.
- Replenish your starter by adding back the same amount you removed, in equal parts flour and water.

Sesame Almond Crackers

NUTRITION Calories: 299 , Fat: 28g , Carb: 4g , Protein: 8g

PREPARATION	COOKING TIME	SERVINGS
10 MINT	24 mins	8

INGREDIENTS

- Tbsp. unsalted butter, softened slightly
- egg whites
- ½ tsp. salt
- ¼ tsp. black pepper
- ¼ cups almond flour
- Tbsp. sesame seeds

DIRECTION

- Preheat the oven to 350F.
- Using a bowl, beat the egg whites, butter, salt, and black pepper.
- Stir in the almond flour and sesame seeds.
- Move the dough out between two pieces of parchment paper to a rectangle.
- Peel off the top parchment paper and place the dough on a sheet pan.
- Cut the dough into crackers with a pizza cutter.
- Bake for 18 to 24 minutes, or until golden, rotating the tray halfway through.
- Serve.

Pizza Dough

NUTRITION Calories 716:, Total Fat 15.7g:, Saturated Fat 2.3g:, Cholesterol 0mg:, Sodium 881g:, Total,Carbohydrate 124.8g:, Dietary Fiber 5.1g:, Total Sugars 4.4 g:, Protein 17.7g

PREPARATION	COOKING TIME	SERVINGS
10 MINT	1 hour 30 mins	2

DIRECTION

- Put ingredients in the bread maker.
- Enable the Dough program and start the cycle.
- Put the finished dough in a greased form or pan and distribute it. Allow standing for 10 minutes.
- Preheat the oven to 400°F. On top of the dough, place the pizza sauce and the filling. Top with grated cheese.
- For 15 to 20 minutes, bake till the edge is browned.

INGREDIENTS

- 1 cup of warm water
- ¾ teaspoon salt
- 2 tablespoons olive oil
- 2 ½ cups flour
- 2 teaspoons sugar
- 2 teaspoons yeast

Pizza Basis

NUTRITION Calories 718;, Total Fat 4.4g;, Saturated Fat 0.6g;, Cholesterol 0mg;, Sodium 1173g;, Total,, Carbohydrate 145.6g;, Dietary Fiber 5.9g; Total Sugars 1.5 g;, Protein 20.9g

INGREDIENTS

- 1 ¼ cups warm water
- 2 cups flour
- 1 cup Semolina flour
- ½ teaspoon sugar
- 1 teaspoon salt
- 1 teaspoon olive oil
- 2 teaspoons yeast

DIRECTION

- Place all the ingredients in the bread maker's bucket in the order recommended by the manufacturer. Select the Dough program.
- After the dough has risen, use it as the base for the pizza.

PREPARATION	COOKING TIME	SERVINGS
10 MINT	1 hour 20 mins	2

Italian Pie Calzone

NUTRITION Calories 247;, Total Fat 9.2g;, Saturated Fat 3.9g;, Cholesterol 22mg;, Sodium 590g;, Total,, Carbohydrate 32g;, Dietary Fiber 1.5g;, Total Sugars 2.8 g;, Protein 8.6g

INGREDIENTS

- 1 ¼ cups water
- 1 teaspoon salt
- 3 cups flour
- 1 teaspoon milk powder
- 1 ½ tablespoons sugar
- 2 teaspoons yeast
- ¾ cup tomato sauce for pizza
- 1 cup pepperoni sausage, finely chopped
- 1 ¼ cups grated mozzarella
- 2 tablespoons butter, melted

DIRECTION

- Put water, salt, bread baking flour, soluble milk, sugar, and yeast in the bread maker's bucket in the order recommended by the manufacturer. Select the Dough setting.
- After the end of the cycle, roll the dough on a lightly floured surface; form a rectangle measuring 45 x 25 cm. Transfer to a lightly oiled baking tray.
- In a small bowl, combine the chopped pepperoni and mozzarella. Spoon the pizza sauce in a strip along the center of the dough. Add the filling of sausage and cheese.
- Make diagonal incisions at a distance of 1 ½ cm from each other at the sides, receding 1 ½ cm from the filling.
- Cross the strips on top of the filling, moistening it with the water. Lubricate with melted butter.
- For 35 to 45 minutes bake at 360 degree F.

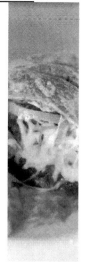

PREPARATION	COOKING TIME	SERVINGS
1 HOURS	1 hour 5 mins	12

Cinnamon Raisin Buns

NUTRITION Calories 308;, Total Fat 9.2g;, Saturated Fat 4.3g;, Cholesterol 31mg;, Sodium 202g;, Total,,,,, Carbohydrate 53.2g;, Dietary Fiber 1.5g;, Total Sugars 27.9 g;, Protein 5.2g

INGREDIENTS

- For dough
- ½ cup milk
- ½ cup of water
- 2 tablespoons butter
- ¾ teaspoon salt
- 3 cups flour
- 2 ¼ teaspoon yeast
- 3 tablespoons sugar
- 1 egg
- For filling
- 3 tablespoons butter, melted
- ¾ teaspoon ground cinnamon
- 1/3 cup sugar
- 1/3 cup raisins
- 1/3 cup chopped walnuts
- For glaze
- 1 cup powdered sugar
- 1 ½ tablespoon melted butter
- ¼ teaspoon vanilla
- 1 ½ tablespoons milk
-

DIRECTION

- In a saucepan, heat ½ cup of milk, water, and 2 tablespoons of butter until they become hot.
- Put the milk mixture, salt, flour, yeast, sugar, and eggs in the bread maker's bucket in the order recommended by the manufacturer. Select the Dough program. Click Start.
- When through with the cycle, take out the dough from the bread maker. On a flour-covered surface, roll the dough into a large rectangle. Lubricate with softened butter.
- Mix the cinnamon and sugar. Sprinkle the rectangle with the mixture. Generously sprinkle with raisins and/or chopped nuts.
- Roll the dough into a roll, starting from the long side. Cut into 12 pieces. Put the buns slit-side down on a greased baking tray (25x35cm).
- Cover and put in the heat until the dough almost doubles, about 30 minutes.
- Preheat the oven to 375 degree F. Mix the powdered sugar, 1 1/2 tablespoon melted butter, vanilla, and 1 ½ tablespoon milk to get a thick frosting; set it aside.
- Bake the buns in a preheated oven for 20 - 25 minutes, until browned. Remove and allow to cool down for 10 minutes. Frost the cooled buns with icing.

PREPARATION	COOKING TIME	SERVINGS
10 MINT	45 mins	12

French Baguettes

NUTRITION Calories 272;, Total Fat 0.8g;, Saturated Fat 0.1g;, Cholesterol 0mg;, Sodium 585g;, Total,,, Carbohydrate 57g;, Dietary Fiber 2.2g;, Total Sugars 1.2g;, Protein 7.9g

INGREDIENTS

- 1½ cups water
- 1½ teaspoons sugar
- 1½ teaspoons salt
- 3½ cups flour
- 1½ teaspoons yeast
- a mixture of different seeds (pumpkin, sunflower, black and white sesame)

DIRECTION

- To prepare the dough for French baguettes in the bread maker, place all the ingredients in the bread maker's container in order: water, salt, and sugar, flour, yeast. Select the Yeast Dough program.
- After 1½ hour, the dough for baguettes is ready.
- Heat the oven to 440°F. Divide the dough into 2 parts. Lubricate the pan with oil. From the dough, form two French baguettes. Put on a baking pan and let it come for 10 minutes.
- Then with a sharp knife, make shallow incisions on the surface of the baguettes. Sprinkle with water and sprinkle with a mixture of seeds. Leave it for another 10 minutes.
- After the oven is warmed, put the pan with French baguettes in the oven for 5-7 minutes, then lower the heat to 360°F and bake for another 20-30 minutes until ready.
- Transfer baguettes to a grate and cool.
- Your crispy, delicious, fragrant French baguettes are ready… Bon Appetit!

PREPARATION	COOKING	SERVINGS
20 HOURS	2 30 mins mins	6

Chapter 13.
Buns & Bread

Keto German Franks Bun

NUTRITION Calories: 16, Calories from fat: 87, Total Fat: 8 g, Total Carbohydrates: 3 g , Net Carbohydrates: 3 g, Protein: 6 g

INGREDIENTS

- 1 1/2 tablespoons vegetable oil
- 1 cup of water
- ½ cup blackberry jelly
- ½ cup peanut butter
- One teaspoon salt
- One tablespoon white sugar
- 2 cups of bread flour
- 1 cup whole-wheat flour
- 1 1/2 teaspoons active dry yeast

DIRECTION

- Position all ingredients in your bread machine pan in the order listed above.
- Close the lid of your bread machine, select DOUGH cycle and press START.
- Once cycle is finish, transfer the dough into a floured surface. Cut the dough in 10 slices long.
- Flatten the dough into 5 x 4 inches. Then firmly roll the dough to form a cylindrical shape size of 5 x 1 inch. Cover and let it rise for an hour or until the dough size doubles.
- Preheat the oven at 350 degrees Fahrenheit. Arrange the dough in a greased baking sheet.
- Place the baking sheet in the oven and bake for 9 minutes or until golden brown.
- Cool then serve with your favorite franks.

PREPARATION	COOKING TIME	SERVINGS
2 HOURS	9 *mins*	10

Buns with Cottage Cheese

NUTRITION Calories: 77 , Fat: 5.2g , Carb: 6.7g , Protein: 5.8g

INGREDIENTS

- eggs
- oz. Almond flour
- 1 oz. Erythritol
- 1/8 tsp. Stevia
- cinnamon and vanilla extract to taste Filling:
- ½ oz. Cottage cheese
- 1 egg
- cinnamon and vanilla extract to taste

DIRECTION

- Prepare the filling by mixing its ingredients in a bowl.
- Combine eggs with almond flour, blend until smooth. Add erythritol, stevia, and flavors to taste.
- Spoon 1 tbsp. Dough into silicone cups. Spoon about 1 tsp. Filling on top, and bake at 365f for 15 minutes.

PREPARATION	COOKING TIME	SERVINGS
10 MINT	15 *mins*	8

Keto Beer Bread

NUTRITION Calories: 118 , Calories from fat: 90, Total Fat: 9, Total Carbohydrates: 3 g , Net Carbohydrates: 3 g, Protein: 6 g

INGREDIENTS

- oz. beer at room temperature
- oz. American cheese, shredded
- oz. Monterey Jack cheese, shredded
- 1 tbsp. sugar
- 1 ½ tsp. salt
- 1 tbsp. butter
- cups almond flour
- tsp. active dry yeast

DIRECTION

- Using a microwave, combine beer and American cheese and warm for 20 seconds.
- Transfer the beer mixture on the bread machine pan and add all the other ingredients as listed above.
- Close the bread machine lid and select WHITE BREAD setting (or BASIC setting and press START button.
- When the cycle ends, cool the bread on a cooling rack.
- Slice then serve with a bowl of chili or beef stew.

PREPARATION	COOKING	SERVINGS
10 MINT	0 *mins*	10

Keto Monterey Jack Jalapeno Bread

NUTRITION Calories: 47 , Calories from fat: 27, Total Fat: 3 g, Total Carbohydrates: 3 g
, Net Carbohydrates: 2 g, Protein: 2 g

INGREDIENTS

- 1 cup water
- tbsps. non-fat milk
- 1 ½ tbsps. sugar
- 1 ½ tsp. salt
- 1 ½ tbsps. butter, cubed
- ¼ cup Monterey Jack cheese, shredded
- 1 small jalapeno pepper
- cups almond flour
- tsp. active dry yeast

DIRECTION

- Get rid of the seeds and stem of the jalapeno and mince finely.
- Add the ingredients in the bread machine pan as listed above.
- Close the lid and select BASIC cycle and light or medium CRUST COLOR, then press START.
- Once the cycle ends, transfer the loaf in a cooling rack before slicing.
- Serve as a side dish for salad or your favorite main course.

PREPARATION	COOKING TIME	SERVINGS
15 MINT	0 *mins*	12

Keto Orange Cranberry Bread

NUTRITION Calories: 141 , Calories from fat: 110, Total Fat: 12 g, Total Carbohydrates: 5 g , Net Carbohydrates: 4 g, Protein: 4 g

INGREDIENTS

- ¼ cup almond flour
- 1 tbsp. baking powder
- ¼ tsp. kosher salt
- large eggs
- 1 ½ cup buttermilk
- tbsp. canola oil
- 1 ½ cup brown sugar
- ½ tbsp. vanilla
- ½ tsp. nutmeg
- ¾ tsp. orange zest
- tbsp. orange juice, fresh
- 1 cup fresh cranberries, chopped

DIRECTION

- Position all the ingredients in your bread machine bucket except for the cranberries.
- Close the bread machine before selecting QUICK BREAD setting on your bread machine then press START.
- Wait for the ping or the fruit and nut signal to open the lid and add the chopped cranberries. Cover the lid again and press START to continue.
- When the cycle finishes, transfer the loaf to a wire rack and let it cool.
- Slice and serve with your favorite salad.

PREPARATION	COOKING TIME	SERVINGS
10 MINT	0 *mins*	10

Keto Rye Sandwich Bread

NUTRITION Calories: 275 , Calories from fat: 144 , Total Fat: 16 g, Total Carbohydrates: 12 , Net, Carbohydrates: 8 g, Protein: 22 g

INGREDIENTS

- ¼ cups warm water
- 2 tbsps. melted butter, unsalted
- 2 tsps. white sugar
- 1 ½ tsp. salt
- 1 tbsp. baking powder
- ¼ tsp. ground ginger
- ¼ cup granulated swerve
- cups vital wheat gluten
- cups super fine almond flour
- ¼ cup dark rye flour
- 1 tsps. Active dry yeast
- 1 tbsp. caraway seeds

DIRECTION

- Position all ingredients in the bread machine bucket and close the lid.
- Select the WHOLE WHEAT cycle in your bread machine setting and choose light color on CRUST COLOR. Press START.
- When the cycle ends, remove the pan from the bread machine and transfer the loaf on a cooling rack.
- Slice and make a pastrami or Rueben sandwich to serve.

PREPARATION	COOKING TIME	SERVINGS
10 MINT	3 *hour*	12

Swiss Whole Meal Cheese Bread

NUTRITION Carbohydrates 5 g , Fats 1 g , Protein 4.1 g , Calories 118

INGREDIENTS

- ¾ cup warm water
- 1 tablespoon sugar
- 1 teaspoon salt
- tablespoons green cheese
- 1 cup flour
- 9/10 cup flour whole-grain, finely ground
- 1 teaspoon yeast
- 1 teaspoon paprika

DIRECTION

- Ingredients are listed in the order in which they are placed in the bread machine.
- Add paprika at the signal.
- The bread is gray, with a porous pulp. And, it does not become stale for a long time. It has a unique flavor, with very interesting cheese notes.

PREPARATION	COOKING TIME	SERVINGS
3 HOURS	0 *mins*	8

Mustard Beer Bread

NUTRITION Carbohydrates 4.2 g , Fats 1 g , Protein 4.1 g , Calories 118

INGREDIENTS

- 1 ¼ cups dark beer
- 1/3 cups flour
- ¾ cup whole meal flour
- 1 tablespoon olive oil
- teaspoons mustard seeds
- 1 ½ teaspoons dry yeast
- 1 teaspoon salt
- teaspoons brown sugar

DIRECTION

- Open a beer bottle and let it stand for 30 minutes to get out the gas.
- In a bread maker's bucket, add the beer, mustard seeds, butter, sifted flour, and whole meal flour.
- From different angles in the bucket, put salt and sugar. In the center of the flour, make a groove and fill with the mustard seeds.
- Start the baking program.

PREPARATION	COOKING TIME	SERVINGS
3 HOURS	0 mins	8

Basic Sweet Yeast Bread

NUTRITION Carbohydrates 2.7 g , Fats 7.6 g , Protein 8.8 g , Calories 338

INGREDIENTS

- 1 egg
- ¼ cup butter
- 1/3 cup sugar
- 1 cup milk
- ½ teaspoon salt
- cups almond flour
- 1 tablespoon active dry yeast
- After beeping:
- fruits/ground nuts

DIRECTION

- Put all of the ingredients to your bread machine, carefully following the instructions of the manufacturer (except fruits/ground nuts).
- Set the program of your bread machine to BASIC/SWEET and set crust type to LIGHT or MEDIUM.
- Press START.
- Once the machine beeps, add fruits/ground nuts.
- Wait until the cycle completes.
- Once the loaf is ready, take the bucket out and let the loaf cool for 5 minutes.
- Gently shake the bucket to remove loaf.
- Move it to a cooling rack, slice and serve.
- Enjoy!

PREPARATION	COOKING TIME	SERVINGS
3 HOURS	0 mins	8

Keto Flaxseed Honey Bread

NUTRITION Calories: 96 , Calories from fat: 36, Total Fat: 4 g, Total Carbohydrates: 5 g , Net Carbohydrates: 3 g, Protein: 8 g

INGREDIENTS

- 1 cup warm water
- small eggs, lightly beaten
- ½ cup oat fiber
- 2/3 cup flaxseed meal
- 1.25 cup vital wheat gluten
- 1 tsp. salt
- tbsp. swerve powdered sweetener
- 1 tsp. honey
- ½ tsp. xanthan gum
- tbsps. Butter, unsalted
- 1 tbsp. dry active yeast

DIRECTION

- Pour the water on the bread bucket. E
- Add the eggs, honey, erythritol, salt, oat fiber, flaxseed meal, wheat gluten, and xanthan in this order. Add softened butter and yeast.
- Place back the bread bucket in your bread machine and close the lid. Select BASIC then select medium darkness on CRUST COLOR. Press START button and wait until the bread cooks.
- Cool bread on a cooling rack before slicing.
- Serve with grilled chicken or any of your favorite grilled meat. Note that nutrition info is only for the bread.

PREPARATION	COOKING TIME	SERVINGS
10 MINT	20 mins	18 slices

Apricot Prune Bread

NUTRITION Carbohydrates 4 g , Fats 8.2 g , Protein 9 g , Calories 364

INGREDIENTS

- 1 egg
- 4/5 cup whole milk
- ¼ cup apricot juice
- ¼ cup butter
- 1/5 cup sugar
- cups almond flour
- 1 tablespoon instant yeast
- ¼ teaspoon salt
- 5/8 cup prunes, chopped
- 5/8 cup dried apricots, chopped

DIRECTION

- Put all of the ingredients to your bread machine, carefully following the instructions of the manufacturer (except apricots and prunes).
- Set the program of your bread machine to BASIC/SWEET and set crust type to LIGHT or MEDIUM.
- Press START.
- Once the machine beeps, add apricots and prunes.
- Wait until the cycle completes.
- Once the loaf is ready, take the bucket out and let the loaf cool for 5 minutes.
- Gently shake the bucket to remove loaf.
- Move it to a cooling rack, slice and serve.
- Enjoy!

PREPARATION	COOKING	SERVINGS
3 HOURS	0 mins	8

Gluten Free Chocolate Zucchini Bread

NUTRITION Calories 185 , Carbohydrates 6 g , Fats 17 g , Protein 5 g

INGREDIENTS

- 1 ½ cups coconut flour
- ¼ cup unsweetened cocoa powder
- ½ cup erythritol
- ½ tsp cinnamon
- 1 tsp baking soda
- 1 tsp baking powder
- ¼ tsp salt
- ¼ cup coconut oil, melted
- eggs
- 1 tsp vanilla
- cups zucchini, shredded

DIRECTION

- Strip the zucchini and use paper towels to drain excess water, set aside.
- Lightly beat eggs with coconut oil then add to bread machine pan.
- Add the remaining ingredients to the pan.
- Set bread machine to gluten free.
- When the bread is done, remove bread machine pan from the bread machine.
- Cool to some extent before transferring to a cooling rack.
- You can store your bread for up to 5 days.

PREPARATION	COOKING TIME	SERVINGS
5 HOUR	0 *mins*	12

Chapter 14.
Bread Machine Recipes

Not Your Everyday Bread

NUTRITION Calories 175 , Carbohydrates 6 g , Fats 14 g , Protein 5 g

INGREDIENTS

- tsp active dry yeast
- 1 tbsp. inulin
- ½ cup warm water
- ¾ cup almond flour
- ¼ cup golden flaxseed, ground
- 2 tbsp. whey protein isolate
- 1 tbsp. psyllium husk finely ground
- 1tsp xanthan gum
- 1 tsp baking powder
- 1 tsp salt
- ¼ tsp cream of tartar
- ¼ tsp ginger, ground
- 1 egg
- egg whites
- 1 tbsp. ghee
- 1 tbsp. apple cider vinegar
- ¼ cup sour cream

DIRECTION

- Pour wet ingredients into bread machine pan.
- Add dry ingredients, with the yeast on top.
- Set bread machine to basic bread setting.
- When the bread is done, remove bread machine pan from the bread machine.
- Cool to some extent before transferring to a cooling rack.
- You can store your bread for up to 5 days.

PREPARATION	COOKING TIME	SERVINGS
7 MINT	0 mins	12

Great Plum Bread

NUTRITION Calories 199, Fat 8, Fiber 3, Carbs 6, Protein 4

INGREDIENTS

- 1 cup plums, pitted and chopped
- 1 and ½ cups coconut flour
- ¼ teaspoon baking soda
- ½ cup ghee, melted
- A pinch of salt
- 1 and ¼ cups swerve
- ½ teaspoon vanilla extract
- 1/3 cup coconut cream
- eggs, whisked

DIRECTION

- Using a bowl, mix the flour with baking soda, salt, swerve, and the vanilla and stir.
- Using a separate bowl, mix the plums with the remaining ingredients and stir.
- Combine the 2 mixtures and stir the batter well.
- Pour into 2 lined loaf pans and bake at temperature 350 degrees f for 50 minutes.
- Cool the bread down, slice and serve them.

PREPARATION	COOKING	SERVINGS
10 MINT	50 mins	8

Lime Bread

NUTRITION Calories 203, Fat 7, Fiber 3, Carbs 4, Protein 6

INGREDIENTS

- 2/3 cup ghee, melted
- cups swerve
- eggs, whisked
- teaspoons baking powder
- 1 cup almond milk
- tablespoons lime zest, grated
- tablespoons lime juice
- cups coconut flour
- Cooking spray

DIRECTION

- Using a bowl, mix the flour with lime zest, baking powder and the swerve and stir.
- In a separate bowl, mix the lime juice with the rest of the ingredients except the cooking spray and stir well.
- Combine the 2 mixtures, stir the batter well and pour into 2 loaf pans greased with cooking spray and bake at 350 degrees f for 50 minutes.
- Cool the bread down, slice and serve.

PREPARATION	COOKING TIME	SERVINGS
10 MINT	50 mins	8

Delicious Cantaloupe Bread

NUTRITION Calories 211, Fat 8, Fiber 3, Carbs 6, Protein 6

INGREDIENTS

- tablespoons stevia
- eggs
- 1 cup coconut oil, melted
- 1 tablespoon vanilla extract
- 1 teaspoon baking powder
- 1 teaspoon baking soda
- teaspoons cinnamon powder
- ½ teaspoon ginger, ground
- cups cantaloupe, peeled and pureed
- ½ cup ghee, melted
- cups almond flour

DIRECTION

- Using a bowl, mix the flour with ginger, cinnamon, baking soda, baking powder, vanilla and the stevia and stir.
- Drop the rest of the ingredients and stir the batter well.
- Pour into 2 lined loaf pans and bake at 360 degrees f for 1 hour.
- Cool the bread down, slice and serve.

PREPARATION	COOKING TIME	SERVINGS
10 MINT	1 hour	8

Delicious Rhubarb Bread

NUTRITION Calories 200, Fat 7, Fiber 2, Carbs 4, Protein 6

INGREDIENTS

- 1 cup almond milk
- 1 teaspoon vanilla extract
- 1 tablespoon lemon juice
- 2/3 cup coconut oil, melted
- 1 egg
- 1 and ½ cups swerve
- an ½ cups coconut flour
- A pinch of salt
- cups rhubarb, chopped
- 1 teaspoon baking soda
- ½ teaspoon cinnamon powder
- 1 tablespoon ghee, melted
- Cooking spray

DIRECTION

- Using a bowl, mix the vanilla with lemon juice, swerve, flour, salt, rhubarb, baking soda, and the cinnamon and stir.
- Drop the rest of the ingredients except the cooking spray, stir the batter and pour into a loaf pan greased with cooking spray.
- Bake at temperature 350 degrees f for 40 minutes, cool down, slice and serve.

PREPARATION	COOKING TIME	SERVINGS
10 MINT	40 mins	10

Carrot Polenta Loaf

NUTRITION 146 Calories, 1 mg cholesterol, 2 g total fat, 186 mg sodium, 27 g carb. 2 fiber, 3.9 g protein

INGREDIENTS

- oz. lukewarm water
- tablespoons extra-virgin olive oil
- 1 tsp salt
- 1 ½ tablespoons sugar
- 1 ½ tablespoons dried thyme
- 1 ½ cups freshly-grated carrots
- 1/2 cup yellow cornmeal
- 1 cup light rye flour
- ½ cups bread flour
- tsp instant active dry yeast

DIRECTION

- 1   Add all ingredients to machine pan.
- 2   Select dough setting.
- 3   When cycle is complete, turn dough onto lightly floured surface.
- 4   Knead the dough and shape into an oval; cover with plastic wrap and let rest for 10 to 15 minutes.
- 5   After resting, turn bottom side up and flatten.
- 6   Make a fold at the top 1/3 of the way to the bottom. Then fold the bottom a 1/3 of the way over the top.
- 7   Preheat oven 400.
- 8   Dust a baking sheet with cornmeal, place dough on and cover in a warm place to rise for 20 minutes.
- 9   After rising, make 3 deep diagonal slashes on the top and brush the top of the bread with cold water.
- 10   Bake until nicely browned for approximately 20 to 25 minutes.

PREPARATION	COOKING	SERVINGS
5MINT	3 hour	1 loaf

Sauerkraut Rye Bread

NUTRITION 74 Calories, 1.8 g total fat (0 g sat. fat), 4 mg Chol., 411 mg sodium, 12 g

INGREDIENTS

- 1 cup sauerkraut – rinsed and drained
- 3/4 cup warm water
- 1 ½ tablespoons molasses
- 1 ½ tablespoons butter
- 1 ½ tablespoons brown sugar
- 1 tsp caraway seed
- 1 ½ tsp salt
- 1 cup rye flour
- cups bread flour
- 1 ½ tsp active dry yeast

DIRECTION

- Add all ingredients to machine pan.
- Select basic bread setting.

PREPARATION	COOKING TIME	SERVINGS
5 MINT	3 hour	1 loaf

Waikiki Cornbread

NUTRITION Calories: 295 , Total Fat: 17.4 g , Cholesterol: 72 mg , Sodium: 498 mg , Total Carbohydrate: 31.3 g , Protein: 4.1 g

INGREDIENTS

- cups buttermilk baking mix
- 1 cup white sugar
- 1/2 teaspoons baking powder
- 1/4 cup yellow cornmeal
- eggs
- 1 1/4 cups milk
- 1 cup butter, melted

DIRECTION

Preheat oven at temperature 350 degrees F (175 degrees C). Lightly grease a 9x13 inch baking pan.
In a giant mixing bowl, combine baking mix, sugar, baking powder and cornmeal.
In a separate bowl, combine eggs, milk and melted butter; beat until creamy. Stir in flour mixture until well combined. Pour batter into prepared pan.
Bake at temperature 350 degrees F (175 degrees C) for 30 minutes, or until a toothpick inserted into the center of the bread comes out clean. Serve warm.

PREPARATION	COOKING TIME	SERVINGS
15 MINT	30 mins	15

Vegetable Spoon Bread

NUTRITION Calories: 234 , Fat: 2 Calories: 226 , Total Fat: 12.2 g , Cholesterol: 53 mg , Sodium: 605 mg , Total Carbohydrate: 24.8 g , Protein: 5.9 g 3g , Carb: 1g

INGREDIENTS

- 1 (10 ounce) package frozen chopped spinach, thawed and squeezed dry
- eggs, beaten
- 1 (8 ounce) can cream-style corn
- 1 cup low-fat sour cream
- 1/4 cup margarine, melted
- 1 (8.5 ounce) package corn muffin mix

DIRECTION

- Preheat the oven at temperature 350 degrees F (175 degrees C). Grease a 9 inch square baking dish.
- In a giant bowl, stir together the spinach, eggs, corn, sour cream and margarine until well blended. Stir in the dry cornbread mix. Dispense into the prepared pan, and spread evenly.
- Bake for 35 minutes in the preheated oven, or until firm and slightly browned on the top.

PREPARATION	COOKING TIME	SERVINGS
10 MINT	35 mins	9

Unleavened Cornbread

NUTRITION Calories: 150 , Total Fat: 5.4 g , Cholesterol: 17 mg , Sodium: 209 mg , Total Carbohydrate: 22.2 g , Protein: 3.1 g

INGREDIENTS

- 1 cup cornmeal
- 1 cup all-purpose flour
- 1/4 cup white sugar
- 1 teaspoon salt
- 1 egg
- 1/4 cup shortening, melted
- 1 cup milk

DIRECTION

- Preheat the oven at temperature 425 degrees F (220 degrees C). Lubricate a 12 cup muffin pan or line with muffin papers.
- Using a large bowl, stir together the cornmeal, flour, sugar and salt. Make a well in the mid and pour in the egg, shortening and milk. Stir until well blended. Spoon batter into the prepared muffin cups.
- Bake for 20 to 25 minutes until a toothpick inserted into the middle of a muffin comes out clean.

PREPARATION	COOKING	SERVINGS
10 MINT	25 mins	12

Vegan Corn Bread

NUTRITION Calories: 218 , Total Fat: 9.1 g , Cholesterol: 0 mg , Sodium: 438 mg , Total Carbohydrate: 30.3 g , Protein: 3.8 g

INGREDIENTS

- 1 cup all-purpose flour
- 1 cup cornmeal
- 1/4 cup turbinado sugar
- 1 tablespoon baking powder
- 1 teaspoon salt
- 1 cup sweetened, plain soy milk
- 1/3 cup vegetable oil
- 1/4 cup soft silken tofu

DIRECTION

- Preheat an oven at temperature 400 degrees F (200 degrees C). Lubricate a 7 inch square baking pan. Whisk together the flour, cornmeal, sugar, baking powder, and salt in a mixing bowl; set aside.
- Place the soy milk, oil, and tofu into a blender. Cover, and puree until smooth. Make a well in the mid of the cornmeal mixture. Pour the pureed tofu into the well, then stir in the cornmeal mixture until just moistened. Dispense the batter into the prepared baking pan.
- Bake in the preheated oven until a toothpick inserted into the center comes out clean, 20 to 25 minutes. Cut into 9 pieces, and serve warm.

PREPARATION	COOKING TIME	SERVINGS
15 MINT	20 mins	9

Herb Focaccia Bread

NUTRITION Calories: 108 , Carbs: 37.4 g , Fiber: 1.6 g , Fat: 7.3 g , Protein: 7.7 g

INGREDIENTS

- Dough:
- 1 cup water
- tablespoons canola oil
- 1 teaspoon salt
- 1 teaspoon dried basil
- cups bread flour
- teaspoons bread machine yeast
- Topping:
- 1 tablespoon canola oil
- ½ cup fresh basil
- cloves garlic (to taste)
- tablespoons grated parmesan cheese
- 1 pinch salt
- 1 tablespoon cornmeal (optional)

DIRECTION

- Put all of the bread ingredients in your bread machine, in the order listed above starting with the water, and finishing with the yeast. Make a well in mid of the flour and place the yeast in the well. Make sure the well doesn't touch any liquid. Put the bread machine to the dough function.
- Check on the dough after about 5 minutes and make sure that it's a soft ball. Put water 1 tablespoon at a time if it's too dry, and add flour 1 tablespoon at a time if it's too wet.
- When dough is ready set it on a lightly floured hard surface. Place a cover it and let it rest for 10 minutes.
- While the dough is resting, chop up the garlic and basil, grease a 13x9 inch pan and evenly distribute cornmeal on top of it.

PREPARATION	COOKING TIME	SERVINGS
3.5 HOURS	0 mins	8

German Black Bread

NUTRITION Calories: 102 , Carbs: 3.8 g , Fiber: 3.4 g , Fat: 1.4 g , Protein: 5.0 g.

INGREDIENTS

- 1 cup water plus 2 table-spoons water
- tablespoons apple cider vinegar
- tablespoons molasses
- 1 tablespoon sugar
- 1 teaspoon salt
- 1 teaspoon instant coffee
- ¼ teaspoon fennel seeds
- 1 tablespoon caraway seeds
- ½ ounce unsweetened chocolate
- ½ cup bran cereal flakes
- ½ cup bread flour
- ½ cup rye flour
- cups whole almond flour
- 1 package active dry yeast

DIRECTION

- Put all of the bread ingredients in your bread machine in the order listed above starting with the water, and finishing with the yeast. Put the bread machine to the whole wheat function.
- Check on the dough after about 5 minutes and make sure that it's a soft ball. Put water 1 tablespoon at a time if it's too dry, and add flour 1 tablespoon at a time if it's too wet.
- When bread is done allow it cool on a wire rack.

PREPARATION	COOKING TIME	SERVINGS
3 50 *hour mins*	0 *mins*	*10*

Jalapeno Loaf

NUTRITION Calories 300, Fat 20, Fiber 3, Carbs 4, Protein 12

INGREDIENTS

- 1 and ½ cups almond flour
- ½ cup flaxseed meal
- A pinch of salt
- teaspoons baking powder
- tablespoons butter, melted
- ½ cup sour cream
- eggs
- drops stevia
- jalapenos, chopped
- ½ cup cheddar, grated
- Cooking spray

DIRECTION

- Using a bowl, mix the flour with flaxseed meal, salt, baking powder, stevia, jalapenos and the cheese and stir.
- Put the remaining ingredients and mix them until you obtain a dough.
- Transfer it to a loaf pan greased with cooking spray and bake at 375 degrees f for 22 minutes.
- Cool the bread down, slice and serve.

PREPARATION	COOKING TIME	SERVINGS
10 MINT	15 *mins*	6

Cheesy Broccoli Bread

NUTRITION Calories 244, Fat 20, Fiber 4, Carbs 6, Protein 6

INGREDIENTS

- *Cooking spray*
- *1 egg*
- *1 tablespoon coconut flour*
- *1 tablespoon almond flour*
- *1 tablespoon almond milk*
- *1 tablespoon butter, melted*
- *¼ teaspoon baking powder*
- *A pinch of salt*
- *1 tablespoon broccoli, chopped*
- *1 tablespoon mozzarella, grated*

DIRECTION

- By means of a bowl, mix the almond flour with the coconut flour, baking powder, salt, broccoli and the mozzarella and stir.
- Put the remaining ingredients except the cooking spray and stir everything really well.
- Grease a loaf pan with cooking spray, pour the bread batter, cook at 400 degrees f for 15 minutes, cool down and serve.

PREPARATION	COOKING TIME	SERVINGS
10 MINT	15 *mins*	2

Artichoke Bread

NUTRITION Calories 211, Fat 12, Fiber 3, Carbs 5, Protein 6

INGREDIENTS

- *oz. canned artichoke hearts*
- *1 garlic clove, minced*
- *1 cup parmesan, grated*
- *1 cup almond flour*
- *½ teaspoon baking powder*
- *1 and ½ cups warm water*

DIRECTION

- Using a bowl, mix the flour with baking powder, and the water and stir well.
- Add the rest of the ingredients, stir the dough well and transfer it to a lined round pan.
- Bake at temperature 360 degrees f for 30 minutes, cool the bread down, slice and serve.

PREPARATION	COOKING TIME	SERVINGS
10 MINT	30 *mins*	10

Dutch Oven Bread

NUTRITION Calories 143, Fat 9, Fiber 3, Carbs 4, Protein 6

INGREDIENTS

- 1 teaspoon baking powder
- 1 teaspoon baking soda
- cups almond flour
- 1 and ½ cups warm water
- A pinch of salt
- 1 teaspoon stevia

DIRECTION

- Using a bowl, mix the water with the flour and stir well.
- Add the rest of the ingredients, stir until you obtain a dough and leave aside for 20 minutes.
- Transfer the dough to a dutch oven and bake the bread at 400 degrees f for 30 minutes.
- Cool the bread down, slice and serve.

PREPARATION	COOKING TIME	SERVINGS
20 MINT	30 mins	6

Keto Spinach Bread

NUTRITION Calories 142, Fat 7, Fiber 3, Carbs 5, Protein 6

INGREDIENTS

- ½ cup spinach, chopped
- 1 tablespoon olive oil
- 1 cup water
- cups almond flour
- A pinch of salt and black pepper
- 1 tablespoon stevia
- 1 teaspoon baking powder
- 1 teaspoon baking soda
- ½ cup cheddar, shredded

DIRECTION

- Using a bowl, mix the flour, with salt, pepper, stevia, baking powder, baking soda and the cheddar and stir well.
- Add the remaining ingredients, stir the batter really well and pour it into a lined loaf pan.
- Cook at temperature 350 degrees f for 30 minutes, cool the bread down, slice and serve.

PREPARATION	COOKING	SERVINGS
10 MINT	30 mins	10

Cinnamon Asparagus Bread

NUTRITION Calories 165, Fat 6, Fiber 3, Carbs 5, Protein 6

INGREDIENTS

- 1 cup stevia
- ¾ cup coconut oil, melted
- 1 and ½ cups almond flour
- eggs, whisked
- A pinch of salt
- 1 teaspoon baking soda
- 1 teaspoon cinnamon powder
- cups asparagus, chopped
- Cooking spray

DIRECTION

- Using a bowl, mix all the ingredients except the cooking spray and stir the batter really well.
- Pour this batter into a loaf pan greased with cooking spray and bake at 350 degrees f for 45 minutes, cool the bread down, slice and serve.

PREPARATION	COOKING TIME	SERVINGS
10 MINT	45 *mins*	8

Beet Bread

NUTRITION Calories 200, Fat 8, Fiber 3, Carbs 5, Protein 6

INGREDIENTS

- 1 cup warm water
- and ½ cups almond flour
- 1 and ½ cups beet puree
- tablespoons olive oil
- A pinch of salt
- 1 teaspoon stevia
- 1 teaspoon baking powder
- 1 teaspoon baking soda

DIRECTION

- Using a bowl, combine the flour with the water and beet puree and stir well.
- Add the rest of the ingredients, stir the dough well and pour it into a lined loaf pan.
- Let the mix to rise in a warm place for 1 hour, and then bake the bread at temperature 375 degrees f for 35 minutes.
- Cool the bread down, slice and serve.

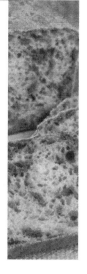

PREPARATION	COOKING TIME	SERVINGS
1 HOURS 10 *mins*	35 *mins*	6

Kale and Cheese Bread

NUTRITION Calories 231, Fat 7, Fiber 2, Carbs 5, Protein 7

INGREDIENTS

- cups kale, chopped
- 1 cup warm water
- 1 teaspoon baking powder
- 1 teaspoon baking soda
- tablespoons olive oil
- teaspoons stevia
- 1 cup parmesan, grated
- cups almond flour
- A pinch of salt
- 1 egg
- tablespoons basil, chopped

DIRECTION

- Using a bowl, mix the flour, salt, parmesan, stevia, baking soda and baking powder and stir.
- Put the rest of the ingredients gradually and stir the dough well.
- Transfer it to a lined loaf pan, cook at 350 degrees f for 1 hour, cool down, slice and serve.

PREPARATION	COOKING TIME	SERVINGS
10 MINT	1 hour	8

Keto Celery Bread

NUTRITION Calories 162, Fat 6, Fiber 2, Carbs 6, Protein 4

INGREDIENTS

- ½ cup celery, chopped
- cups almond flour
- 1 teaspoon baking powder
- 1 teaspoon baking soda
- A pinch of salt
- tablespoons coconut oil, melted
- ½ cup celery puree

DIRECTION

- Using a bowl, mix the flour with salt, baking powder and baking soda and stir.
- Add the rest of the ingredients, stir the dough well, cover the bowl and keep in a warm place for 2 hours.
- Move the dough to a lined loaf pan and cook at 400 degrees f for 35 minutes.
- Cool the bread down, slice and serve.

PREPARATION	COOKING TIME	SERVINGS
2 HOURS 10 mins	35 mins	6

Easy Cucumber Bread

NUTRITION Calories 243, Fat 12, Fiber 3, Carbs 6, Protein 7

INGREDIENTS

- 1 cup erythritol
- 1 cup coconut oil, melted
- 1 cup almonds, chopped
- 1 teaspoon vanilla extract
- A pinch of salt
- A pinch of nutmeg, ground
- ½ teaspoon baking powder
- A pinch of cloves
- eggs
- 1 teaspoon baking soda
- 1 tablespoon cinnamon powder
- cups cucumber, peeled, deseeded and shredded
- cups coconut flour
- Cooking spray

DIRECTION

- Using a bowl, mix the flour with cucumber, cinnamon, baking soda, cloves, baking powder, nutmeg, salt, vanilla extract and the almonds and stir well.
- Put the rest of the ingredients except the coconut flour, stir well and transfer the dough to a loaf pan greased with cooking spray.
- Bake at temperature of 325 degrees f for 50 minutes, cool the bread down, slice and serve.

PREPARATION	COOKING TIME	SERVINGS
10 MINT	50 mins	6

Chapter 15.
Nut and Seed Bread

Red Bell Pepper Bread

NUTRITION Calories 100, Fat 5, Fiber 1, Carbs 4, Protein 4

INGREDIENTS

- 1 and ½ cups red bell peppers, chopped
- 1 teaspoon baking powder
- 1 teaspoon baking soda
- tablespoons warm water
- 1 and ¼ cups parmesan, grated
- A pinch of salt
- cups almond flour
- tablespoons ghee, melted
- 1/3 cup almond milk
- 1 egg

DIRECTION

- Using a bowl, mix the flour with salt, parmesan, baking powder, baking soda and the bell peppers and stir well.
- Put the rest of the ingredients and stir the bread batter well.
- Transfer it to a lined loaf pan and bake at 350 degrees f for 30 minutes.
- Cool the bread down, slice and serve.

PREPARATION	COOKING TIME	SERVINGS
10 MINT	30 *mins*	12

Flax and Sunflower Seed Bread

NUTRITION Calories: 140 calories;, Sodium: 169 , Total Carbohydrate: 22.7 , Cholesterol: 4 , Protein: 4.2 , Total Fat: 4.2

INGREDIENTS

- 1 1/3 cups water
- Two tablespoons butter softened
- Three tablespoons honey
- 2/3 cups of bread flour
- One teaspoon salt
- One teaspoon active dry yeast
- 1/2 cup flax seeds
- 1/2 cup sunflower seeds

DIRECTION

- With the manufacturer's suggested order, add all the ingredients (apart from sunflower seeds) to the bread machine's pan.
- The select basic white cycle, then press start.
- Just in the knead cycle that your machine signals alert sounds, add the sunflower seeds.

PREPARATION	COOKING	SERVINGS
5 MINT	25 *mins*	8

Honey and Flaxseed Bread

NUTRITION Calories: 174 calories;, Protein: 7.1 , Total Fat: 4.9 , Sodium: 242 , Total Carbohydrate: 30.8 , Cholesterol: 1

INGREDIENTS

- 1 1/8 cups water
- 1 1/2 tablespoons flaxseed oil
- Three tablespoons honey
- 1/2 tablespoon liquid lecithin
- cups whole wheat flour
- 1/2 cup flax seed
- Two tablespoons bread flour
- Three tablespoons whey powder
- 1 1/2 teaspoons sea salt
- Two teaspoons active dry yeast

DIRECTION

- In the bread machine pan, put in all of the ingredients following the order recommended by the manufacturer.
- Choose the Wheat cycle on the machine and press the Start button to run the machine.

PREPARATION	COOKING TIME	SERVINGS
5 MINT	25 mins	8

Seven Grain Bread

NUTRITION Calories: 285 calories;, Total Fat: 5.2 , Sodium: 629 , Total Carbohydrate: 50.6 , Cholesterol: 24 , Protein: 9.8

INGREDIENTS

- 1 1/3 cups warm water
- One tablespoon active dry yeast
- Three tablespoons dry milk powder
- Two tablespoons vegetable oil
- Two tablespoons honey
- Two teaspoons salt
- One egg
- 1 cup whole wheat flour
- 1/2 cups bread flour
- 3/4 cup 7-grain cereal

DIRECTION

- Follow the order of putting the ingredients into the pan of the bread machine recommended by the manufacturer.
- Choose the Whole Wheat Bread cycle on the machine and press the Start button to run the machine.

PREPARATION	COOKING TIME	SERVINGS
5 MINT	25 mins	8

Pumpkin and Sunflower Seed Bread

NUTRITION Calories: 148 calories; , Total Carbohydrate: 24.1 , Cholesterol: 0 , Protein: 5.1 , Total Fat: 4.8 , Sodium: 158

INGREDIENTS

- 1 (.25 ounce) package instant yeast
- 1 cup of warm water
- 1/4 cup honey
- Four teaspoons vegetable oil
- cups whole wheat flour
- 1/4 cup wheat bran (optional)
- One teaspoon salt
- 1/3 cup sunflower seeds
- 1/3 cup shelled, toasted, chopped pumpkin seeds

DIRECTION

- Into the bread machine, put the ingredients according to the order suggested by the manufacturer.
- Next is setting the machine to the whole wheat setting, then press the start button.
- You can add the pumpkin and sunflower seeds at the beep if your bread machine has a signal for nuts or fruit.

PREPARATION	COOKING TIME	SERVINGS
5 MINT	25 mins	8

Wheat Bread with Flax Seed

NUTRITION Calories: 168 calories, Total Carbohydrate: 22.5 , Cholesterol: 1 , Protein: 5.5 , Total Fat: 7.3 , Sodium: 245

INGREDIENTS

- 1 (.25 ounce) package active dry yeast
- 1 1/4 cups whole wheat flour
- 3/4 cup ground flax seed
- 1 cup bread flour
- One tablespoon vital wheat gluten
- Two tablespoons dry milk powder
- One teaspoon salt
- 1 1/2 tablespoons vegetable oil
- 1/4 cup honey
- 1 1/2 cups water

DIRECTION

- In the bread machine pan, put the ingredients following the order recommendation of the manufacturer.
- Make sure to select the cycle and then press Start.

PREPARATION	COOKING	SERVINGS
5 MINT	25 mins	8

High Fiber Bread

NUTRITION Calories: 101 calories;, Total Fat: 2.1 , Sodium: 100 , Total Carbohydrate: 18.2 ,

INGREDIENTS

- 1 2/3 cups warm water
- Four teaspoons molasses
- One tablespoon active dry yeast
- 2/3 cups whole wheat flour
- 3/4 cup ground flax seed
- 2/3 cup bread flour
- 1/2 cup oat bran
- 1/3 cup rolled oats
- 1/3 cup amaranth seeds
- One teaspoon salt

DIRECTION

- In the bread machine pan, put in the water, molasses, yeast, wheat flour, ground flaxseed, bread flour, oat bran, rolled oats, amaranth seeds, and salt in the manufacturer's suggested order of ingredients. Choose the Dough cycle on the machine and press the Start button; let the machine finish the whole Dough cycle.
- Put the dough on a clean surface that is covered with a little bit of flour. Shape the dough into two loaves and put it on a baking stone. Use a slightly wet cloth to shelter the loaves and allow it to rise in volume for about 1 hour until it has doubled in size.
- Preheat the oven to 375°F.
- Put in the warm-up oven and bake for 20-25 minutes until the top part of the loaf turns golden brown. Let the loaf slide onto a clean working surface and tap the loaf's bottom part gently. The bread is done if you hear a hollow sound when tapped.

PREPARATION	COOKING TIME	SERVINGS
5 MINT	25 mins	8

High Protein Bread

NUTRITION Calories: 137 calories, Total Fat: 2.4 , Sodium: 235 , Total Carbohydrate: 24.1 , Cholesterol: 0 , Protein: 6.5

INGREDIENTS

- Two teaspoons active dry yeast
- 1 cup bread flour
- 1 cup whole wheat flour
- 1/4 cup soy flour
- 1/4 cup powdered soy milk
- 1/4 cup oat bran
- One tablespoon canola oil
- One tablespoon honey
- One teaspoon salt
- 1 cup of water

DIRECTION

- Into the bread machine's pan, put the ingredients by following the order suggested by the manufacturer.
- Set the machine to either the regular setting or the basic medium.
- Push the Start button.

PREPARATION	COOKING TIME	SERVINGS
5 MINT	25 mins	8

High Flavor Bran Head

NUTRITION Calories: 146 calories, Total Fat: 2.4 , Sodium: 254 , Total Carbohydrate: 27.9 , Cholesterol: 1 , Protein: 4.6

INGREDIENTS

- 1 1/2 cups warm water
- Two tablespoons dry milk powder
- Two tablespoons vegetable oil
- Two tablespoons molasses
- Two tablespoons honey
- 1 1/2 teaspoons salt
- 1/4 cups whole wheat flour
- 1 1/4 cups bread flour
- 1 cup whole bran cereal
- Two teaspoons active dry yeast

DIRECTION

- In the pan of your bread machine, move all the ingredients directed by the machine's maker.
- Set the machine to either the whole grain or whole wheat setting.

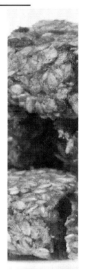

PREPARATION	COOKING TIME	SERVINGS
5 MINT	25 mins	8

Whole Wheat Bread with Sesame Seeds

NUTRITION Calories: 153 calories, Sodium: 235 , Total Carbohydrate: 28.3 , Cholesterol: 0 , Protein: 5 , Total Fat: 2.3

INGREDIENTS

- 1/2 cup water
- Two teaspoons honey
- One tablespoon vegetable oil
- 3/4 cup grated zucchini
- 3/4 cup whole wheat flour
- cups bread flour
- One tablespoon chopped fresh basil
- Two teaspoons sesame seeds
- One teaspoon salt
- 1 1/2 teaspoons active dry yeast

DIRECTION

- Follow the order of putting the ingredients into the bread machine pan recommended by the manufacturer.
- Choose the Basic Bread cycle or the Normal setting on the machine.

PREPARATION	COOKING TIME	SERVINGS
5 MINT	25 mins	8

Bagels with Poppy Seeds

NUTRITION Calories: 50 calories, Total Fat: 1.3 , Sodium: 404 , Total Carbohydrate: 8.8 , Cholesterol: 0 , Protein: 1.4

INGREDIENTS

- 1 cup of warm water
- 1 1/2 teaspoons salt
- Two tablespoons white sugar
- cups bread flour
- 1/4 teaspoons active dry yeast
- quarts boiling water
- Three tablespoons white sugar
- One tablespoon cornmeal
- One egg white
- Three tablespoons poppy seeds

DIRECTION

- In the bread machine's pan, pour in the water, salt, sugar, flour, and yeast following the order of ingredients suggested by the manufacturer. Choose the Dough setting on the machine.
- Once the machine has finished the whole cycle, place the dough on a clean surface covered with a little bit of flour; let it rest. While the dough is resting on the floured surface, put 3 quarts of water in a big pot and let it boil. Add in 3 tablespoons of sugar and mix.
- Divide the dough evenly into nine portions and shape each into a small ball. Press down each dough ball until it is flat. Use your thumb to make a shack in the center of each flattened dough. Increase the whole's size in the center and smoothen out the dough around the whole area by spinning the dough on your thumb or finger. Use a clean cloth to cover the formed bagels and let it sit for 10 minutes.
- Cover the bottom part of an ungreased baking sheet evenly with cornmeal. Place the bagels gently into the boiling water. Let it boil for 1 minute and flip it on the other side halfway through. Let the bagels drain quickly on a clean towel. Place the boiled bagels onto the prepared baking sheet. Coat the topmost of each bagel with egg white and top it off with your preferred toppings.
- Put the bagels into the preheated 375°F (190°C) oven and bake for 20-25 minutes until it turns nice brown.

PREPARATION	COOKING TIME	SERVINGS
5 MINT	25 mins	8

Moroccan Ksra

NUTRITION Calories: 111 calories, Total Fat: 1.6 , Sodium: 219 , Total Carbohydrate: 20.2 , Cholesterol: 0 , Protein: 3.6

INGREDIENTS

- 7/8 cup water
- 1/4 cups bread flour
- 3/4 cup semolina flour
- One teaspoon anise seed
- 1 1/2 teaspoons salt
- 1/2 teaspoon white sugar
- Two teaspoons active dry yeast
- One tablespoon olive oil
- One tablespoon sesame seed

DIRECTION

- In a bread machine, put the first set of ingredients according to the manufacturer's recommendation. Set to DOUGH cycle and select Start. In this procedure, refrain from mixing in the sesame seeds and olive oil.
- When the dough cycle signal stops, take the dough from the machine and deflate by punching down. Cut the dough into two halves and form it into balls. Pat the balls into a 3/4-inch thickness. Put the flattened dough on a floured baking sheet. Cover the baking sheet with towels and let it stand for about 30 minutes to rise to double.
- Set the oven to 200 degrees C (400 degrees F) to preheat. Spread the top of the loaves with olive oil using a brush and garnish with sesame seeds, if preferred. Using a fork, puncture the top of each loaf all over.
- Place the pans in the heated oven, then bake for 20 to 25 minutes, or until colors are golden and they sound hollow when tapped. Serve either warm or cold.

PREPARATION	COOKING TIME	SERVINGS
5 MINT	25 mins	8

Bruce's Honey Sesame Bread

NUTRITION Calories: 62 calories, Total Carbohydrate: 8.4 , Cholesterol: 1 , Protein: 1.7 , Total Fat: 3.1 , Sodium: 295

INGREDIENTS

- 1 1/4 cups water
- 1/4 cup honey
- One tablespoon powdered buttermilk
- 1 1/2 teaspoons salt
- cups bread flour
- Three tablespoons wheat bran
- 1/2 cup sesame seeds, toasted
- 1/4 teaspoons active dry yeast

DIRECTION

- Into the bread machine's pan, place all the ingredients by following the order endorsed by your machine's manufacturer.
- Set the mechanism to the Basic Bread cycle

PREPARATION	COOKING TIME	SERVINGS
5 MINT	25 mins	8

Bread Sticks with Sesame Seeds

NUTRITION Calories: 154, Total Fat: 3.5 , Sodium: 278 , Total Carbohydrate: 26 , Cholesterol: 5 , Protein: 4.5

INGREDIENTS

- 1 1/3 cups warm water
- Three tablespoons butter softened
- cups bread flour
- Two teaspoons salt
- 1/4 cup white sugar
- 1/4 cup sesame seeds
- Two tablespoons dry milk powder
- 1/2 teaspoons active dry yeast

DIRECTION

- Into the bread machine pan, set the ingredients according to the order given by the manufacturer. Put the machine to the Dough cycle and then push the Start button. Use cooking spray to spritz two baking sheets.
- Preheat the oven. After the dough cycle comes to an end, place the dough onto a lightly oiled surface. Separate the dough into 18 pieces. Fold every piece on a board oiled from the middle of the amount to the outside edges. It is to create breadticks. Transfer the breadticks onto the prepared pans placing at least one inch apart.
- Bake for around 15 minutes using

PREPARATION	COOKING TIME	SERVINGS
5 MINT	25 mins	8

Apricot Cake Bread

NUTRITION Calories: 144 , Fat (g): 3.6 , Protein (g): 3.9 , Carbs: 25.6

INGREDIENTS

- *Water, lukewarm*
- *Egg, at room temperature*
- *Orange juice*
- *Butter, unsalted, softened*
- *Dried apricots, snipped*
- *All-purpose flour*
- *Sugar*
- *Baking powder*
- *Baking soda*
- *Salt*
- *Chopped nuts*

DIRECTION

- Take a medium bowl, place apricots in it, pour in water, and let soak for 30 minutes.
- Then remove apricots from the water, reserve the water, and chop apricots into pieces.
- Gather the remaining ingredients needed for the bread.
- Power on bread machine that has about 2 pounds of the bread pan.
- Put all the ingredients into the bread machine pan, except for apricots and nuts in the order mentioned in the ingredients list.
- Press the "Bread" button, press the start button, let mixture knead for 5 minutes, add chopped apricots and nuts and continue kneading for 5 minutes until all the pieces have thoroughly combined and incorporated.
- Select the "basic/white" cycle, press the up/down arrow to do baking to 4 hours, choose light or medium color for the crust, and press the start button.
- When the timer of the bread machine beeps, open the machine.
- It should come out spotless, else bake for another 10 to 15 minutes.
- Cut bread into eight slices and then serve.

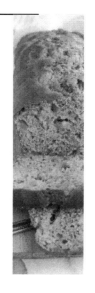

PREPARATION	COOKING TIME	SERVINGS
20 MINT	4 hour 30 mint	8

Nutty Wheat Bread

NUTRITION Calories: 187 , Fat (g): 7 , Protein (g): 5 , Carbs: 28

INGREDIENTS

- *Water, lukewarm*
- *Olive oil*
- *Honey*
- *Molasses*
- *Whole wheat flour*
- *Bread flour*
- *Dry yeast, active*
- *Salt*
- *Chopped pecans*
- *Chopped walnuts*

DIRECTION

- Gather all the ingredients needed for the bread.
- Power on bread machine that has about 2 pounds of the bread pan.
- Add all the ingredients in the order listed in the ingredients list into the bread machine pan except for pecans and nuts.
- Press the "Dough" switch, press the start button, let mixture knead for 5 minutes, add pecans and nuts, and then continue kneading for another 5 minutes until all the ingredients have thoroughly combined and incorporated.
- Then select the "basic/white" cycle, press the up/down arrow to make the baking time to 4 hours.
- Select light or medium color for the crust, and press the start button.
- Then put the bread on a wire rack for 1 hour or more until cooled.
- Cut bread into twelve slices and then serve.

PREPARATION	COOKING TIME	SERVINGS
10 MINT	4 hour	8

Cherry and Almond Bread

NUTRITION Calories: 125 , Fat (g): 3 , Protein (g): 4 , Carbs: 20.4

INGREDIENTS

- Milk, lukewarm
- Butter, unsalted, softened
- Egg, at room temperature
- Bread flour
- Dried cherries
- Slivered almonds, toasted
- Salt
- Dry yeast, active
- Sugar

DIRECTION

- Gather all the ingredients needed for the bread.
- Power on bread machine that has about 2 pounds of the bread pan.
- Add all the ingredients in the order mentioned in the ingredients list into the bread machine pan.
- Press the "Dough" button, key the left button, and let mixture knead for 5 to 10 minutes.
- Then select the "basic/white" down arrow to set baking time to 4 hours, select light or medium color for the crust, and press the start button.
- Then prudently lift out the bread and put it on a wire rack for 1 hour or more until cooled.
- Cut bread into sixteen slices and then serve.

PREPARATION	COOKING TIME	SERVINGS
10 MINT	4 hour	8

Hazelnut Yeast Bread

NUTRITION Calories: 139 , Fat (g): 6 , Protein (g): 5 , Carbs: 18

INGREDIENTS

- Milk, lukewarm
- Butter, unsalted, melted
- Egg, at room temperature
- Almond extract, unsweetened
- Salt
- Bread flour
- Sugar
- Dry yeast, active
- Chopped hazelnuts, toasted

DIRECTION

- Gather all the ingredients needed for the bread.
- Then power on bread machine that has about 2 pounds of the bread pan.
- Add all the ingredients in the order stated in the ingredients list into the bread machine pan except for nuts.
- Press the "Dough" button, press the start button, let mixture knead for 5 minutes, add nuts, and then knead for another 5 minutes until all the ingredients have thoroughly combined and incorporated.
- Then select the "basic/white" cycle, or press the up/down arrow to set baking time to 3 hours.
- Select light or medium color for the crust, and then press the start button.
- Put it on a wire rack for 1 hour or more until cooled.
- Cut bread into sixteen slices and then serve

PREPARATION	COOKING TIME	SERVINGS
10 MINT	3 hour	16

Date-Nut Yeast Bread

NUTRITION Calories: 123 , Fat (g): 2 , Protein (g): 4 , Carbs: 24

INGREDIENTS

- Water, lukewarm
- Butter, unsalted, softened
- Bread flour
- Dry yeast, active
- Brown sugar
- Salt
- Dates, chopped
- Walnuts, chopped

DIRECTION

- Gather all the ingredients needed for the bread.
- Power on bread machine that has about 2 pounds of the bread pan.
- Add all the ingredients in the order cited in the ingredients list into the bread machine pan.
- Press the "Dough" button, push the start button.
- Allow the mixture to knead for 5 to 10 minutes until all the pieces have been thoroughly combined and incorporated.
- Select the "basic/white" cycle, or press the up/down arrow to set baking day to 4 hours.
- Select light or medium color for the crust, and then press the start button.
- Then handover it to a wire rack for one hour or more until cooled.
- Cut bread into twelve slices and then serve.

PREPARATION	COOKING TIME	SERVINGS
10 MINT	4 *hour*	12

Cranberry Walnut Bread

NUTRITION Calories: 134 , Fat (g): 3 , Protein (g): 4 , Carbs: 24

INGREDIENTS

- Water, lukewarm
- Butter, unsalted, softened
- Bread flour
- Dry yeast, active
- Brown sugar
- Salt
- Ground cinnamon
- Chopped walnuts
- Dried cranberries

DIRECTION

- Gather all the ingredients needed for the bread.
- Power on bread machine that has about 2 pounds of the bread pan.
- Add all the ingredients except for nuts and cranberries into the bread machine pan in the order mentioned in the ingredients list.
- Press the "Dough" button, press the start button, let mixture knead for 5 minutes, then add walnuts and cranberries and continue kneading for 5 minutes until all the ingredients have thoroughly combined and incorporated.
- Select the "basic/white" cycle, press the up/down arrow to set baking time to 4 hours.
- Select light or medium color for the crust, and press the start button.
- Then carefully lift the bread, and transfer it to a wire rack for 1 hour or additional until cooled.
- Cut bread into slices and then serve.

PREPARATION	COOKING TIME	SERVINGS
10 MINT	4 *hour*	16

Walnut Bread with Dry Yeast

NUTRITION Calories: 135 , Fat (g): 5 , Protein (g): 5 , Carbs: 19

INGREDIENTS

- Water, lukewarm
- Egg, at room temperature
- Butter, unsalted, softened
- Bread flour
- Dry yeast, active
- Dry milk powder, nonfat
- Sugar
- Salt
- Chopped walnuts, toasted

DIRECTION

- Gather all the ingredients needed for the bread.
- Then power on bread machine that has about 2 pounds of the bread pan.
- Add all the ingredients in the order revealed in the ingredients list into the bread machine pan.
- Press the "Dough" button, press the start button, and let mixture knead for 5 to 10 minutes until all the ingredients have thoroughly combined and incorporated.
- Select the "basic/white" cycle, key the up/down arrow to set baking time to 4 hours.
- Select light or medium color for the crust, and press the start button.
- Then sensibly lift out the bread, and put it on a wire rack for 1 hour or more until cooled.
- Cut bread into twelve slices and then serve.

PREPARATION	COOKING TIME	SERVINGS
10 MINT	4 hour	12

Pumpkin Bread with Walnuts

NUTRITION Calories: 166 , Fat (g): 9 , Protein (g): 3 , Carbs: 19

INGREDIENTS

- Olive oil
- Pumpkin puree
- Eggs, at room temperature
- All-purpose flour
- Baking powder
- Baking soda
- Ground ginger
- Sugar
- Salt
- Ground cinnamon
- Ground nutmeg
- Chopped walnuts

DIRECTION

- Gather all the ingredients needed for the bread.
- Power on bread machine that has about 2 pounds of the bread pan.
- Take a large mixing bowl, add eggs to it and then beat in sugar, oil, and pumpkin puree using an electric mixer until smooth and well blended.
- Beat in salt, all the spices, baking powder, and soda, and then beat in flour, ½-cup at a time, until incorporated.
- Pour the batter into the bread pan, top with nuts, select the "cake/quick bread" cycle, or press the up/down arrow to set baking time to 1 hour.
- Choose light or medium color for the crust, and then press the start button.
- Then carefully get out the bread and hand it to a wire rack for 1 hour or more until cooled.
- Cut bread into sixteen slices and then serve.

PREPARATION	COOKING TIME	SERVINGS
10 MINT	1 hour	16

Chapter 16.
Vegetable Bread

Orange Date Bread

NUTRITION Calories: 80 | Carbohydrates: 14g| Fat: 2g | Protein: 1g

INGREDIENTS

- 2 cups all-purpose flour
- 1 cup dates, chopped
- ¾ cup of sugar
- ½ cup walnuts, chopped
- Two tablespoons orange rind, grated
- 1 ½ teaspoons baking powder
- One teaspoon baking soda
- ½ cup of orange juice
- ½ cup of water
- One tablespoon vegetable oil
- One teaspoon vanilla extract

DIRECTION

- Put the wet ingredients then the dry ingredients into the bread pan.
- Press the "Quick" or "Cake" mode of the bread machine.
- Allow all cycles to be finished.
- Remove the pan from the machine, but keep the bread in the pan for 10 minutes more.
- Take out the bread from the pan, and let it cool down completely before slicing.

PREPARATION	COOKING TIME	SERVINGS
20 MINT	1.5 hour	1 ounce (28.3g)

Banana-Lemon Loaf

NUTRITION Calories: 120 | Carbohydrates: 15g | Fat: 6g | Protein: 2g

INGREDIENTS

- 2 cups all-purpose flour
- 1 cup bananas, very ripe and mashed
- 1 cup walnuts, chopped
- 1 cup of sugar
- One tablespoon baking powder
- One teaspoon lemon peel, grated
- ½ teaspoon salt
- Two eggs
- ½ cup of vegetable oil
- Two tablespoons lemon juice

DIRECTION

- Put all ingredients into a pan in this order: bananas, wet ingredients, and then dry ingredients.
- Press the "Quick" or "Cake" setting of your bread machine.
- Allow the cycles to be completed.
- Take out the pan from the machine. The cooldown for 10 minutes before slicing the bread enjoy.

PREPARATION	COOKING TIME	SERVINGS
15 MINT	1.5 hour	1 ounce (28.3g)

Zero-Fat Carrot Pineapple Loaf

NUTRITION Calories: 70 | Carbohydrates: 16g | Fat: 0g | Protein: 1g

INGREDIENTS

- 2 ½ cups all-purpose flour
- ¾ cup of sugar
- ½ cup pineapples, crushed
- ½ cup carrots, grated
- ½ cup raisins
- Two teaspoons baking powder
- ½ teaspoon ground cinnamon
- ½ teaspoon salt
- ¼ teaspoon allspice
- ¼ teaspoon nutmeg
- ½ cup applesauce
- One tablespoon molasses

DIRECTION

- Put first the wet ingredients into the bread pan before the dry ingredients.
- Press the "Quick" or "Cake" mode of your bread machine.
- Allow the machine to complete all cycles.
- Take out the pan from the machine, but wait for another 10 minutes before transferring the bread into a wire rack.
- Cooldown the bread before slicing.

PREPARATION	COOKING TIME	SERVINGS
20 MINT	1.5 hour	1 ounce (28.3g)

Autumn Treasures Loaf

NUTRITION Calories: 80 | Carbohydrates: 12g | Fat: 3g | Protein: 1g

INGREDIENTS

- 1 cup all-purpose flour
- ½ cup dried fruit, chopped
- ¼ cup pecans, chopped
- ¼ cup of sugar
- Two tablespoons baking powder
- One teaspoon salt
- ¼ teaspoon of baking soda
- ½ teaspoon ground nutmeg
- 1 cup apple juice
- ¼ cup of vegetable oil
- Three tablespoons aquafaba
- One teaspoon of vanilla extract

DIRECTION

- Add all wet ingredients first to the bread pan before the dry ingredients.
- Turn on the bread machine with the "Quick" or "Cake" setting.
- Wait for all cycles to be finished.
- Remove the bread pan from the machine.
- After 10 minutes, transfer the bread from the pan into a wire rack.
- Slice the bread only when it has completely cooled down.

PREPARATION	COOKING TIME	SERVINGS
15 MINT	1.5 hour	1 ounce (28.3g)

Pumpkin Raisin Bread

NUTRITION Calories: 70 | Carbohydrates: 12g | Fat: 2g | Protein: 1g

INGREDIENTS

- ½ cup all-purpose flour
- ½ cup whole-wheat flour
- ½ cup pumpkin, mashed
- ½ cup raisins
- ¼ cup brown sugar
- Two tablespoons baking powder
- One teaspoon salt
- One teaspoon pumpkin pie spice
- ¼ teaspoon baking soda
- ¾ cup apple juice
- ¼ cup of vegetable oil
- Three tablespoons aquafaba

DIRECTION

- Place all ingredients in the bread pan in this order: apple juice, pumpkin, oil, aquafaba, flour, sugar, baking powder, baking soda, salt, pumpkin pie spice, and raisins.
- Select the "Quick" or "Cake" mode of your bread machine.
- Let the machine finish all cycles.
- Remove the pan from the machine.
- After 10 minutes, transfer the bread to a wire rack.
- Slice the bread only when it has completely cooled down.

PREPARATION	COOKING TIME	SERVINGS
15 MINT	1.5 hour	1 ounce (28.3g)

Oatmeal Walnut Bread

NUTRITION Calories: 80 | Carbohydrates: 11g | Fat: 3g | Protein: 2g

INGREDIENTS

- ¾ cup whole-wheat flour
- ¼ cup all-purpose flour
- ½ cup brown sugar
- 1/3 cup walnuts, chopped
- ¼ cup oatmeal
- ¼ teaspoon of baking soda
- Two tablespoons baking powder
- One teaspoon salt
- 1 cup Vegan buttermilk
- ¼ cup of vegetable oil
- Three tablespoons aquafaba

DIRECTION

- Add into the bread pan the wet ingredients then followed by the dry ingredients.
- Use the "Quick" or "Cake" setting of your bread machine.
- Allow the cycles to be completed.
- Take out the pan from the machine.
- Wait for 10 minutes, then remove the bread from the pan.
- Once the bread has cooled down, slice it and serve.

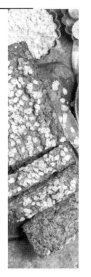

PREPARATION	COOKING TIME	SERVINGS
15 MINT	1.5 hour	1 ounce (28.3g)

Hawaiian Bread

NUTRITION Calories: 169 | Carbohydrates: 30g | Fat: 3g | Protein: 4g

INGREDIENTS

- 3 cups bread flour
- 2 ½ tablespoons brown sugar
- ¾ teaspoon salt
- Two teaspoons quick-rising yeast
- One egg
- ¾ cup pineapple juice
- Two tablespoons almond milk
- Two tablespoons vegetable oil

DIRECTION

- Pour all wet ingredients first into the bread pan before adding the dry ingredients.
- Set the bread machine to "Basic" or "Normal" mode with a light crust colour setting.
- Allow the machine to finish the mixing, kneading, and baking cycles.
- Take out the pan from the machine.
- Transfer the bread to a wire rack.
- After one hour, slice the bread and serve.

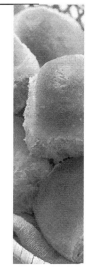

PREPARATION	COOKING TIME	SERVINGS
10MINT	3 hour	1 ounce (56.7g)

Sweet Potato Bread

NUTRITION Calories: 111 | Carbohydrates: 21g | Fat: 2g | Protein: 3g

INGREDIENTS

- 4 cups bread flour
- 1 cup sweet potatoes, mashed
- ½ cup brown sugar
- Two teaspoons yeast
- 1 ½ teaspoon salt
- ½ teaspoon cinnamon
- ½ cup of water
- Two tablespoons vegetable oil
- One teaspoon vanilla extract

DIRECTION

- Add the wet ingredients first, then follow by dry ingredients to the bread pan.
- Use the "Normal" or "Basic" mode of the bread machine.
- Select the light or medium crust colour setting.
- Once the cycles are finished, take out the machine's bread, Cooldown the bread on a wire rack before slicing and serving.

PREPARATION	COOKING TIME	SERVINGS
10MINT	3 hour	2 ounce (56.7g)

Vegan Cinnamon Raisin Bread

NUTRITION Calories: 130 | Carbohydrates: 26g | Fat: 2g | Protein: 3g

INGREDIENTS

- Two ¼ cups oat flour
- ¾ cup raisins
- ½ cup almond flour
- ¼ cup of coconut sugar
- 2 ½ teaspoons cinnamon
- One teaspoon baking powder
- ½ teaspoon baking soda
- ¼ teaspoon salt
- ¾ cup of water
- ½ cup of soy milk
- ¼ cup maple syrup
- Three tablespoons coconut oil
- One teaspoon vanilla extract

DIRECTION

- Put all wet ingredients first into the bread pan, followed by the dry ingredients.
- Set the bread machine to "Quick" or "Cake" mode.
- Wait until the mixing and baking cycles are done.
- Remove the pan from the machine.
- Wait for another 10 minutes before transferring the bread to a wire rack.
- After the bread has completely cooled down, slice it and serve.

PREPARATION	COOKING TIME	SERVINGS
10MINT	3 hour	2 ounce (56.7g)

Black Forest Loaf

NUTRITION *Calories: 136 | Carbohydrates: 27g | Fat: 2g | Protein: 3g*

INGREDIENTS

- 1 ½ cups bread flour
- 1 cup whole wheat flour
- 1 cup rye flour
- Three tablespoons cocoa
- One tablespoon caraway seeds
- Two teaspoons yeast
- 1 ½ teaspoons salt
- One ¼ cups water
- 1/3 cup molasses
- 1 ½ tablespoon canola oil

DIRECTION

- Combine the ingredients in the bread pan by putting the wet ingredients first, followed by the dry ones.
- Press the "Normal" or "Basic" mode and light the bread machine's crust colour setting.
- After the cycles are completed, take out the bread from the machine.
- Cooldown and then slice the bread.

PREPARATION	COOKING TIME	SERVINGS
20 MINT	3 hour	2 ounce (56.7g)

Beer Bread

NUTRITION Calories: 130 | Carbohydrates: 25g | Fat: 1g | Protein: 4g

INGREDIENTS

- 3 cups bread flour
- Two tablespoons sugar
- Two ¼ teaspoons yeast
- 1 ½ teaspoons salt
- 2/3 cup beer
- 1/3 cup water
- Two tablespoons vegetable oil

DIRECTION

- Add all ingredients into a pan in this order: water, beer, oil, salt, sugar, flour, and yeast.
- Start the bread machine with the "Basic" or "Normal" mode on and light to medium crust colour.
- Let the machine complete all cycles.
- Take out the pan from the machine.
- Transfer the beer bread into a wire rack to cool it down for about an hour.
- Cut into 12 slices, and serve.

PREPARATION	COOKING TIME	SERVINGS
10-15 MINT	2.5-3 hour	2 ounce (56.7g)

Onion and Mushroom Bread

NUTRITION Calories: 120 | Carbohydrates: 25g | Fat: 0g | Protein: 5g

INGREDIENTS

- 4 ounces mushrooms, chopped
- 4 cups bread flour
- Three tablespoons sugar
- Four teaspoons fast-acting yeast
- Four teaspoons dried onions, minced
- 1 ½ teaspoons salt
- ½ teaspoon garlic powder
- ¾ cup of water

DIRECTION

- Pour the water first into the bread pan, and then add all of the dry ingredients.
- Press the "Fast" cycle mode of the bread machine.
- Wait until all cycles are completed.
- Transfer the bread from the pan into a wire rack.
- Wait for one hour before slicing the bread into 12 pieces.
- Serving Size: 2 ounces per slice

PREPARATION	COOKING TIME	SERVINGS
10MINT	1 hour	2 ounce (56.7g)

Mashed Potato Bread

NUTRITION Calories: 140, Carbohydrates: 26 g

INGREDIENTS

- 2 1/3 cups bread flour
- ½ cup mashed potatoes
- One tablespoon sugar
- 1 ½ teaspoons yeast
- ¾ teaspoon salt
- ¼ cup potato water
- One tablespoon ground flax seeds
- Four teaspoons oil

DIRECTION

- Put the ingredients into the pan in this order: potato water, oil, flax seeds, mashed potatoes, sugar, salt, flour, and yeast.
- Ready the bread machine by pressing the "Basic" or "Normal" mode with a medium crust colour setting.
- Allow the bread machine to finish all cycles.
- Remove the bread pan from the machine.
- Carefully take the bread from the pan.
- Put the bread on a wire rack, then cool down before slicing.

PREPARATION	COOKING TIME	SERVINGS
40 MINT	2.5-3 hour	2 ounce (56.7g) per slice

Low-Carb Multigrain Bread

NUTRITION Calories: 60 | Carbohydrates: 9g | Fat: 2g | Protein: 1g

INGREDIENTS

- ¾ cup whole-wheat flour
- ¼ cup cornmeal
- ¼ cup oatmeal
- Two tablespoons 7-grain cereals
- Two tablespoons baking powder
- One teaspoon salt
- ¼ teaspoon baking soda
- ¾ cup of water
- ¼ cup of vegetable oil
- ¼ cup of orange juice
- Three tablespoons aquafaba

DIRECTION

- In the bread pan, add the wet ingredients first, then the dry ingredients.
- Press the "Quick" or "Cake" mode of your bread machine.
- Wait until all cycles are through.
- Remove the bread pan from the machine.
- Let the bread rest for 10 minutes in the pan before taking it out to cool down further.
- Slice the bread after an hour has passed.

PREPARATION	COOKING TIME	SERVINGS
15 MINT	1.5 hour	1 ounce (28.3g)

Healthy Celery Loaf

NUTRITION Calories: 73 Cal , Fat: 4 g , Carbohydrates: 8 g , Protein: 3 g , Fiber: 1 g

INGREDIENTS

- 1 can (10 ounces) cream of celery soup
- tablespoons low-fat milk, heated
- 1 tablespoon vegetable oil
- 1¼ teaspoons celery salt
- ¾ cup celery, fresh/sliced thin
- 1 tablespoon celery leaves, fresh, chopped
- 1 whole egg
- ¼ teaspoon sugar
- cups bread flour
- ¼ teaspoon ginger
- ½ cup quick-cooking oats
- tablespoons gluten
- teaspoons celery seeds
- 1 pack of active dry yeast

DIRECTION

- Add all of the ingredients to your bread machine, carefully following the instructions of the manufacturer
- Set the program of your bread machine to Basic/White Bread and set crust type to Medium
- Press START
- Wait until the cycle completes
- Once the loaf is ready, take the bucket out and let the loaf cool for 5 minutes
- Gently shake the bucket to remove the loaf
- Transfer to a cooling rack, slice and serve
- Enjoy!

PREPARATION	COOKING TIME	SERVINGS
2 HOUR 40 MINT	50 mint	1 loaf

Zucchini Herbed Bread

NUTRITION Calories: 153 Cal , Fat: 1 g , Carbohydrates: 28 g , Protein: 5 g , Fiber: 2 g

INGREDIENTS

- ½ cup water
- teaspoon honey
- 1 tablespoons oil
- ¾ cup zucchini, grated
- ¾ cup whole wheat flour
- cups bread flour
- 1 tablespoon fresh basil, chopped
- teaspoon sesame seeds
- 1 teaspoon salt
- 1½ teaspoon active dry yeast

DIRECTION

- Add all of the ingredients to your bread machine, carefully following the instructions of the manufacturer
- Set the program of your bread machine to Basic/White Bread and set crust type to Medium
- Press START
- Wait until the cycle completes
- Once the loaf is ready, take the bucket out and let the loaf cool for 5 minutes
- Gently shake the bucket to remove the loaf
- Transfer to a cooling rack, slice and serve
- Enjoy!

Serena Bakes Simply

PREPARATION	COOKING TIME	SERVINGS
2 HOUR 20 MINT	50 mint	1 loaf

Broccoli and Cauliflower Bread

NUTRITION Calories: 156 Cal , Fat: 8 g , Carbohydrates: 17 g , Protein: 5 g , Fiber: 2 g

INGREDIENTS

- ¼ cup water
- tablespoons olive oil
- 1 egg white
- 1 teaspoon lemon juice
- 2/3 cup grated cheddar cheese
- tablespoons green onion
- ½ cup broccoli, chopped
- ½ cup cauliflower, chopped
- ½ teaspoon lemon pepper seasoning
- cups bread flour
- 1 teaspoon bread machine yeast

DIRECTION

- Add all of the ingredients to your bread machine, carefully following the instructions of the manufacturer
- Set the program of your bread machine to Basic/White Bread and set crust type to Medium
- Press START
- Wait until the cycle completes
- Once the loaf is ready, take the bucket out and let the loaf cool for 5 minutes
- Gently shake the bucket to remove the loaf
- Transfer to a cooling rack, slice and serve
- Enjoy!

PREPARATION	COOKING TIME	SERVINGS
2 HOUR 20 MINT	50 mint	1 loaf

Potato Bread

NUTRITION Calories: 35calories; , Total Carbohydrate: 19 g , Total Fat: 0 g , Protein: 4 g

INGREDIENTS

- 1 3/4 teaspoon active dry yeast
- tablespoon dry milk
- 1/4 cup instant potato flakes
- tablespoon sugar
- cups bread flour
- 1 1/4 teaspoon salt
- tablespoon butter
- 1 3/8 cups water

DIRECTION

- Put all the liquid ingredients in the pan. Add all the dry ingredients, except the yeast. Form a shallow hole in the middle of the dry ingredients and place the yeast.
- Secure the pan in the machine and close the lid. Choose the basic setting and your desired color of the crust. Press starts.
- Allow the bread to cool before slicing.

PREPARATION	COOKING TIME	SERVINGS
2 HOUR	45 mint	2 loaves

Golden Potato Bread

NUTRITION Calories: 90calories;, Total Carbohydrate: 15 g , Total Fat: 2 g , Protein: 4 g ,
Protein: 4 g

INGREDIENTS

- teaspoon bread machine yeast
- cups bread flour
- 1 1/2 teaspoon salt
- tablespoon potato starch
- 1 tablespoon dried chives
- tablespoon dry skim milk powder
- 1 teaspoon sugar
- tablespoon unsalted butter, cubed
- 3/4 cup mashed potatoes
- 1 large egg, at room temperature
- 3/4 cup potato cooking water, with a temperature of 80 to 90 degrees F (26 to 32 degrees C)

DIRECTION

- Prepare the mashed potatoes. Peel the potatoes and put them in a saucepan. Pour enough cold water to cover them. Turn the heat to high and bring to a boil. Turn the heat to low and continue cooking the potatoes until tender. Transfer the cooked potatoes to a bowl and mash. Cover the bowl until the potatoes are ready to use. Reserve cooking water and cook until it reaches the needed temperature.
- Put the ingredients in the bread pan in this order: potato cooking water, egg, mashed potatoes, butter, sugar, milk, chives, potato starch, salt, flour, and yeast.
- Place the pan in the machine and close the lid. Turn it on. Choose the sweet setting and your preferred crust color. Start the cooking process.
- Gently unmold the baked bread and leave to cool on a wire rack.
- Slice and serve.

PREPARATION	COOKING TIME	SERVINGS
2 HOUR 40 MINT	50 mint	2 loaves

Spinach Bread

NUTRITION Calories: 121 calories;, Total Carbohydrate: 20.5 g , Cholesterol: 4 mg , Total Fat: 2.5 g , Protein: 4 g , Sodium: 184 mg

INGREDIENTS

- 1 cup water
- 1 tablespoon vegetable oil
- 1/2 cup frozen chopped spinach, thawed and drained
- cups all-purpose flour
- 1/2 cup shredded Cheddar cheese
- 1 teaspoon salt
- 1 tablespoon white sugar
- 1/2 teaspoon ground black pepper
- 1/2 teaspoons active dry yeast

DIRECTION

- In the pan of bread machine, put all ingredients according to the suggested order of manufacture. Set white bread cycle.

PREPARATION	COOKING TIME	SERVINGS
2 HOUR 20 MINT	40 mint	1 loaf

Onion Potato Bread

NUTRITION Calories: 160calories; , Total Carbohydrate: 44 g , Total Fat: 2 g , Protein: 6 g

INGREDIENTS

- tablespoon quick rise yeast
- cups bread flour
- 1 1/2 teaspoon seasoned salt
- tablespoon sugar
- 2/3 cup baked potatoes, mashed
- 1 1/2 cup onions, minced
- large eggs
- tablespoon oil
- 3/4 cup hot water, with the temperature of 115 to 125 degrees F (46 to 51 degrees C)

DIRECTION

- Put the liquid ingredients in the pan. Add the dry ingredients, except the yeast. Form a shallow well in the middle using your hand and put the yeast.
- Place the pan in the machine, close the lid and turn it on. Select the express bake 80 setting and start the machine.
- Once the bread is cooked, leave on a wire rack for 20 minutes or until cooled.

PREPARATION	COOKING TIME	SERVINGS
1 HOUR 20 MINT	45 mint	2 loaves

Curd Bread

NUTRITION Calories: 277 calories; Total Carbohydrate: 48.4 g , Cholesterol: 9 g , Total Fat: 4.7g , Protein: 9.4 g, Sodium: 547 mg , Sugar: 3.3 g

INGREDIENTS

- ¾ cup lukewarm water
- 2/3 cups wheat bread machine flour
- ¾ cup cottage cheese
- Tablespoon softened butter
- Tablespoon white sugar
- 1½ teaspoon sea salt
- 1½ Tablespoon sesame seeds
- Tablespoon dried onions
- 1¼ teaspoon bread machine yeast

DIRECTION

- Place all the dry and liquid ingredients in the pan and follow the instructions for your bread machine.
- Pay particular attention to measuring the ingredients. Use a measuring cup, measuring spoon, and kitchen scales to do so.
- Set the baking program to BASIC and the crust type to MEDIUM.
- If the dough is too dense or too wet, adjust the amount of flour and liquid in the recipe.
- When the program has ended, take the pan out of the bread machine and let cool for 5 minutes.
- Shake the loaf out of the pan. If necessary, use a spatula.
- Wrap the bread with a kitchen towel and set it aside for an hour. Otherwise, you can cool it on a wire rack.

PREPARATION	COOKING TIME	SERVINGS
4 HOUR	15 mint	12

Curvy Carrot Bread

NUTRITION Calories: 142 calories;, Total Carbohydrate: 32.2 g , Cholesterol: 0 g , Total Fat: 0.8 g , Protein: 2.33 g

INGREDIENTS

- ¾ cup milk, lukewarm
- tablespoons butter, melted at room temperature
- 1 tablespoon honey
- ¾ teaspoon ground nutmeg
- ½ teaspoon salt
- 1 ½ cups shredded carrot
- cups white bread flour
- ¼ teaspoons bread machine or active dry yeast

DIRECTION

- Take 1 ½ pound size loaf pan and first add the liquid ingredients and then add the dry ingredients.
- Place the loaf pan in the machine and close its top lid.
- Plug the bread machine into power socket. For selecting a bread cycle, press "Quick Bread/Rapid Bread" and for selecting a crust type, press "Light" or "Medium".
- Start the machine and it will start preparing the bread.
- After the bread loaf is completed, open the lid and take out the loaf pan.
- Allow the pan to cool down for 10-15 minutes on a wire rack. Gently shake the pan and remove the bread loaf.
- Make slices and serve.

PREPARATION	COOKING TIME	SERVINGS
2 HOUR	15 *mint*	*12*

Beetroot Prune Bread

NUTRITION Calories: 443 calories; , Total Carbohydrate: 81.1 g , Total Fat: 8.2 g , Protein: 9.9 g , Sodium: 604 mg , Fiber: 4.4 g , Sugar: 11.7 g

INGREDIENTS

- 1½ cups lukewarm beet broth
- 5¼ cups all-purpose flour
- 1 cup beet puree
- 1 cup prunes, chopped
- tablespoons extra virgin olive oil
- tablespoons dry cream
- 1 tablespoon brown sugar
- teaspoons active dry yeast
- 1 tablespoon whole milk
- teaspoons sea salt

DIRECTION

- Prepare all of the ingredients for your bread and measuring means (a cup, a spoon, kitchen scales).
- Carefully measure the ingredients into the pan, except the prunes.
- Place all of the ingredients into the bread bucket in the right order, following the manual for your bread machine.
- Close the cover.
- Select the program of your bread machine to BASIC and choose the crust color to MEDIUM.
- Press START.
- After the signal, put the prunes to the dough.
- Wait until the program completes.
- When done, take the bucket out and let it cool for 5-10 minutes.
- Shake the loaf from the pan and let cool for 30 minutes on a cooling rack.
- Slice, serve and enjoy the taste of fragrant homemade bread.

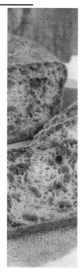

PREPARATION	COOKING TIME	SERVINGS
3 HOUR	30 *mint*	*20*

Potato Rosemary Bread

NUTRITION Calories: 106 calories; , Total Carbohydrate: 21 g , Total Fat: 1 g , Protein: 2.9 g , Sodium: 641 mg ,Fiber: 1 g , Sugar: 0.8 g

INGREDIENTS

- cups bread flour, sifted
- 1 tablespoon white sugar
- 1 tablespoon sunflower oil
- 1½ teaspoons salt
- 1½ cups lukewarm water
- 1 teaspoon active dry yeast
- 1 cup potatoes, mashed
- teaspoons crushed rosemary

DIRECTION

- Prepare all of the ingredients for your bread and measuring means (a cup, a spoon, kitchen scales).
- Carefully measure the ingredients into the pan, except the potato and rosemary.
- Place all of the ingredients into the bread bucket in the right order, following the manual for your bread machine
- Close the cover.
- Select the program of your bread machine to BREAD with FILLINGS and choose the crust color to MEDIUM.
- Press START.
- After the signal, put the mashed potato and rosemary to the dough.
- Wait until the program completes.
- When done, take the bucket out and let it cool for 5-10 minutes.
- Shake the loaf from the pan and let cool for 30 minutes on a cooling rack.
- Slice, serve and enjoy the taste of fragrant homemade bread.

PREPARATION	COOKING TIME	SERVINGS
3 HOUR	30 mint	20

Chapter 17.
Basic Bread

Gluten-Free Bread

NUTRITION Calories: 126 | Carbohydrates: 21g | Fat: 2g | Protein: 3 g

INGREDIENTS

- 2 cups rice flour, Potato starch
- 1 1/2 cup Tapioca flour
- 1/2 cup Xanthan gum
- 2 1/2 teaspoons 2/3 cup powdered milk or 1/2 non-dairy substitute
- 1 1/2 teaspoons salt
- 1 1/2 teaspoons egg substitute (optional)
- Three tablespoons Sugar
- 1 2/3 cups lukewarm water
- 1 1/2 tablespoons dry yeast, granules
- Four tablespoons butter, melted or margarine
- One teaspoon Vinegar
- Three eggs, room temperature

DIRECTION

- Add yeast to the bread pan.
- Add all the flours, xanthan/ gum, milk powder, salt, and sugar.
- Beat the eggs, and mix with water, butter, and vinegar.
- Choose white bread setting at medium or use a 3-4-hour set.

PREPARATION	COOKING TIME	SERVINGS
2 HOUR 40 MINT	50 mint	1 loaf

Oat Bread

NUTRITION Calories: 130 | Carbohydrates: 26 g | Fat: 2 g | Protein: 3 g

INGREDIENTS

- cup Oats
- 1⅜ to 1½ cups Water
- tablespoons Butter or margarine
- ¼ cup Honey
- teaspoons Salt
- cups Bread flour red star brand
- 2½ teaspoons Active dry yeast

DIRECTION

- Place all Ingredients in bread pan, using the least amount of liquid listed in the recipe. Select medium crust setting and press start.
- Observe the dough as it kneads. After 5 to 10 minutes, if it appears dry and stiff or if your machine sounds as if it's straining to knead it, add more liquid 1 tablespoon at a time until dough forms a smooth, soft, pliable ball that is slightly tacky to the touch.
- After the baking cycle ends, remove bread from pan, place on cake rack, and allow to cool 1 hour before slicing.

PREPARATION	COOKING TIME	SERVINGS
1 HOUR 30 MINT	40 mint	2-3 loaves

Green Olive Bread

NUTRITION Calories: 136 | Carbohydrates: 27g | Fat: 2g | Protein: 3g

INGREDIENTS

- 1 3/8 cups wheat flour
- 1 1/2 tablespoons flavorless oil
- 1 1/2 tablespoons sugar
- 2 tablespoons dry yeast
- 1/4 cup warm water
- 1/3 cup and a half water Zevi
- 1 cup of green olives

DIRECTION

- In a big bowl add water, sugar and yeast, stir until dissolved.
- Add half a cup of water and olive oil, stir until dissolved.
- Add half cup of water and mix it.
- Add all of the other ingredients and mix it.
- Put all of the ingredients on the table and add olive oil and water.
- And mixed until smooth.
- Put the dough on a surface that has been oiled and sprinkled with wheat flour.
- Place the dough in the doughmaker.
- Bake the dough for 40 minutes at full temperature
- When the dough is ready, it will produce a very nice sound and there will be a golden color.
- Leave in the container on the bread maker for about 60 minutes.
- Transfer the bread on a plate.

PREPARATION	COOKING TIME	SERVINGS
30-40 MINT	1 hour	8

All-Purpose White Bread

NUTRITION Calories: 130 | Carbohydrates: 25g | Fat: 1g | Protein: 4g

INGREDIENTS

- ¾ cup water at 80 degrees F
- One tablespoon melted butter cooled
- One tablespoon sugar
- ¾ teaspoon salt
- Two tablespoons skim milk powder
- 2 cups white bread flour
- ¾ teaspoon instant yeast

DIRECTION

- Add all of the ingredients to your bread machine, carefully following the instructions of the manufacturer.
- Set the program of your bread machine to Basic/White Bread and set crust type to Medium.
- Press START.
- Wait until the cycle completes.
- Once the loaf is ready, take the bucket out and let the loaf cool for 5 minutes.
- Gently shake the bucket to remove the loaf.
- Put to a cooling rack, slice, and serve.

PREPARATION	COOKING TIME	SERVINGS
2 HOUR 10 MINT	40 mint	1 loaf

Mustard-flavoured General Bread

NUTRITION Calories: 340 Cal , Fat: 10 g , Carbohydrates: 54 g , Protein: 10 g , Fiber: 1 g

INGREDIENTS

- 1¼ cups milk
- Three tablespoons sunflower milk
- Three tablespoons sour cream
- Two tablespoons dry mustard
- One whole egg, beaten
- ½ sachet sugar vanilla
- 4 cups flour
- One teaspoon dry yeast
- Two tablespoons sugar
- Two teaspoon salt

DIRECTION

- Take out the bread maker's bucket and pour in milk and sunflower oil; stir and then add sour cream and beaten egg.
- Add flour, salt, sugar, mustard powder, vanilla sugar, and mix well.
- Make a small groove in the flour and sprinkle the yeast.
- Transfer the bucket to your bread maker and cover.
- Set the program of your bread machine to Basic/White Bread and set crust type to Medium.
- Press START.
- Wait until the cycle completes.
- Once the loaf is ready, take the bucket out and let it cool for 5 minutes.
- Gently shake the bucket to remove the loaf.
- Transfer to a cooling rack, slice, and serve.

PREPARATION	COOKING TIME	SERVINGS
2 HOUR 10 MINT	40 mint	2 loaves

Oatmeal Bread

NUTRITION Calories: 269 calories; , Total Carbohydrate: 49 g , Total Fat: 4 g , Protein: 8 g

INGREDIENTS

- Three teaspoons bread machine yeast
- Four teaspoons vital wheat gluten
- 4 cups bread flour
- One teaspoon salt
- 1 cup instant or regular oatmeal
- Two tablespoon maple syrup
- Two tablespoons unsalted butter, cubed
- 1/3 cup water, with a temperature of 80 to 90 degrees F (26 to 32 degrees C)
- 1 1/2 cups buttermilk, with a temperature of 80 to 90 degrees F (26 to 32 degrees C)

DIRECTION

- Put the pan's ingredients in this order: buttermilk, water, butter, maple syrup, oatmeal, salt, flour, gluten, and yeast.
- Make secure the pan in the machine, close the lid and turn it on.
- Choose the basic setting and your preferred crust colour and press start.
- Transfer the baked bread to a wire rack and allow to cool before slicing.

PREPARATION	COOKING TIME	SERVINGS
3 HOUR	45 mint	2 loaves

Country White Bread

NUTRITION Calories: 105 calories;, Total Carbohydrate: 0 g , Total Fat: 0 g , Protein: 0 g

INGREDIENTS

- Two teaspoons active dry yeast
- 1 1/2 tablespoon sugar
- 4 cups bread flour
- 1 1/2 teaspoon salt
- One large egg
- 1 1/2 tablespoon butter
- 1 cup warm milk, with a temperature of 110 to 115 degrees F (43 to 46 degrees C)

DIRECTION

- Put all the liquid ingredients in the pan. Add all the dry ingredients except the yeast. Use your hand to form a hole in the middle of the dry ingredients. Put the yeast in the spot.
- Secure the pan in the chamber and close the lid. Choose the basic setting and your preferred crust colour—press start.
- Once done, transfer the baked bread to a wire rack. Slice once cooled.

PREPARATION	COOKING TIME	SERVINGS
3 HOUR	45 mint	2 loaves

Anadama Bread

NUTRITION ories: 130 calories; , Total Carbohydrate: 25 g , Total Fat: 2 g , Protein: 3 g

INGREDIENTS

- 1/2 cup sunflower seeds
- Two teaspoons bread machine yeast
- 4 1/2 cups bread flour
- 3/4 cup yellow cornmeal
- Two tablespoons unsalted butter, cubed
- 1 1/2 teaspoon salt
- 1/4 cup dry skim milk powder
- 1/4 cup molasses
- 1 1/2 cups water, with a temperature of 80 to 90 degrees F (26 to 32 degrees C)

DIRECTION

- Put all the pan's ingredients, except the sunflower seeds, in this order: water, molasses, milk, salt, butter, cornmeal, flour, and yeast.
- Put the pan in the machine and cover the lid.
- Put the sunflower seeds in the fruit and nut dispenser.
- Turn the machine on and choose the basic setting and your desired colour of the crust—press start.

PREPARATION	COOKING TIME	SERVINGS
3 HOUR	45 mint	2 loaves

Apricot Oat

NUTRITION *Calories: 80 calories;, Total Carbohydrate: 14.4 g , Cholesterol: 5 mg , Total Fat: 2.3 g , Protein,1.3 g, Sodium: 306 mg*

INGREDIENTS

- 4 1/4 cups bread flour
- 2/3 cup rolled oats
- One tablespoon white sugar
- Two teaspoons active dry yeast
- 1 1/2 teaspoons salt
- One teaspoon ground cinnamon
- Two tablespoons butter cut up
- 1 2/3 cups orange juice
- 1/2 cup diced dried apricots
- Two tablespoons honey, warmed

DIRECTION

- Into the bread machine's pan, put the bread ingredients in the order suggested by the manufacturer. Then pout in dried apricots before the knead cycle completes.
- Immediately remove bread from a machine when it's done and then glaze with warmed honey. Let to cool thoroughly before serving.

PREPARATION	COOKING TIME	SERVINGS
1 HOUR 25 MINT	25 *mint*	*1 loaf*

Homemade Wonderful Bread

NUTRITION *Calories: 162 calories;, Total Carbohydrate: 31.6 g , Cholesterol: < 1 mg , Total Fat: 1.8 g Protein: 4.5 g , Sodium: 339 mg*

INGREDIENTS

- 2 1/2 teaspoons active dry yeast
- 1/4 cup warm water
- One tablespoon white sugar
- 4 cups all-purpose flour
- 1/4 cup dry potato flakes
- 1/4 cup dry milk powder
- Two teaspoons salt
- 1/4 cup white sugar
- Two tablespoons margarine
- 1 cup of warm water(45 degrees C)

DIRECTION

- Prepare the yeast, 1/4 cup warm water and sugar to whisk and then let it sit in 15 minutes.
- Take all ingredients together with yeast mixture to put in the pan of bread machine according to the manufacturer's recommended order. Choose basic and light crust settings.

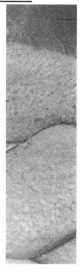

PREPARATION	COOKING TIME	SERVINGS
3 HOUR 25 MINT	15 *mint*	*2 loaves*

Buttermilk White Bread

NUTRITION Calories: 34 calories; ,Total Carbohydrate: 5.7 g , Cholesterol: 1 mg , Total Fat: 1 g , Protein: 1 g , Sodium: 313 mg

INGREDIENTS

- • 1 1/8 cups water
- • Three teaspoon honey
- • One tablespoon margarine
- • 1 1/2 teaspoon salt
- • 3 cups bread flour
- • Two teaspoons active dry yeast
- • Four teaspoons powdered buttermilk

DIRECTION

- Into the bread machine's pan, place the ingredients in the order suggested by the manufacturer: select medium crust and white bread settings. You can use a fcw yeasts during the hot and humid months of summer.

PREPARATION	COOKING TIME	SERVINGS
2 HOUR 50 MINT	25 mint	1 loaf

Honey White Bread

NUTRITION Calories: 172 Cal, Carbohydrates: 28.9 g, Cholesterol: 9 mg, Fat: 3.9 g ,Protein: 5 g

INGREDIENTS

- 1 cup milk
- Three tablespoons unsalted butter, melted
- Two tablespoons honey
- 3 cups bread flour
- 3/4 teaspoon salt
- 3/4 teaspoon vitamin c powder
- 3/4 teaspoon ground ginger
- 1 1/2 teaspoons active dry yeast

DIRECTION

- Follow the order as directed in your bread machine manual on how to assemble the ingredients. Use the setting for the Basic Bread cycle.

PREPARATION	COOKING TIME	SERVINGS
3 HOUR 25 MINT	15 mint	1 loaf

Chapter 18
Pleasure Bread

Mediterranean Semolina Bread

NUTRITION Calories 243; Total Fat 8.1g; Saturated Fat 4.9g; Cholesterol 20g; Sodium 203mg; Total Carbohydrate 37g; Dietary Fiber 1.5g; Total Sugars 2.8g; Protein 5.3g, Vitamin D 5mcg, Calcium 10mg, Iron 2mg, Potassium 80mg

PREPARATION	COOKING TIME	SERVINGS
2 HOUR	1½ HOUR	1½-pound loaf / 16 slices

DIRECTION

- Prepare all of the ingredients for your bread and measuring means (a cup, a spoon, kitchen scales).
- Carefully measure the ingredients into the pan.
- Put all the ingredients into a bread bucket in the right order. Follow your manual for the bread machine.
- Close the cover.
- Select your bread machine's program to ITALIAN BREAD / SANDWICH mode and choose the crust colour to MEDIUM.
- Press START. Wait until the program completes.
- When done, take the bucket out and let it cool for 5-10 minutes.
- Shake the loaf from the pan and let cool for 30 minutes on a cooling rack.
- Slice and serve.

INGREDIENTS

- 1 cup lukewarm water (80 degrees F)
- One teaspoon salt
- 2½ tablespoons butter, melted
- 2½ teaspoons white sugar
- 2¼ cups all-purpose flour
- 1/3 cups semolina
- 1½ teaspoons active dry yeast

Crisp White Bread

NUTRITION Calories 113; Total Fat 1.4g; Saturated Fat 0.8g; Cholesterol 3g; Sodium 158mg; Total sCarbohydrate 21.6g; Dietary Fiber 0.7g; Total Sugars 2.1g; Protein 3.3g, Vitamin D 1mcg, Calcium 24mg, Iron 1mg, Potassium 33mg

PREPARATION	COOKING TIME	SERVINGS
2 HOUR 30 MINT	1 hour 30 mins	1-pound loaf / 10 slices

DIRECTION

- Prepare all of the ingredients for your bread and measuring means (a cup, a spoon, kitchen scales).
- Carefully measure the ingredients into the pan.
- Put all the ingredients into a bread bucket in the right order, following the manual for your bread machine.
- Close the cover. Select your bread machine program to BASIC / WHITE BREAD and choose the crust colour to MEDIUM.
- Press START. Wait until the program completes.
- When done, take the bucket out and let it cool for 5-10 minutes.
- Shake the loaf from the pan and let cool for 30 minutes on a cooling rack.
- Slice and serve.

INGREDIENTS

- ¾ cup lukewarm water (80 degrees F)
- One tablespoon butter, melted
- One tablespoon white sugar
- ¾ teaspoon sea salt
- Two tablespoons of milk powder
- 2 cups wheat flour
- ¾ teaspoon active dry yeast

Mustard Sour Cream Bread

NUTRITION Calories 340; Total Fat 9.2g; Saturated Fat 1.9g; Cholesterol 26g; Sodium 614mg; Total Carbohydrate 54.6g; Dietary Fiber 2.2g; Total Sugars 5.5g; Protein 9.3g

PREPARATION	COOKING TIME	SERVINGS
1 HOUR	1 hour	2½ pounds

DIRECTION

- Prepare all of the ingredients for your bread and measuring means (a cup, a spoon, kitchen scales).
- Carefully measure the ingredients into the pan.
- Put all the ingredients into a bread bucket in the right order, follow your manual for the bread machine.
- Cover it. Select the program of your bread machine to BASIC and choose the crust colour to MEDIUM.
- Press START. Wait until the program completes.
- When done, take the bucket out and let it cool for 5-10 minutes.
- Shake the loaf from the pan and let cool for 30 minutes on a cooling rack.
- Slice, serve and enjoy the taste of fragrant homemade bread.

INGREDIENTS

- 1¼ cups (320 ml) lukewarm milk
- Three tablespoons sunflower oil
- Three tablespoons sour cream
- Two tablespoons dry mustard
- One egg
- ½ sachet sugar vanilla
- 4 cups (690 g) wheat flour
- One teaspoon active dry yeast
- Two tablespoons white sugar
- Two teaspoons sea salt

Buttermilk Bread

NUTRITION Calories 183; Total Fat 2.2g; Saturated Fat 0.9g; Cholesterol 4g; Sodium 223mg; Total, Carbohydrate 35.4g; Dietary Fiber 1.3g; Total Sugars 2.1g; Protein 4.8g, Vitamin D 1mcg, Calcium 18mg, Iron 2mg, Potassium 69mg

PREPARATION	COOKING TIME	SERVINGS
2 HOUR 30 MINT	1 hour 30 mins	1-pound loaf / 10 slices

INGREDIENTS

- 2/3 cup lukewarm buttermilk (80 degrees F)
- One tablespoon butter, melted
- One tablespoon white sugar
- ¾ teaspoon salt
- ¼ teaspoon baking powder
- 1¾ cups all-purpose flour
- 1 1/8 teaspoons instant yeast

DIRECTION

- Prepare all of the ingredients for your bread and measuring means (a cup, a spoon, kitchen scales).
- Carefully measure the ingredients into the pan.
- Put all the ingredients into a bread bucket in the right order. Follow your manual for the bread machine.
- Close the cover.
- Select the program of your bread machine to BASIC and choose the crust colour to MEDIUM.
- Press START.
- Wait until the program completes.
- When done, take the bucket out and let it cool for 5-10 minutes.
- Shake the loaf from the pan and let cool for 30 minutes on a cooling rack.
- Slice, serve and enjoy the taste of fragrant homemade bread.

Tomato Paprika Bread

NUTRITION Calories 133; Total Fat 4.2g; Saturated Fat 2.6g; Cholesterol 10g; Sodium 177mg; Total Carbohydrate 20.5g; Dietary Fiber 1.2g; Total Sugars 1.9g; Protein 3.1g, Vitamin D 3mcg, Calcium 7mg, Iron 1mg, Potassium 87mg

PREPARATION	COOKING TIME	SERVINGS
2 HOUR	1 hour	1-pound loaf / 10 slices

DIRECTION

- Prepare all of the ingredients for your bread and measuring means (a cup, a spoon, kitchen scales).
- Carefully measure the ingredients into the pan, except the tomatoes.
- Put all the ingredients into a bread bucket in the right order. Follow your manual for the bread machine.
- Close the cover.
- Select your bread machine program to BASIC and choose the crust colour to MEDIUM or DARK.
- Press START. After the signal, put the chopped tomatoes into the dough.
- Wait until the program completes.
- When done, take the bucket out and let it cool for 5-10 minutes.
- Shake the loaf from the pan and let cool for 30 minutes on a cooling rack.
- Slice, serve and enjoy the taste of fragrant homemade bread.

INGREDIENTS

- 1½ teaspoons active dry yeast
- 3 cups bread flour
- Two tablespoons white sugar
- One teaspoon salt
- 1½ tablespoons butter, melted
- 1 cup lukewarm water
- Two teaspoons ground paprika
- 1 cup dried tomatoes, chopped

Honey Rye Bread

NUTRITION Calories 177; Total Fat 2.7g; Saturated Fat 0.6g; Cholesterol 20g; Sodium 300mg; Total Carbohydrate 33.1g; Dietary Fiber 2.0g; Total Sugars 3.4g; Protein 5.1g

PREPARATION	COOKING TIME	SERVINGS
2 HOUR	1 ½ HOUR	1½ pound / 16 slices

INGREDIENTS

- Two ¼ cups (350 g) wheat flour
- ¼ cup (50 g) rye flour
- 1 cup (200 ml) lukewarm water
- One egg
- One tablespoon olive oil
- One teaspoon salt
- 1 ½ tablespoon liquid honey
- One teaspoon active dry yeast

DIRECTION

- Prepare all of the ingredients for your bread and measuring means (a cup, a spoon, kitchen scales).
- Carefully measure the ingredients into the pan.
- Put all the ingredients into a bread bucket in the right order. Follow your manual for the
- Close the cover. Select your bread machine program to BASIC and choose the crust colour to MEDIUM or DARK.
- Press START. Wait until the program completes.
- When done, take the bucket out and let it cool for 5-10 minutes.
- Shake the loaf from the pan and let cool for 30 minutes on a cooling rack.
- Slice, serve and enjoy the taste of fragrant homemade bread.

Bran Bread

NUTRITION Calories 307; Total Fat 5.1g; Saturated Fat 0.9g; Cholesterol 33g; Sodium 480mg; Total Carbohydrate 54g; Dietary Fiber 7.9g; Total Sugars 1.8g; Protein 10.2g

PREPARATION	COOKING TIME	SERVINGS
2 HOUR	1 hour	1 pound / 10 slices

DIRECTION

- Prepare all of the ingredients for your bread and measuring means (a cup, a spoon, kitchen scales).
- Carefully measure the ingredients into the pan.
- Put all the ingredients into a bread bucket in the right order. Follow your manual for the bread machine.
- Close the cover. Select your bread machine's program to FRENCH BREAD and choose the crust colour to MEDIUM.
- Press START.
- Wait until the program completes.
- When done, take the bucket out and let it cool for 5-10 minutes.
- Slice, serve and enjoy the taste of fragrant homemade bread.

INGREDIENTS

- 2 ½ cups (320 g) all-purpose flour, sifted
- One whole egg
- ¾ cup (40 g) bran
- 1 cup (240 ml) lukewarm water
- One tablespoon sunflower oil
- Two teaspoons brown sugar
- One teaspoon of sea salt
- One teaspoon active dry yeast

Honey Beer Bread

NUTRITION Calories 210; Total Fat 1.6g; Saturated Fat 0.2g; Cholesterol 0g; Sodium 135mg; Total Carbohydrate 42.3g; Dietary Fiber 1.8g; Total Sugars 2.6g; Protein 5.9g, Vitamin D 0mcg, Calcium 10mg, Iron 3mg, Potassium 91mg

PREPARATION	COOKING TIME	SERVINGS
2 HOUR	1 20 hour mint	1½-pound loaf / 14 slices

INGREDIENTS

- 1 1/6 cups light beer, without foam
- Two tablespoons of liquid honey
- One tablespoon olive oil
- One teaspoon of sea salt
- One teaspoon cumin
- 2¾ cups bread flour
- 1½ teaspoons active dry yeast

DIRECTION

- Prepare all of the ingredients for your bread and measuring means (a cup, a spoon, kitchen scales).
- Carefully measure the ingredients into the pan.
- Put all ingredients into a bread bucket in the right order, follow your manual for the bread machine.
- Close the cover. Select the program of your bread machine to BASIC and choose the crust colour to MEDIUM.
- Press START. Wait until the program completes.
- When done, take the bucket out and let it cool for 5-10 minutes.
- Shake the loaf from the pan and let cool for 30 minutes on a cooling rack.
- Slice, serve and enjoy the taste of fragrant homemade bread

Chapter 18. Pleasure Bread

Egg and Milk Bread

NUTRITION *Calories: 319 Cal, Fat: 5.6 g, Cholesterol: 56 g, Sodium: 495 mg, Carbohydrates: 56.7 g, Fiber: 1.8 g*

PREPARATION	COOKING TIME	SERVINGS
2 HOUR	1 *hour*	1½ pound / 16 *slices*

INGREDIENTS

- 4 cups (520 g) bread flour, sifted
- 1 cup (230 ml) lukewarm milk
- Two whole eggs
- One teaspoon active dry yeast
- 1 ½ teaspoons salt
- Two ¼ tablespoons white sugar
- 1 ½ tablespoons butter, melted

DIRECTION

- Prepare all of the ingredients for your bread and measuring means (a cup, a spoon, kitchen scales).
- Carefully measure the ingredients into the pan.
- Put all the ingredients into a bread bucket in the right order, follow your manual for the bread machine.
- Close the cover. Select the program of your bread machine to BASIC and choose the crust colour to MEDIUM.
- Press START. Wait until the program completes.
- When done, take the bucket out and let it cool for 5-10 minutes.
- Shake the loaf from the pan and let cool for 30 minutes on a cooling rack.
- Slice, serve and enjoy the taste of fragrant homemade bread

Honey Pound Cake

NUTRITION *Calories: 117, Sodium: 183 mg, Dietary Fiber: 0.3 g, Fat: 6.9 g, Carbs: 12.3 g, Protein: 1.9 g.*

PREPARATION	COOKING TIME	SERVINGS
5 MINT	2 *hour* 50 *mins*	12-16

DIRECTION

- Bring the butter to room temperature and cut into 1/2-inch cubes.
- Add all ingredients to the bread machine in the order listed (butter, honey, milk, eggs, sugar, and flour).
- Press Sweetbread setting follow by light crust colour, then press Start. Take out the cake on the bread pan using a rubber spatula as soon as it's finished. Cool on a rack and serve with your favorite fruit.

INGREDIENTS

- 1 cup butter, unsalted
- 1/4 cup honey
- Two tablespoons whole milk
- Four eggs, beaten
- 1 cup of sugar
- 2 cups flour

Carrot Cake Bread

NUTRITION Calories: 151, Sodium: 69 mg, Dietary Fiber: 1.2 g, Fat: 7.2 g, Carbs: 20.1 g, Protein: 2.4 g.

PREPARATION	COOKING TIME	SERVINGS
5 MINT	1 hour 20 mins	12-16

DIRECTION

- Coat the inside of the bread pan with non-stick cooking spray.
- Add all of the ingredients, in the order listed, to the bread pan.
- Select Express Bake, medium crust colour, and press Start. While the batter is mixing, scrape the bread pan's sides with a rubber spatula to incorporate ingredients fully.
- When baked, remove from bread pan and place on a wire rack to cool completely before slicing and serving.

INGREDIENTS

- Non-stick cooking spray
- 1/4 cup vegetable oil
- Two large eggs, room temperature
- 1/2 teaspoon pure vanilla extract
- 1/2 cup sugar
- 1/4 cup light brown sugar
- 1/4 cup of crushed pineapple with juice (from a can or fresh)
- 1 1/4 cups unbleached, all-purpose flour
- One teaspoon baking powder
- 1/4 teaspoon baking soda
- 1/4 teaspoon salt
- One teaspoon ground cloves
- 3/4 teaspoon ground cinnamon
- 1 cup freshly grated carrots
- 1/3 cup chopped pecans
- 1/3 cup golden raisins

Insane Coffee Cake

NUTRITION Calories: 148, Sodium: 211 mg, Dietary Fiber: 0.9 g, Fat: 3.9 g, Carbs: 24.9 g, Protein: 3.5 g.

PREPARATION	COOKING TIME	SERVINGS
15 MINTS	2 hour	10-12

DIRECTION

- Set the topping ingredients set aside, then add the other ingredients to the bread pan in the order above.
- Set the bread machine to the Dough process.
- Butter a 9-by-9-inch glass baking dish and pour the dough into the container. Cover with a towel and rise for about 10 minutes.
- Preheat an oven to 375°F.
- Brush the dough with the melted butter.
- Put brown sugar and cinnamon in a bowl, mix it well, and then put a sprinkle on top of the coffee cake.
- Let the topped dough rise, uncovered, for another 30 minutes.
- Place in oven and bake for 35 minutes or until a wooden toothpick inserted into the center comes out clean and dry.
- When baked, let the coffee cake rest for 10 minutes. Carefully remove the coffee cake from the dish with a rubber spatula, slice and serve.

INGREDIENTS

- 7/8 cup of milk
- 1/4 cup of sugar
- One teaspoon salt
- One egg yolk
- One tablespoon butter
- 2 1/4 cups bread flour
- Two teaspoons of active dry yeast
- For the topping:
- Two tablespoons butter, melted
- Two tablespoons brown sugar
- One teaspoon cinnamon

Lemon Cake

NUTRITION Calories: 290, Sodium: 77 mg, Dietary Fiber: 0.6 g, Fat: 9.3 g, Carbs: 42.9 g, Protein: 4 g.

PREPARATION	COOKING TIME	SERVINGS
5 MINT	2 hour 50 mins	12

DIRECTION

1. Prepare the glaze by whisking the powder sugar and lemon juice together in a small mixing bowl and set aside.
2. Add all remaining ingredients to the baking pan in the order listed.
3. Select the Sweetbread, medium colour crust, and press Start.
4. When baked, transfer the baking pan to a cooling rack.
5. When the cake has cooled, gently shake the cake out into a serving plate. Glaze the cold cake and serve.

INGREDIENTS

- Three large eggs, beaten
- 1/3 cup 2% milk
- 1/2 cup butter, melted
- 2 cups all-purpose flour
- Three teaspoons baking powder
- 1 1/3 cup sugar
- One teaspoon vanilla extract
- Two lemons, zested
- For the glaze:
- 1 cup powdered sugar
- Two tablespoons lemon juice, freshly squeezed

Chocolate Marble Cake

NUTRITION Calories: 172, Sodium: 218 mg, Dietary Fiber: 1.6 g, Fat: 4.3 g, Carbs: 30.1 g, Protein: 3 g.

PREPARATION	COOKING TIME	SERVINGS
15 MINTS	3 hour 45 mints	12-16

DIRECTION

- Set the chocolate chips aside and add the other ingredients to your bread maker's pan.
- Program the machine for Sweetbread and then press Start.
- Check the dough after 15 minutes of kneading; you should have a smooth ball, soft but not sticky.
- Add the chocolate chips about 3 minutes before the end of the second kneading cycle.
- Once baked, remove with a rubber spatula and cool on a rack before serving.

INGREDIENTS

- 1 1/2 cups water
- 1 1/2 teaspoons vanilla extract
- 1 1/2 teaspoons salt
- 3 1/2 cups bread flour
- 1 1/2 teaspoons instant yeast
- 1 cup semi-sweet chocolate chips

Pumpkin Spice Cake

NUTRITION Calories: 195, Sodium: 64 mg, Dietary Fiber: 1.3 g, Fat: 7.1 g, Carbs: 31.2 g, Protein: 2.8 g.

	PREPARATION	COOKING TIME		SERVINGS
DIRECTION	5 MINT	2 hour	50 mins	12

DIRECTION

- Grease bread maker pan and kneading blade generously with shortening.
- Add all ingredients to the pan in the order listed above.
- Select the Rapid cycle and press Start.
- Open the lid three minutes into the cycle,
- Carefully scrape the pan's downsides with a rubber spatula; close the lid to continue the process.
- Cool the baked cake for 10 minutes on a wire rack before slicing.

INGREDIENTS

- 1 cup of sugar
- 1 cup canned pumpkin
- 1/3 cup vegetable oil
- One teaspoon vanilla extract
- Two eggs
- 1 1/2 cups all-purpose flour
- Two teaspoons baking powder
- 1/4 teaspoon salt
- One teaspoon ground cinnamon
- 1/4 teaspoon ground nutmeg
- 1/8 teaspoon ground cloves
- Shortening, for greasing pan

Cinnamon Pecan Coffee Cake

NUTRITION Calories: 488 Cal, Sodium: 333 mg, Fiber: 2.5 g, Fat: 32.8 g

	PREPARATION	COOKING TIME	SERVINGS
DIRECTION	15 MINTS	2 hour	10-12

DIRECTION

- Add butter, sugar, eggs, sour cream and vanilla to the bread maker baking pan, followed by the dry ingredients.
- Select the Cake cycle and press Start, then Prepare toppings and set aside.
- When the kneading cycle is done, about 20 minutes, sprinkle 1/2 cup of topping on top of the dough and continue baking.
- During the last hour of baking time, sprinkle the remaining 1/2 cup of topping on the cake. Bake until complete.
Cool it on a wire rack for 10 minutes and serve warm.

INGREDIENTS

- 1 cup butter, unsalted
- 1 cup of sugar
- Two eggs
- 1 cup sour cream
- One teaspoon vanilla extract
- 2 cups all-purpose flour
- One teaspoon baking powder
- One teaspoon baking soda
- 1/2 teaspoon salt
- For the topping:
- 1/2 cup brown sugar
- 1/4 cup sugar
- 1/2 teaspoon cinnamon
- 1/2 cup pecans, chopped

Lemon Blueberry Quick Bread

NUTRITION Calories: 462, Sodium: 332 mg, Dietary Fiber: 1 g, Fat: 32.1 g, Carbs: 41.8 g, Protein: 4 g.

PREPARATION	COOKING TIME	SERVINGS
20 MINT	2 hour	10-12

DIRECTION

- Spray bread maker pan with non-stick cooking spray and lightly flour.
- Combine crumb topping ingredients and set aside.
- In a small bowl, put the whisk together with flour, baking powder and salt and set aside.
- In a large bowl, put the sugar and lemon zest, then mix them. Add butter and beat until light and fluffy. Add eggs, vanilla and milk.
- Add flour mixture and mix until combined. Stir in blueberries and spread batter evenly into bread maker pan.
- Top with crumb topping; select Sweetbread, light colour crust, and press Start.
- When the cake is made, cool it on a wire rack for 15 minutes and serves warm.

INGREDIENTS

- 2 cups all-purpose flour
- 1 1/2 teaspoons baking powder
- 1/2 teaspoon salt
- One tablespoon lemon zest
- 1 cup of sugar
- 1/2 cup unsalted butter, softened
- Two large eggs
- Two teaspoons pure vanilla extract
- 1/2 cup whole milk
- 1 1/2 cups blueberries
- For the crumb topping:
- 1/3 cup sugar
- Three tablespoons all-purpose flour
- Two tablespoons butter, melted
- Non-stick cooking spray

Chapter 20.
Meat Bread

French Ham Bread

NUTRITION Calories 287 , Total Fat 5.5g , Saturated Fat 1.1g , Cholesterol 11g , Sodium 557mg , Total, Carbohydrate 47.2g , Dietary Fiber 1.7g , Total Sugars 6.4g , Protein 11.4g

PREPARATION	COOKING TIME	SERVINGS
30-45MINT	2 hour	8

DIRECTION

- Cut ham into cubes of 0.5-1 cm (approximately ¼ inch).
- Put all ingredients in the bread maker from the following order: water, olive oil, salt, sugar, flour, milk powder, ham, and yeast.
- Put all the ingredients according to the instructions in your bread maker.
- Basil put in a dispenser or fill it later, at the signal in the container.
- Turn on the bread maker.
- After the end of the baking cycle, leave the bread container
- In the bread maker to keep warm for 1 hour.
- Then your delicious bread is ready!

INGREDIENTS

- 3 1/3 cups wheat flour
- 1 cup ham
- ½ cup of milk powder
- 1 ½ tablespoons sugar
- One teaspoon yeast, fresh
- One teaspoon salt
- One teaspoon dried basil
- 1 1/3 cups water
- Two tablespoons olive oil

Onion Bacon Bread

NUTRITION Calories 391, Total Fat 9.7g , Saturated Fat 2.7g , Cholesterol 38g , Sodium 960mg , Total Carbohydrate 59.9g , Dietary Fiber 2.8g , Total Sugars 4.3g , Protein 14.7g

PREPARATION	COOKING TIME	SERVINGS
1 hour 30 mins	1 hour 30 mins	8

DIRECTION

- Cut the bacon.
- Put all ingredients into the machine.
- Set it to the Basic program.
- Enjoy this tasty bread!

INGREDIENTS

- 1 ½ cups water
- Two tablespoons sugar
- Three teaspoons dry yeast
- 4 ½ cups flour
- One egg
- Two teaspoons salt
- One tablespoon oil
- Three small onions, chopped
- 1 cup bacon

Meat Bread

NUTRITION Calories 283, Total Fat 6.2g , Saturated Fat 1.4g , Cholesterol 50g , Sodium 484mg , Total Carbohydrate 38.4g , Dietary Fiber 1.6g , Total Sugars 2g , Protein 17.2g

PREPARATION   COOKING TIME   SERVINGS

DIRECTION   1 hour   30 mins   1 hour   30 mins   8

- Pre-cook the meat. You can use a leg or fillet.
- Separate meat from the bone and cut it into small pieces.
- Pour all ingredients into the bread maker according to the instructions.
- Add chicken pieces now.
- The program is Basic.
- This bread is perfectly combined with dill and butter.

INGREDIENTS

- 2 cups boiled chicken
- 1 cup milk 3 cups flour
- One tablespoon dry yeast one egg
- One teaspoon sugar
- ½ tablespoon salt
- Two tablespoons oil

Onion Bacon Bread

NUTRITION Calories 208 , Total Fat 3.8g , Saturated Fat 0.5g , Cholesterol 8g , Sodium 487mg , Total Carbohydrate 35.9g , Dietary Fiber 4.2g , Total Sugars 2.7g , Protein 7.2g

PREPARATION COOKING TIME   SERVINGS

DIRECTION   1 hour   30 mins   1 hour   30 mins   8

- Grind onion and fry until golden brown.
- Cut the fish into small pieces and the pepper into cubes.
- Load all the ingredients in the bucket.
- Turn on the baking program.
- Bon Appetit!

INGREDIENTS

- 2 ½ cups flour
- ½ cup bran
- 1 1/3 cups water
- 1 ½ teaspoons salt
- 1 ½ teaspoons sugar
- 1 ½ tablespoon mustard oil
- One ¼ teaspoons dry yeast
- Two teaspoons powdered milk
- 1 cup chopped bell pepper
- ¾ cup chopped smoked fish
- One onion

Sausage Bread

NUTRITION Calories 234 , Total Fat 5.1g , Saturated Fat 1.2g , Cholesterol 9g , Sodium 535mg , Total Carbohydrate 38.7g , Dietary Fiber 1.4g , Total Sugars 2.7g , Protein 7.4g

PREPARATION	COOKING TIME	SERVINGS
2 HOUR	2 hour	8

DIRECTION

- Fold all the ingredients in the order that is recommended specifically for your model.
- Set the required parameters for baking bread.
- When ready, remove the delicious hot bread.
- Wait until it cools down and enjoy sausage.

INGREDIENTS

- 1 ½ teaspoons dry yeast
- 3 cups flour
- One teaspoon sugar
- 1 ½ teaspoons salt
- 1 1/3 cups whey
- One tablespoon oil
- 1 cup chopped smoked sausage

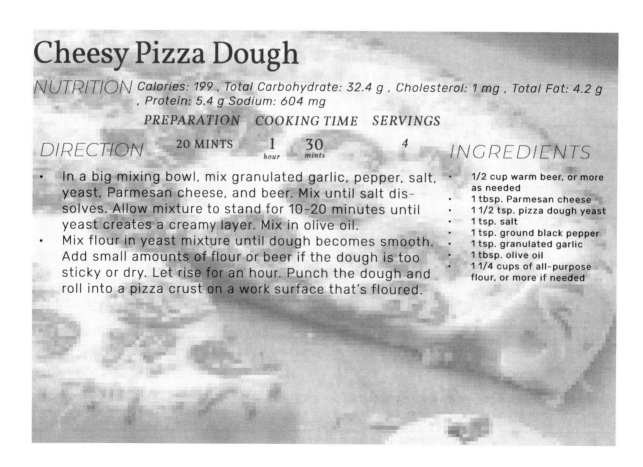

Cheesy Pizza Dough

NUTRITION Calories: 199 , Total Carbohydrate: 32.4 g , Cholesterol: 1 mg , Total Fat: 4.2 g , Protein: 5.4 g Sodium: 604 mg

PREPARATION	COOKING TIME	SERVINGS
20 MINTS	1 hour 30 mints	4

DIRECTION

- In a big mixing bowl, mix granulated garlic, pepper, salt, yeast, Parmesan cheese, and beer. Mix until salt dissolves. Allow mixture to stand for 10-20 minutes until yeast creates a creamy layer. Mix in olive oil.
- Mix flour in yeast mixture until dough becomes smooth. Add small amounts of flour or beer if the dough is too sticky or dry. Let rise for an hour. Punch the dough and roll into a pizza crust on a work surface that's floured.

INGREDIENTS

- 1/2 cup warm beer, or more as needed
- 1 tbsp. Parmesan cheese
- 1 1/2 tsp. pizza dough yeast
- 1 tsp. salt
- 1 tsp. ground black pepper
- 1 tsp. granulated garlic
- 1 tbsp. olive oil
- 1 1/4 cups of all-purpose flour, or more if needed

Cheese Sausage Bread

NUTRITION Calories 260 , Total Fat 5.6g , Saturated Fat 1.4g , Cholesterol 8g , Sodium 355mg , Total Carbohydrate 43.8g , Dietary Fiber 1.6, Total Sugars 1.7g , Protein 7.7g

	PREPARATION	COOKING TIME	SERVINGS
DIRECTION	2 HOUR	2 hour	8

DIRECTION

- Cut the sausage into small cubes.
- Grate the cheese on a grater
- Chop the garlic.
- Add all ingredients to the machine according to the instructions.
- Turn on the baking program, and let it do the work

INGREDIENTS

- One teaspoon dry yeast
- 3 ½ cups flour
- One teaspoon salt
- One tablespoon sugar
- 1 ½ tablespoon oil
- Two tablespoons smoked sausage
- Two tablespoons grated cheese
- One tablespoon chopped garlic
- 1 cup of water

Collards & Bacon Grilled Pizza

NUTRITION Calories: 498, Total Carbohydrate: 50 g , Cholesterol: 33 mg , Total Fat: 28 g Fiber: 6 g , Protein: 19 g Sodium: 573 mg , Sugar: 3 g Saturated Fat: 7 g

	PREPARATION	COOKING TIME	SERVINGS
DIRECTION	15 MINTS	15 mins	4

DIRECTION

- Heat grill to medium-high.
- Roll out dough to an oval that's 12 inches on a surface that's lightly floured. Move to a big baking sheet that's lightly floured. Put Cheddar, collards, oil, and dough on the grill.
- Grease grill rack. Move to grill the crust. Cover the lid and cook for 1-2 minutes until it becomes light brown and puffed. Use tongs to flip over the crust—spread oil on the crust and top with Cheddar and collards. Close lid and cook until cheese melts for another 2-3 minutes or the crust is light brown at the bottom.
- Put pizza on the baking sheet and top using bacon

INGREDIENTS

- 1 lb. whole-wheat pizza dough
- 3 tbsps. garlic-flavoured olive oil
- 2 cups thinly sliced cooked collard greens
- 1 cup shredded Cheddar cheese
- ¼ cup crumbled cooked bacon

Crazy Crust Pizza Dough

NUTRITION Calories: 86, Total Carbohydrate: 13.1 g , Cholesterol: 48 mg , Total Fat: 1.8 g , Protein: 3.9 g, Sodium: 317 mg

PREPARATION	COOKING TIME	SERVINGS
10 MINT	45 mins	8

DIRECTION

- Heat the oven to 200 degrees C or 400 degrees F. Grease a baking sheet or rimmed pizza pan lightly.
- Mix the black pepper, oregano, salt, and flour in a big bowl. Stir in milk and eggs thoroughly. Put butter in the pan and tilt it until it is evenly coated. Put whatever toppings you want on the top of the batter.
- Bake it in the oven and set for 20-25 minutes until the crust is cooked
- Take the crust out of the oven. Drizzle pizza sauce on and top with cheese. Bake for around 10 minutes until the cheese melts.

INGREDIENTS

- 1 cup all-purpose flour
- 1 tsp. salt
- 1 tsp. dried oregano
- 1/8 tsp. black pepper
- Two eggs, lightly beaten
- 2/3 cup milk

Double Crust Stuffed Pizza

NUTRITION Calories: 410 Cal, Carbohydrates: 32.5 g, Fat: 21.1 g, Protein: 22.2 g

PREPARATION	COOKING TIME	SERVINGS
30 MINTS	2 hour 45 mints	8

DIRECTION

- In a large bowl or work bowl of a stand mixer, mix warm water and white sugar. Sprinkle with yeast and let the mixture stand for 5 minutes until the yeast starts to form creamy foam and softens. Stir in 1 tbsp. Of olive oil.
- Mix flour with 1/2 tsp. of salt. Add half flour mixture into the yeast mixture and mix until no dry spots are visible. Whisk in remaining flour, a half cup at a time, mixing well every after addition. Put the dough on a lightly floured surface once it has pulled together. Knead the dough for 8 minutes until elastic and smooth. You can use the dough hook in a stand mixer to mix it.
- Transfer it into a lightly oiled bowl and flip to coat the dough with oil. Use a light cloth to cover the dough. Rise it in a warm place for 1 hour until the volume doubles.
- In a small saucepan, mix 1 tsp of olive oil, brown sugar, crushed tomatoes, garlic powder, and salt. Cover the saucepan and let it cook in low heat for 30 minutes until the tomatoes begin to break down.
- Set the oven to 450°F for preheating. Flatten the dough and place it on a lightly floured surface. Divide the dough into two equal portions. Roll one part into a 12-inches thin circle, then Roll the other piece into a 9-inches thicker circle.
- Press the the12-inches dough round into an ungreased 9-inches springform pan. Top the dough with a cup of cheese. Form sausage into a 9-inches patty and place it on top of the cheese. Arrange the pepperoni, green pepper, mushrooms, red pepper, and the remaining cheese on top of the sausage patty. Place the 9-inches dough around on the top, pinching its edges to seal. Make vent holes on the top of the crust by cutting several 1/2-inch. Pour the sauce evenly on the crust, leaving an only 1/2-inch border at the edges.
- Bake the pizza inside the preheated oven for 40-45 minutes until the cheese is melted, then check sausage is cooked through when the crust is fixed. Let the pizza rest for 15 minutes. Before serving, cut the pizza into wedges.

INGREDIENTS

- 1 1/2 tsp. white sugar
- 1 cup of warm water (100 degrees F or 40 degrees C)
- 1 1/2 tsp. active dry yeast
- 1 tbsp. olive oil
- 1/2 tsp. salt
- 2 cups all-purpose flour
- 1 (8 oz.) can crushed tomatoes
- 1 tbsp. packed brown sugar
- 1/2 tsp. garlic powder
- 1 tsp. olive oil
- 1/2 tsp. salt
- 3 cups shredded mozzarella cheese, divided
- 1/2 lb. bulk Italian sausage
- 1 (4 oz.) package sliced pepperoni
- 1 (8 oz.) package sliced fresh mushrooms
- 1/2 green bell pepper, chopped
- 1/2 red bell pepper, chopped

Deep Dish Pizza Dough

NUTRITION Calories: 328 , Total Carbohydrate: 38.5 g , Cholesterol: 0 mg , Total Fat: 17.5 g Protein: 4.4 g , Sodium: 583 mg

PREPARATION	COOKING TIME	SERVINGS
15 MINT	2 hour 15 mins	8

DIRECTION

- Dissolve sugar and yeast in a bowl with water. Stand the mixture for 5 minutes until the yeast starts to form creamy foam and softens.
- In a bowl, mix bread flour, salt, corn oil, and 2 cups of all-purpose flour. Add the yeast mixture. Knead the mixture in a work surface using 1/2 of the all-purpose flour until well-incorporated. Place the dough in a warm area, then rise for 2 hours until its size doubles.

INGREDIENTS

- 1 (.25 oz.) package active dry yeast
- 1/3 cup white sugar
- 2/3 cup water
- 2 cups all-purpose flour
- 1 cup bread flour
- 1/4 cup corn oil
- 2 tsp. salt
- 6 tbsps. vegetable oil
- 1/2 cup all-purpose flour, or if it's needed

Chapter 21.
Multi-Grain Bread

French Crusty Loaf Bread

NUTRITION Calories 186, Fat 1.2 g, carbs 31.4 g, sodium 126 mg, protein 5.7 g

INGREDIENTS

- *16 slice bread (2 pounds)*
- *2 cups + 2 tablespoons water, lukewarm between 80 and 90 degrees F*
- *Four teaspoons sugar*
- *Two teaspoons table salt*
- *6 1/2 cups white bread flour*
- *Two teaspoons bread machine yeast*
- *12 slice bread (1 ½ pound)*
- *1 1/2 cups + 1 tablespoon water, lukewarm between 80 and 90 degrees F*
- *Three teaspoons sugar*
- *1 1/2 teaspoons table salt*
- *4 3/4 cups white bread flour*
- *1 1/2 teaspoons bread machine yeast*

DIRECTION

- Choose the size of loaf you would like to make and measure your ingredients.
- Put the ingredients to the bread pan in the order list above.
- Place the pan in the machine and close the lid.
- Switch on the bread maker. Select the French setting, then the loaf size, and finally, the crust colour. Start the cycle.
- When the process is finished and the bread is baked, remove the pan from the machine. Use a potholder as the handle. Rest for a few minutes.
- Take out the bread from the pan and let it cool on a wire rack for at least 10 minutes before slicing.

PREPARATION	COOKING TIME	SERVINGS
1 HOUR	1 hour	1 loaf

100% Whole Wheat Bread

NUTRITION Calories: 147, Fat: 5.8 g , Carbohydrates: 22.1 g , Sodium: 138 mg , Protein: 3.4 g

INGREDIENTS

- *16 slice bread (2 pounds)*
- *1¼ cups lukewarm water*
- *Two tablespoons vegetable oil or olive oil*
- *¼ cup honey or maple syrup*
- *1½ teaspoons table salt*
- *3½ cups whole wheat flour*
- *¼ cup sesame, sunflower, or flax seeds (optional)*
- *1½ teaspoons bread machine yeast*
- *12 slice bread (1½ pounds)*
- *1 cup lukewarm water*
- *1½ tablespoons vegetable oil or olive oil*
- *Three tablespoons honey or maple syrup*
- *One teaspoon table salt*
- *Two 2/3 cups whole wheat flour*
- *Three tablespoons sesame, sunflower, or flax seeds (optional)*
- *One teaspoon bread machine yeast*

DIRECTION

- Choose the size of loaf you would like to make and measure your ingredients.
- Put the ingredients to the bread pan in the order listed above.
- Put the pan in the bread machine and cover it.
- Turn on the bread maker. Select the Whole Wheat/Wholegrain setting, then the loaf size, and finally, the crust colour. Start the process.
- When the process is finished, and the bread is baked, remove the pan from the machine. Use a potholder as the handle. Rest for a few minutes.
- Take out the bread from the pan and allow to cool on a wire rack for at least 10 minutes before slicing.

PREPARATION	COOKING TIME	SERVINGS
2 HOUR	1 hour	1 loaf

Baguette Style French Bread

NUTRITION Calories 87, Fat 0.8 g, carbs 16.5 g, sodium 192 mg, protein 3.4 g

INGREDIENTS

- Two baguettes of 1-pound each
- Ingredients for bread machine
- One 2/3 cups water, lukewarm between 80 and 90 degrees F
- One teaspoon table salt
- Four 2/3 cups white bread flour
- Two 2/3 teaspoons bread machine yeast or rapid rise yeast
- Two baguettes of ¾-pound each
- Ingredients for bread machine
- One ¼ cups water, lukewarm between 80 and 90 degrees F
- ¾ teaspoon table salt
- 3 ½ cups white bread flour
- Two teaspoons bread machine

DIRECTION

- Choose the size of crusty bread you would like to make and measure your ingredients.
- Add the ingredients for the bread machine to the pan in the order listed above.
- Put the pan in the bread machine and close the lid. Switch on the bread maker. Select the dough setting.
- When the dough cycle is completed, remove the pan and lay the dough on a floured working surface.
- Knead the dough a few times and add flour if needed, so it is not too sticky to handle. Cut the dough in half and form a ball with each half.
- Grease a baking sheet with olive oil. Dust lightly with cornmeal.
- Preheat the oven to 375 degrees and place the oven rack in the middle position.
- Using a rolling pin dusted with flour, roll one of the dough balls into a 12-inch by 9 -inch rectangle for the 2 pounds bread size or a 10-inch by 8-inch rectangle for the 1 ½ pound bread size. Starting on the longer side, roll the dough tightly. Pinch the ends and the seam with your fingers to seal. Roll the dough in a back in forth movement to make it into an excellent French baguette shape.
- Repeat the process with the second dough ball.
- Place loaves of bread onto the baking sheet with the seams down and brush with some olive oil with enough space in between them to rise. Dust top of both loaves with a little bit of cornmeal. Cover with a clean towel and place in a warm area with any air draught. Let rise for 10 to 15 minutes, or until loaves doubled in size.
- Mix the egg white and one tablespoon of water and lightly brush over both loaves of bread.
- Place in the oven and bake for 20 minutes. Remove from oven and brush with remaining egg wash on top of both loaves of bread. Place back into the range, taking care of turning around the baking sheet. Bake for another 5 to 10 minutes or until the baguettes are golden brown. Let rest on a wired rack for 5-10 minutes before serving.

PREPARATION	COOKING TIME	SERVINGS
2 HOUR	1 hour	2 loaves

Oat Molasses Bread

NUTRITION Calories 160, Fat 7.1 g, carbs 18 g, sodium 164 mg, protein 5.1 g

INGREDIENTS

- 16 slice bread (2 pounds)
- 1 1/3 cups boiling water
- ¾ cup old-fashioned oats
- Three tablespoons butter
- One large egg, lightly beaten
- Two teaspoons table salt
- ¼ cup honey
- 1½ tablespoons dark molasses
- 4 cups white bread flour
- 2½ teaspoons bread machine yeast
- 12 slice bread (1½ pounds)
- 1 cup boiling water
- ½ cup old-fashioned oats
- Two tablespoons butter
- One large egg, lightly beaten
- 1½ teaspoons table salt
- Three tablespoons honey
- One tablespoon dark molasses
- 3 cups white bread flour
- Two teaspoons bread machine yeast

DIRECTION

- Add the boiling water and oats to a mixing bowl. Allow the oats to soak well and cool down completely. Do not drain the water.
- Choose the size of bread you would like to make, then measure your ingredients.
- Add the soaked oats, along with any remaining water, to the bread pan.
- Put the remaining ingredients in the bread pan in the order listed above.
- Place the pan in the bread machine, then cover.
- Press on the machine. Select the Basic setting, then the loaf size, and finally, the crust colour. Start the cycle.
- When the process is finished, then when the bread is baked, then remove the pan. Use a pot-holder as the handle. Rest for a while
- Take out the bread from the pan and place it in a wire rack. Let it cool for at least 10 minutes before slicing.

PREPARATION	COOKING TIME	SERVINGS
2 HOUR	1 hour	1 loaf

Whole Wheat Corn Bread

NUTRITION Calories 146, Fat 5.7 g, carbs 19.3 g, sodium 124 mg, protein 4.8 g

INGREDIENTS

- 16 slice bread (2 pounds)
- 1 1/3 cups lukewarm water
- Two tablespoons light brown sugar
- One large egg, beaten
- Two tablespoons unsalted butter, melted
- 1½ teaspoons table salt
- ¾ cup whole wheat flour
- ¾ cup cornmeal
- 2¾ cups white bread flour
- 2½ teaspoons bread machine yeast
- 12 slice bread (1½ pounds)
- 1 cup lukewarm water
- 1½ tablespoons light brown sugar
- One medium egg, beaten
- 1½ tablespoons unsalted butter, melted
- 1½ teaspoons table salt
- ½ cup whole wheat flour
- ½ cup cornmeal
- 2 cups of white bread flour
- 1½ teaspoons bread machine yeast

DIRECTION

- Choose the size of loaf you would like to make and measure your ingredients.
- Put the ingredients in a pan in the order list above.
- Put the pan in the bread machine and cover it.
- Switch on the bread maker. Select the Basic setting, then the loaf size, and finally, the crust colour. Start the process.
- When the process is finished, when the bread is baked, remove the pan from the machine. Use a potholder as the handle. Rest for a while.
- Take out the bread from the pan and allow to cool on a wire rack for at least 10 minutes before slicing.

PREPARATION	COOKING TIME	SERVINGS
2 HOUR	1 hour	1 loaf

Chapter 22. Holiday Bread

162

Wheat Bran Bread

NUTRITION Calories: 147 Cal, Fat: 2.8 g, Carbohydrates: 24.6 g, Sodium: 312 mg

INGREDIENTS

- 16 slice bread (2 pounds)
- 1½ cups lukewarm milk
- Three tablespoons unsalted butter, melted
- ¼ cup of sugar
- Two teaspoons table salt
- ½ cup wheat bran
- 3½ cups white bread flour
- Two teaspoons bread machine yeast
- 12 slice bread (1½ pounds)
- 1 1/8 cups lukewarm milk
- 2¼ tablespoons unsalted butter, melted
- Three tablespoons sugar
- 1½ teaspoons table salt
- 1/3 cup wheat bran
- 2 2/3 cups of white bread flour
- 1½ teaspoons bread machine yeast

DIRECTION

- Choose the size of loaf you would like to make and measure your ingredients.
- Put the ingredients to the bread pan in the order listed above.
- Put the pan in the bread machine and close the lid.
- Switch on the bread maker. Select the Basic setting, then the loaf size, and finally, the crust colour. Start the process.
- When the process is finished, and the bread is baked, remove the pan from the machine. Use a potholder as the handle. Rest for a few minutes.

PREPARATION	COOKING TIME	SERVINGS
2 HOUR	1 hour	1 loaf

Pumpkin Bread

NUTRITION Calories 13, Total Fat 3.6 g, Saturated Fat 2.1 g , Cholesterol 9 mg , Sodium 149 mg, Total Carbs 22.4 g , Fiber 1.1 g, Sugar 2.9 g , Protein 2.9 g

INGREDIENTS

- ½ cup plus 2 tablespoons warm water
- ½ cup canned pumpkin puree
- ¼ cup butter, softened
- ¼ cup non-fat dry milk powder
- 2¾ cups bread flour
- ¼ cup brown sugar
- ¾ teaspoon salt
- 1 teaspoon ground cinnamon
- ½ teaspoon ground ginger
- 1/8 teaspoon ground nutmeg
- 2¼ teaspoons active dry yeast

DIRECTION

- Place all ingredients in the baking pan of the bread machine in the order recommended by the manufacturer.
- Place the baking pan in the bread machine and close the lid.
- Select Basic setting.
- Press the start button.
- Carefully, remove the baking pan from the machine and then invert the bread loaf onto a wire rack to cool completely before slicing.
- With a sharp knife, cut bread loaf into desired-sized slices and serve.

PREPARATION	COOKING TIME	SERVINGS
5 MINT	1 hour	14

Pumpkin Cranberry Bread

NUTRITION Calories 199,Total Fat 6 g, Saturated Fat 0.7 g , Cholesterol 0 mg , Sodium

INGREDIENTS

- ¾ cup water
- 2/3 cup canned pumpkin
- 3 tablespoons brown sugar
- 2 tablespoons vegetable oil
- 2 cups all-purpose flour
- 1 cup whole-wheat flour
- 1¼ teaspoon salt
- ½ cup sweetened dried cranberries
- ½ cup walnuts, chopped
- 1¾ teaspoons active dry yeast

DIRECTION

- Place all ingredients in the baking pan of the bread machine in the order recommended by the manufacturer.
- Place the baking pan in the bread machine and close the lid.
- Select Basic setting.
- Press the start button.
- Carefully, remove the baking pan from the machine and then invert the bread loaf onto a wire rack to cool completely before slicing.
- With a sharp knife, cut bread loaf into desired-sized slices and serve.

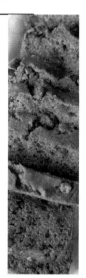

PREPARATION	COOKING TIME	SERVINGS
10 MINT	4 hour	12

Cranberry Orange Bread

NUTRITION Calories 166, Total Fat 2.7 g, Saturated Fat 1 g , Cholesterol 3 mg , Sodium 309 mg, Total Carbs 30.4 g , Fiber 1.3 g, Sugar 5.8 g , Protein 4.4 g

INGREDIENTS

- 3 cups all-purpose flour
- 1 cup dried cranberries
- ¾ cup plain yogurt
- ½ cup warm water
- 3 tablespoons honey
- 1 tablespoon butter, melted
- 2 teaspoons active dry yeast
- 1½ teaspoons salt
- 1 teaspoon orange oil

DIRECTION

- Place all ingredients in the baking pan of the bread machine in the order recommended by the manufacturer.
- Place the baking pan in the bread machine and close the lid.
- Select Basic setting and then Light Crust.
- Press the start button.
- Carefully, remove the baking pan from the machine and then invert the bread loaf onto a wire rack to cool completely before slicing.
- With a sharp knife, cut bread loaf into desired-sized slices and serve.

PREPARATION	COOKING TIME	SERVINGS
10 MINT	3 hour	12

Cranberry Bread

NUTRITION *Calories: 80 calories;, Total Carbohydrate: 14.4 g , Cholesterol: 5 mg , Total*

INGREDIENTS

- 4 1/4 cups bread flour
- 2/3 cup rolled oats
- One tablespoon white sugar
- Two teaspoons active dry yeast
- 1 1/2 teaspoons salt
- One teaspoon ground cinnamon
- Two tablespoons butter cut up
- 1 2/3 cups orange juice
- 1/2 cup diced dried apricots
- Two tablespoons honey, warmed

DIRECTION

- Into the bread machine's pan, put the bread ingredients in the order suggested by the manufacturer. Then pout in dried apricots before the knead cycle completes.
- Immediately remove bread from a machine when it's done and then glaze with warmed honey. Let to cool thoroughly before serving.

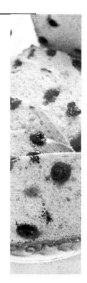

PREPARATION	COOKING TIME	SERVINGS
10 MINT	3 hour	16

Orange Bread

NUTRITION *Calories 197, Total Fat 2.9 g, Saturated Fat 0.6 g , Cholesterol 0 mg , Sodium 162 mg, Total Carbs 36.9 g , Fiber 2.6 g, Sugar 5.6 g , Protein 6.1 g*

INGREDIENTS

- 1¼ cups water
- 3 tablespoons powdered milk
- 1½ tablespoons vegetable oil
- 3 tablespoons honey
- 2½ cups bread flour
- ¾ cup amaranth flour
- 1/3 cup whole-wheat flour
- ¾ teaspoon salt
- 3 tablespoons fresh orange zest, grated finely
- 2¼ teaspoons active dry yeast

DIRECTION

- Place all ingredients in the baking pan of the bread machine in the order recommended by the manufacturer.
- Place the baking pan in the bread machine and close the lid.
- Select Basic setting.
- Press the start button.
- Carefully, remove the baking pan from the machine and then invert the bread loaf onto a wire rack to cool completely before slicing.
- With a sharp knife, cut bread loaf into desired-sized slices and serve.

PREPARATION	COOKING TIME	SERVINGS
10 MINT	3 hour	12

Banana Chocolate Chip Bread

NUTRITION Calories 215, Total Fat 8.2 g, Saturated Fat 5 g , Cholesterol 38 mg , Sodium

INGREDIENTS

- ½ cup warm milk
- 2 eggs
- ½ cup butter, melted
- 1 teaspoon vanilla extract
- 3 medium ripe bananas, peeled and mashed
- 1 cup granulated white sugar
- 2 cups all-purpose flour
- ½ teaspoon salt
- 2 teaspoons baking powder
- 1 teaspoon baking soda
- ½ cup chocolate chips

DIRECTION

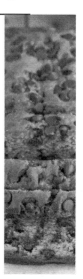

- 1. Add ingredients (except for cranberries) in the baking pan of the bread machine in the order recommended by the manufacturer.
- 2. Place the baking pan in the bread machine and close the lid.
- 3. Select Quick Bread setting.
- 4. Press the start button.
- 5. Wait for the bread machine to beep before adding the chocolate chips.
- 6. Carefully, remove the baking pan from the machine and then invert the bread loaf onto a wire rack to cool completely before slicing.
- 7. With a sharp knife, cut bread loaf into desired-sized slices and serve.

PREPARATION	COOKING TIME	SERVINGS
10 MINT	1 hour 40 mint	16

Raisin Cinnamon Swirl Bread

NUTRITION Calories 297, Total Fat 10.6 g, Saturated Fat 6.3 g , Cholesterol 41 mg , Sodium 277 mgTotal Carbs 46.2 g , Fiber 1.7 g, Sugar 16.5 g , Protein 5.6 g

INGREDIENTS

- ¼ cup milk
- 1 large egg, beaten
- Water, as required
- ¼ cup butter, softened
- 1/3 cup white sugar
- 1 teaspoon salt
- 3½ cups bread flour
- 2 teaspoons active dry yeast
- ½ cup raisins

DIRECTION

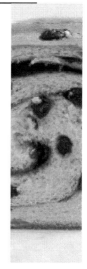

- For bread: Place milk and egg into a small bowl.
- Add enough water to make 1 cup of mixture.
- Place the egg mixture into the baking pan of the bread machine.
- Place the remaining ingredients (except for raisins) on top in the order recommended by the manufacturer.
- Place the baking pan in the bread machine and close the lid.
- Select Dough cycle.
- Press the start button.
- Wait for the bread machine to beep before adding the raisins.
- After Dough cycle completes, remove the dough from the bread pan and place onto lightly floured surface.
- Roll the dough into a 10x12-inch rectangle.
- For swirl: Mix together the sugar and cinnamon.
- Brush the dough rectangle with 1 egg white, followed by the melted butter.
- Now, sprinkle the dough with cinnamon sugar, leaving about a 1-inch border on each side.
- From the short side, roll the dough and pinch the ends underneath. Grease loaf pan and place the dough.
- With a kitchen towel, cover the loaf pan and place in warm place for 1 hour or until doubled in size.
- Preheat your oven to 350°F.
- Brush the top of dough with remaining egg white.
- Bake for approximately 35 minutes or until a wooden skewer inserted in the center comes out clean.
- Remove the bread pan and place onto a wire rack to cool for about 15 minutes.
- Cool bread before slicing

PREPARATION	COOKING TIME	SERVINGS
15 MINT	3 hour	12

Gingerbread

NUTRITION Calories 202, Total Fat 4 g, Saturated Fat 2.2 g , Cholesterol 23 mg , Sodium 184 mg, Total Carbs 36.8 g , Fiber 1.3 g, Sugar 7.7 g , Protein 5 g

INGREDIENTS

- 3/4 cup milk
- 1/4 cup molasses
- 1 egg
- 3 tablespoons butter
- 3 1/3 cups bread flour
- 1 tablespoon brown sugar
- ¾ teaspoon salt
- ¾ teaspoon ground cinnamon
- ¾ teaspoon ground ginger
- 2¼ teaspoons active dry yeast
- 1/3 cup raisins

DIRECTION

- Place all ingredients (except for raisins) in the baking pan of the bread machine in the order recommended by the manufacturer.
- Place the baking pan in the bread machine and close the lid.
- Select Basic setting and then Light Crust.
- Press the start button.
- Wait for the bread machine to beep before adding the raisins.
- Carefully, remove the baking pan from the machine and then invert the bread loaf onto a wire rack to cool completely before slicing.
- With a sharp knife, cut bread loaf into de-sired-sized slices and serve.

PREPARATION	COOKING TIME	SERVINGS
10 MINT	2 hour	12

Chapter 23.
Keto Bread Recipes

Toast Bread

NUTRITION carbohydrates 5 g fats 2.7 g protein 5.2 g calories 203 fiber 1 g

INGREDIENTS

- 1 ½ teaspoons yeast
- cups almond flour
- tablespoons sugar
- 1 teaspoon salt
- 1 ½ tablespoon butter
- 1 cup water

DIRECTION

- Pour water into the bowl; add salt, sugar, soft butter, flour, and yeast.
- I add dried tomatoes and paprika.
- Put it on the basic program.
- The crust can be light or medium.

PREPARATION	COOKING TIME	SERVINGS
3 ½ HOURS	3 ½ HOURS	8

Simple Milk Bread

NUTRITION carbohydrates 4 g fats 7 g protein 3 g calories 85 Fiber 1.5 g

INGREDIENTS

- cups almond flour
- tbsp. inulin
- 1 tbsp. whole milk
- ½ tsp. salt
- tsp. active yeast
- 1 ¼ cups warm water
- 1 tbsp. olive oil

DIRECTION

- Use a small mixing bowl to combine all dry Ingredients, except for the yeast.
- In the bread machine pan add all wet Ingredients.
- Add all of your dry Ingredients, from the small mixing bowl, in the bread machine pan. Top with the yeast.
- Set the bread machine to the basic bread setting.
- When the bread is done, remove bread machine pan from the bread machine.
- Let cool slightly before transferring to a cooling rack.
- The bread can be stored for up to 5 days on the counter and for up to 3 months in the freezer.

PREPARATION	COOKING TIME	SERVINGS
3 MINT	3 mint	8

Walnut Bread

NUTRITION carbohydrates 4 g fats 6.7 g protein 8.3 g calories 257 fiber 1.3 g

INGREDIENTS

- cups almond flour
- ½ cup water
- ½ cup milk
- eggs
- ½ cup walnuts
- 1 tablespoon vegetable oil
- 1 tablespoon sugar
- 1 teaspoon salt
- 1 teaspoon yeast

DIRECTION

- All products must be room temperature.
- Pour water, milk, and vegetable oil into the bucket and add in the eggs.
- Now pour in the sifted almond flour. In the process of kneading bread, you may need a little more or less flour – it depends on its moisture.
- Pour in salt, sugar, and yeast. If it is hot in the kitchen (especially in summer), pour all three Ingredients into the different ends of the bucket so that the dough does not have time for peroxide.
- Now the first kneading dough begins, which lasts 15 minutes. In the process, we monitor the state of the ball. It should be soft, but at the same time, keep its shape and not spread. If the ball does not want to be collected, add a little flour, since the moisture of this product is different for everyone. If the bucket is clean and all the flour is incorporated into the dough, then everything is done right. If the dough is still lumpy and even crumbles, you need to add a little more liquid.
- Close the lid and then prepare the nuts. They need to be sorted and lightly fried in a dry frying pan; the pieces of nuts will be crispy. Then let them cool and cut with a knife to the desired size. When the bread maker signals, pour in the nuts and wait until the spatula mixes them into the dough.
- Remove the bucket and take out the walnut bread. Completely cool it on a grill so that the bottom does not get wet.

PREPARATION	COOKING TIME	SERVINGS
4 HOUR	4 hour	10

Bulgur Bread

NUTRITION carbohydrates 3 g fats 3 g protein 8.9 g calories 255 fiber 1.2 g

INGREDIENTS

- ½ cup bulgur
- 1/3 cup boiling water
- 1 egg
- 1 cup water
- 1 tablespoon butter
- 1 ½ tablespoon milk powder
- 1 tablespoon sugar
- teaspoons salt
- ¼ cups flour
- 1 teaspoon dried yeast

DIRECTION

- Bulgur pour boiling water into a small container and cover with a lid. Leave to stand for 30 minutes.
- Cut butter into small cubes.
- Stir the egg with water in a measuring container. The total volume of eggs with water should be 300 ml.
- Put all the Ingredients in the bread maker in the order that is described in the instructions for your bread maker. Bake in the basic mode, medium crust.

PREPARATION	COOKING TIME	SERVINGS
3 HOUR	3 hour	8

Milk Almond Bread

NUTRITION carbohydrates 5 g fats 4.5 g protein 10.1 g calories 352 fiber 1.5 g

INGREDIENTS

- 1 ¼ cup milk
- ¼ cups almond flour
- tablespoons butter
- teaspoons dry yeast
- 1 tablespoon sugar
- teaspoons salt

DIRECTION

- Pour the milk into the form and ½ cup of water. Add flour.
- Put butter, sugar, and salt in different corners of the mold. Make a groove in the flour and put in the yeast.
- Bake on the basic program.
- Cool the bread.

PREPARATION	COOKING TIME	SERVINGS
3 ½ HOURS	3 ½ HOURS	8

Italian Blue Cheese Bread

NUTRITION carbohydrates 5 g fats 4.6 g protein 6 g calories 194 fiber 1.5 g

INGREDIENTS

- whole eggs
- ¼ teaspoon sea salt
- 1 cup olive oil
- 1 cup white sugar
- 1 tablespoon vanilla sugar
- teaspoon cinnamon
- ½ cup nuts, ground
- cups bread flour, well sifted
- 1 tablespoon baking powder
- 1¼ cup zucchini, grated

DIRECTION

- Mix all the Ingredients. Start baking.

PREPARATION	COOKING TIME	SERVINGS
3 *hour*	3 *hour*	8

Zucchini bread

NUTRITION Carbohydrates 4 g, Fats 31 g, Protein 8.6 g , Calories 556 , Fiber 1.3 g

INGREDIENTS

- whole eggs
- ¼ teaspoon sea salt
- 1 cup olive oil
- 1 cup white sugar
- 1 tablespoon vanilla sugar
- teaspoon cinnamon
- ½ cup nuts, ground
- cups bread flour, well sifted
- 1 tablespoon baking powder
- 1¼ cup zucchini, grated

DIRECTION

- scales).
- Carefully measure the ingredients into the pan, except the zucchini and nuts.
- Place all of the ingredients into the bread bucket in the right order, following the manual for your bread machine.
- Close the cover.
- Select the program of your bread machine to CAKE and choose the crust color to LIGHT.
- Press START.
- After the signal, put the grated zucchini and nuts to the dough.
- Wait until the program completes.
- When done, take the bucket out and let it cool for 5-10 minutes.
- Shake the loaf from the pan and let cool for 30 minutes on a cooling rack.
- Slice, serve, and enjoy the taste of fragrant homemade bread.

PREPARATION	COOKING TIME	SERVINGS
2 *hour* 10 *mint*	2 *hour* 10 *mint*	8

French ham bread

NUTRITION *Carbohydrates 2 g, Fats 5.5 g , Protein 11.4 g , Calories 287 , Fiber 1 g*

INGREDIENTS

- 1/3 cups Almond flour
- 1 cup ham
- ½ cup milk powder
- 1 ½ tablespoons sugar
- 1 teaspoon yeast, fresh
- 1 teaspoon salt
- 1 teaspoon dried basil
- 1 1/3 cups water
- tablespoons olive oil

DIRECTION

- Cut ham into cubes of 0.5-1 cm (approximately ¼ inch).
- Put the ingredients in the bread maker in the following order: water, olive oil, salt, sugar, flour, milk powder, ham, and yeast.
- Put all the ingredients according to the instructions to your bread maker.
- Basil put in a dispenser or fills it later, at the signal in the container.
- Turn on the bread machine.
- After the end of the baking cycle, leave the bread container in the bread maker to keep warm for 1 hour.
- Then your delicious bread is ready!

PREPARATION		COOKING TIME		SERVINGS
3 hour	30 mint	3 hour	30 mint	8

Cheese sausage bread

NUTRITION *Carbohydrates 4 g , Fats 5.6 g , Protein 7.7 g , Calories 260 , Fiber 1.3 g*

INGREDIENTS

- 1 teaspoon dry yeast
- ½ cups flour
- 1 teaspoon salt
- 1 tablespoon sugar
- 1 ½ tablespoon oil
- tablespoons smoked sausage
- tablespoons grated cheese
- 1 tablespoon chopped garlic
- 1 cup water

DIRECTION

- Cut the sausage into small cubes.
- Grate the cheese on a grater; chop the garlic.
- Add the ingredients to the bread machine according to the instructions.
- Turn on the baking program, and let it do the work.

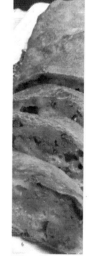

PREPARATION	COOKING TIME	SERVINGS
4 HOUR	4 hour	8

Sausage bread

NUTRITION Carbohydrates 4 g , Fats 5.1 g , Protein 7.4 g , Calories 234 , Fiber 1.3 g

INGREDIENTS

- 1 ½ teaspoon dry yeast
- cups flour
- 1 teaspoon sugar
- 1 ½ teaspoons salt
- 1 1/3 cups whey
- 1 tablespoon oil
- 1 cup chopped smoked sausage

DIRECTION

- Fold all the ingredients in the order that is recommended specifically for your model.
- Set the required parameters for baking bread.
- When ready, remove the delicious hot bread.
- Wait for it to cool down and enjoy with sausage.

PREPARATION	COOKING TIME	SERVINGS
4 HOUR	4 hour	8

Bread with Beef

NUTRITION Carbohydrates 6 g , Fats 21 g , Protein 13 g , Calories 299 , Fiber 1.6 g

INGREDIENTS

- oz. beef
- 15 oz. almond flour
- oz. rye flour
- 1 onion
- teaspoons dry yeast
- tablespoons olive oil
- 1 tablespoon sugar
- Sea salt
- Ground black pepper

DIRECTION

- Pour the warm water into the 15 oz. of the wheat flour and rye flour and leave overnight.
- Chop the onions and cut the beef into cubes.
- Fry the onions until clear and golden brown and then mix in the bacon and fry on low heat for 20 minutes until soft.
- Combine the yeast with the warm water, mixing until smooth consistency and then combine the yeast with the flour, salt and sugar, but don't forget to mix and knead well.
- Add in the fried onions with the beef and black pepper and mix well.
- Pour some oil into a bread machine and place the dough into the bread maker. Cover the dough with the towel and leave for 1 hour.
- Close the lid and turn the bread machine on the basic/white bread program.
- Bake the bread until the medium crust and after the bread is ready take it out and leave for 1 hour covered with the towel and only then you can slice the bread.

PREPARATION	COOKING TIME	SERVINGS
2 HOUR	2 hour	6

Coconut milk bread

NUTRITION Carbohydrates 6 g , Fats 15.3 g , Protein 9.5 g , Calories 421 , Fiber 1.6 g

INGREDIENTS

- 1 whole egg
- ½ cup lukewarm milk
- ½ cup lukewarm coconut milk
- ¼ cup butter, melted and cooled
- tablespoons liquid honey
- cups almond flour, sifted
- 1 tablespoon active dry yeast
- 1 teaspoon salt
- ½ cup coconut chips

DIRECTION

- Prepare all of the ingredients for your bread and measuring means (a cup, a spoon, kitchen scales).
- Carefully measure the ingredients into the pan, except the coconut chips.
- Place all of the ingredients, into the bread bucket in the right order, following the manual for your bread machine.
- Close the cover.
- Select the program of your bread machine to SWEET and choose the crust color to MEDIUM.
- Press START.
- After the signal, add the coconut chips into the dough.
- Wait until the program completes.
- When done, take the bucket out and let it cool for 5-10 minutes.
- Shake the loaf from the pan and let cool for 30 minutes on a cooling rack.
- Slice, serve, and enjoy the taste of fragrant home-made bread.

PREPARATION	COOKING TIME	SERVINGS
3 hour	3 hour	10

Cream Cheese Bread

NUTRITION 98 Cal, 7.9 g Fat, 3.5 g Protein, 2.6 g Carb, 0.4 g Fiber, 2.2 g Net Carb

INGREDIENTS

- ¼ cup / 60 grams butter, grass-fed, unsalted
- 1 cup and 3 tablespoons / 140 grams cream cheese, softened
- egg yolks, pasteurized
- 1 teaspoon vanilla extract, unsweetened
- 1 teaspoon baking powder
- ¼ teaspoon of sea salt
- tablespoons monk fruit powder
- ½ cup / 65 grams peanut flour
-

DIRECTION

- Gather all the ingredients for the bread and plug in the bread machine having the capacity of 2 pounds of bread recipe.
- Take a large bowl, place butter in it, beat in cream cheese until thoroughly combined and then beat in egg yolks, vanilla, baking powder, salt, and monk fruit powder until well combined.
- Add egg mixture into the bread bucket, top with flour, shut the lid, select the "basic/white" cycle or "low-carb" setting and then press the up/down arrow button to adjust baking time according to your bread machine; it will take 3 to 4 hours.
- Then press the crust button to select light crust if available, and press the "start/stop" button to switch on the bread machine.
- When the bread machine beeps, open the lid, then take out the bread basket and lift out the bread.
- Let bread cool on a wire rack for 1 hour, then cut it into twelve slices and serve.

PREPARATION	COOKING TIME	SERVINGS
10 MINT	4 hour	1 ½ pounds / 12 slices

Egg Butter Bread

NUTRITION Carbohydrates 3 g , Fats 5.6 g , Protein 9.6 g , Calories 319 , Fiber 1.3 g

INGREDIENTS

- cups almond flour
- 1 cup milk
- eggs
- 1 teaspoon yeast
- 1 ½ teaspoons salt
- ¼ tablespoons sugar
- 1 ½ tablespoon butter

DIRECTION

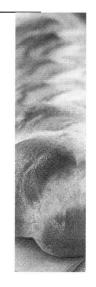

- Lay the products in the bread pan according to the instructions for your device. At me in the beginning liquid, therefore we pour warm milk, and we will add salt.
- Then add the eggs (pre-loosen with a fork) and melted butter, which must be cooled to a warm state.
- Now add the sifted almond flour.
- Top the yeast - dry active ones, since they do not require pre-activation with liquid.
- In the end, mix the yeast with sugar.
- Select the Basic program (on mine, it is 1 of 12). The time will automatically be set for 3 hours. When the batch begins, this is the most crucial moment. Kneading on this program lasts precisely 10 minutes, from which a ball of all products is produced. Not porridge, not liquid, not a rough dense lump – namely a softball.
- Ideally, it is formed after the first 4-5 minutes of kneading; then you can help the bread maker. First, scrape off the flour from the walls, which the blade sometimes does not entirely grasp and thus interferes with the dough. Second, you need to look carefully, as different flours from different manufacturers have different degrees of humidity so that it may take a little more - about 2-3 tablespoons. This is when you see that the dough cannot condense and gather in a ball.
- Very rarely, but sometimes it happens that there is not enough liquid and the dough turns into lumps. If so, add a little more water and thereby help the bread maker knead the dough.
- After exactly 3 hours, you will hear the signal, but much sooner, your home will be filled with the fantastic aroma of homemade bread. Turn off the appliance, open the lid, and take out the bowl of bread. Handsome!
- Take out the hot egg bread, and remove the paddle if it does not stay in the bowl, but is at the bottom of the loaf. Cool the loaves on a grate. In general, it is always advised to cool the bread on its side.
- This bread is quite tall - 12 cm.
- Only when the loaf completely cools, you can cut the egg bread!
- Help yourself!

PREPARATION	COOKING TIME	SERVINGS
3 HOUR	3 hour	8

Almond Meal Bread

NUTRITION 104 Cal, 8.8 g Fat, 4 g Protein, 2.1 g Carb, 1.8 g Fiber, 0.3 g Net Carb

INGREDIENTS

- eggs, pasteurized
- ¼ cup / 60 ml melted coconut oil
- 1 tablespoon apple cider vinegar
- ¼ cups / 215 grams almond meal
- 1 teaspoon baking soda
- ¼ cup / 35 grams ground flaxseed meal
- 1 teaspoon onion powder
- 1 tablespoon minced garlic
- 1 teaspoon of sea salt
- 1 teaspoon chopped sage leaves
- 1 teaspoon fresh thyme
- 1 teaspoon chopped rosemary leaves

DIRECTION

- Gather all the ingredients for the bread and plug in the bread machine having the capacity of 2 pounds of bread recipe.
- Take a large bowl, crack eggs in it and then beat in coconut oil and vinegar until well blended.
- Take a separate large bowl, place the almond meal in it, add remaining ingredients, and stir until well mixed.
- Add egg mixture into the bread bucket, top with flour mixture, shut the lid, select the "basic/white" cycle or "low-carb" setting and then press the up/down arrow button to adjust baking time according to your bread machine; it will take 3 to 4 hours.
- Then press the crust button to select light crust if available, and press the "start/stop" button to switch on the bread machine.
- When the bread machine beeps, open the lid, then take out the bread basket and lift out the bread.
- Let bread cool on a wire rack for 1 hour, then cut it into ten slices and serve.

PREPARATION	COOKING TIME	SERVINGS
10 MINT	4 hour	1 ½ pounds / 10 slices

Simple Macadamia Nut Bread

NUTRITION *155 Cal, 14.3 g Fat, 5.6 g Protein, 3.9 g Carb, 3 g Fiber, 0.9 g Net Carb*

INGREDIENTS

- 1 cup / 135 grams macadamia nuts
- eggs, pasteurized
- ½ teaspoon apple cider vinegar
- ¼ cup / 30 grams coconut flour
- ½ teaspoon baking soda

DIRECTION

- Gather all the ingredients for the bread and plug in the bread machine having the capacity of 1 pound of bread recipe.
- Place nuts in a blender, pulse for 2 to 3 minutes until mixture reaches a consistency of butter, and then blend in eggs and vinegar until smooth.
- Stir in flour and baking soda until well mixed.
- Add the batter into the bread bucket, shut the lid, select the "basic/white" cycle or "low-carb" setting and then press the up/down arrow button to adjust baking time according to your bread machine; it will take 3 to 4 hours.
- Then press the crust button to select light crust if available, and press the "start/stop" button to switch on the bread machine.
- When the bread machine beeps, open the lid, then take out the bread basket and lift out the bread.
- Let bread cool on a wire rack for 1 hour, then cut it into eight slices and serve.

PREPARATION	COOKING TIME	SERVINGS
10 MINT	4 hour	*1 pound / 8 slices*

Keto Zucchini Bread

NUTRITION *Calories 270,, Fat 15, Fiber 3, Carbs 5, Protein 9*

INGREDIENTS

- ounces almond flour
- ounces coconut flour
- 1/2 teaspoon salt
- 1/2 teaspoon pepper
- teaspoons heating powder
- 1 teaspoon thickener
- enormous eggs
- 2/3 cup margarine dissolved
- ounces cheddar ground
- ounces zucchini ground and fluid crushed out
- ounces bacon diced

DIRECTION

- Preheat broiler to 175C/350F.
- In an enormous bowl include the almond flour, coconut flour, salt, pepper, preparing powder and thickener. Blend well.
- Include the eggs and softened spread and blend well.
- Overlap through ¾ of the cheddar, alongside the zucchini and bacon.
- Spoon into your lubed 9in clay portion dish (if utilizing a meat dish, line with material paper) and prepare for 35 minutes, expel from the stove and top with the rest of the cheddar.
- Prepare for another 10-15 minutes, until the cheddar has caramelized and a stick confesses all.
- Leave to cool for 20 minutes.
- Cut into 12 cuts and appreciate warm.

PREPARATION	COOKING TIME	SERVINGS
15 MINT	58 mint	*12*

Cheesy Garlic Bread

NUTRITION 250 Cal, 14.5 g Fat, 7.2 g Protein, 3 g Carb, 1.6 g Fiber, 1.4 g Net Carb

INGREDIENTS

- For the Bread:
- eggs, pasteurized
- cups / 200 grams almond flour
- 1/2 teaspoon xanthan gum
- 1 teaspoon garlic powder
- 1 teaspoon salt
- 1 teaspoon parsley
- 1 teaspoon Italian seasoning
- 1 teaspoon dried oregano
- 1 stick of butter, grass-fed, unsalted, melted
- 1 cup / 100 grams grated mozzarella cheese
- tablespoons ricotta cheese
- 1 cup / 235 grams grated cheddar cheese
- 1/3 cup / 30 grams grated parmesan cheese
- For the Topping:
- ½ stick of butter, grass-fed, unsalted, melted
- 1 teaspoon garlic powder

DIRECTION

- For the Bread:
- eggs, pasteurized
- cups / 200 grams almond flour
- 1/2 teaspoon xanthan gum
- 1 teaspoon garlic powder
- 1 teaspoon salt
- 1 teaspoon parsley
- 1 teaspoon Italian seasoning
- 1 teaspoon dried oregano
- 1 stick of butter, grass-fed, unsalted, melted
- 1 cup / 100 grams grated mozzarella cheese
- tablespoons ricotta cheese
- 1 cup / 235 grams grated cheddar cheese
- 1/3 cup / 30 grams grated parmesan cheese
- For the Topping:
- ½ stick of butter, grass-fed, unsalted, melted
- 1 teaspoon garlic powder

PREPARATION	COOKING TIME	SERVINGS
10 MINT	4 hour	2 pounds / 16 slices

Low-Carb Bread

NUTRITION Calories 270, Fat 15, Fiber 3, Carbs 5, Protein 9

INGREDIENTS

- tablespoons almond flour
- 1/2 tablespoon coconut flour
- 1/4 teaspoon heating powder
- 1 egg
- 1/2 tablespoon liquefied margarine or ghee
- 1 tablespoon unsweetened milk of decision

DIRECTION

- Blend all fixings in a little bowl and speed until smooth.
- Oil a 3×3-inch glass microwave-safe bowl or shape with spread, ghee, or coconut oil
- Empty your blend into your well-lubed bowl or shape and microwave on high for 90 seconds.
- Cautiously expel your bread from the glass dish or shape.
- Cut, toast, and liquefy spread on top, whenever wanted.

PREPARATION	COOKING TIME	SERVINGS
5 MINT	31 mine	I

Keto Bread

NUTRITION Calories 270,, Fat 15, Fiber 3, Carbs 5,, Protein 9

INGREDIENTS

- 1/3 cups Almond flour
- 1 cup ham
- ½ cup milk powder
- 1 ½ tablespoons sugar
- 1 teaspoon yeast, fresh
- 1 teaspoon salt
- 1 teaspoon dried basil
- 1 1/3 cups water
- tablespoons olive oil

DIRECTION

- Cut ham into cubes of 0.5-1 cm (approximately ¼ inch).
- Put the ingredients in the bread maker in the following order: water, olive oil, salt, sugar, flour, milk powder, ham, and yeast.
- Put all the ingredients according to the instructions to your bread maker.
- Basil put in a dispenser or fills it later, at the signal in the container.
- Turn on the bread machine.
- After the end of the baking cycle, leave the bread container in the bread maker to keep warm for 1 hour.
- Then your delicious bread is ready!

PREPARATION	COOKING TIME	SERVINGS
15 MINT	40 *mint*	6

Low-Carb "Rye" Bread

NUTRITION Calories 270, Fat 15, Fiber 3, Carbs 5,, Protein 9

INGREDIENTS

- Pressed cups ground flaxseed (300g/10.6 oz.)
- 1 cup coconut flour (120g/4.2 oz.)
- tablespoons caraway seeds (or rosemary)
- 1 tablespoon + 1 teaspoon heating powder (I utilized my very own sans gluten preparing blend: 1 tsp. heating soft drink added to the dry blend + 2 tsp. cream of tartar added to the egg whites)
- 1 tbsp. Erythritol (10g/0.4 oz.) or 5 drops fluid stevia
- 1/4 cup ground chia seeds (32g/1.1 oz.) or 1 tbsp. (thickener isn't paleo-accommodating)
- 1 teaspoon salt or more to taste (pink Himalayan stone salt)

DIRECTION

- Move the broiler rack to the middle situation of the stove, and preheat to 175 °C/350 °F. Add the dry fixings to a huge bowl and altogether speed to join (ground flaxseed, coconut flour, caraway, heating pop, Erythritol, salt, and thickener or ground chia seeds). It is particularly critical to appropriate the thickener (or ground chia seeds) uniformly. Low-Carb "Rye" Bread
- Separate the egg yolks from the egg whites and keep the egg whites aside. Include relaxed ghee or spread and toasted sesame oil into the eggs yolks.
- Note: Although the first formula doesn't request isolating the eggs, I found that doing so makes the bread more "feathery". Low-Carb "Rye" Bread
- "Cream" the egg yolks and the ghee (spread or olive oil) until smooth. In a different bowl, whisk the egg whites until they make delicate pinnacles and "fix" them with the cream of tartar. Low-Carb "Rye" Bread
- Add the dry blend to the bowl with the egg yolk blend and procedure well. It's a thick player and will meet up gradually. Set aside the effort to ensure everything is completely blended. Low-Carb "Rye" Bread
- Include the vinegar and blend in well. Low-Carb "Rye" Bread
- Include warm water and procedure until joined. Low-Carb "Rye" Bread
- Include the egg whites and tenderly crease them in. Do whatever it takes not to empty the player totally. Low-Carb "Rye" Bread
- Oil a huge portion container with some ghee or margarine and include the player. Smooth the player out equally in the skillet and "cut" it on top utilizing a spatula to make a wave impact.
- Note: If you utilize a silicon portion container, you won't have to oil it. Low-Carb "Rye" Bread
- Prepare for a roughly 50-an hour (relies upon the stove). At the point when the bread is prepared, expel from portion dish to a cooling rack, and permit to cool completely. Low-Carb "Rye" Bread

PREPARATION	COOKING TIME	SERVINGS
22 MINT	1 *hour*	5

Keto Almond Bread

NUTRITION *Calories; 21g, Fat; 4.7g , Carbs; 44.2g , Protein; 0, .5g Sugars*

INGREDIENTS

- ½ cup spread
- Tbsp. coconut oil
- eggs
- cups almond flour

DIRECTION

- Preheat the broiler to 355 .
- Line a portion container with material paper.
- Blend the eggs in a bowl on high for as long as two minutes.
- Include the almond flour, liquefied coconut oil and dissolved spread to the eggs. Keep on blending.
- Scratch the blend into the portion container.
- Heat for 45-50 minutes or until a toothpick tells the truth

PREPARATION	COOKING TIME	SERVINGS
10 MINT	55 *mint*	8

Sourdough Keto Baguettes

NUTRITION *398 Calories;, Fat; 4.7g , Carbs; 44.2g , Protein; 0.5g Sugars*

INGREDIENTS

- DryIngredients:
- 1/2 cup almond flour (150 g/5.3 oz.)
- 1/3 cup psyllium husk powder (40 g/1.4 oz.)
- 1/2 cup coconut flour (60 g/2.1 oz.)
- 1/2 stuffed cup flax supper (75 g/2.6 oz.)
- 1 tsp. preparing pop
- 1 tsp. salt (pink Himalayan or ocean salt)
- WetIngredients:
- huge egg whites
- huge eggs
- 3/4 cup low-fat buttermilk (180 g/6.5 oz.) - full-fat would make them excessively overwhelming and they may not rise
- 1/4 cup white wine vinegar or apple juice vinegar (60 ml/2 fl oz.)
- 1 cup tepid water (240 ml/8 fl oz.)

DIRECTION

- Preheat the broiler to 180 °C/360 °F (fan helped). Utilize a kitchen scale to gauge every one of the fixings cautiously. Blend all the dry fixings in a bowl (almond flour, coconut flour, ground flaxseed, psyllium powder, heating pop and salt).
- In a different bowl, blend the eggs, egg whites, and buttermilk.
- The explanation you shouldn't utilize just entire eggs is that the bread wouldn't ascend with such a large number of egg yolks in. Try not to squander them - use them for making Homemade Mayo, Easy Hollandaise Sauce or Lemon Curd. For a similar explanation, utilize low-fat (not full-fat) buttermilk. Sourdough Keto Baguettes
- Include the egg blend and procedure well utilizing a blender until the mixture is thick. Include vinegar and tepid water and procedure until all-around joined.
- Sourdough Keto Baguettes
- Don't over-process the mixture. Utilizing a spoon, make 8 ordinary or 16 smaller than usual rolls and spot them on a preparing plate fixed with material paper or a non-stick tangle. They will rise, so make a point to leave some space between them. Alternatively, score the loaves slantingly and make 3-4 cuts. Sourdough Keto Baguettes
- Spot in the stove and cook for 10 minutes. At that point, decrease the temperature to 150 °C/300 °F and heat for another 30-45 minutes (little loaves will set aside less effort to cook). Sourdough Keto Baguettes
- Expel from the stove, let the plate chill off and place the rolls on a rack to chill off to room temperature. Store them at room temperature on the off chance that you intend to utilize them in the following couple of days or store in the cooler for as long as 3 months.
- Prepared products that utilization psyllium consistently result is marginally wet surface. If necessary, cut the rolls down the middle and spot in a toaster or in the broiler before serving. Sourdough Keto Baguettes
- Tip: To spare time, blend all the dry fixings ahead and store in a ziplock sack and include a mark with the number of servings. At the point when fit to be prepared, simply include the wet fixings!

PREPARATION	COOKING TIME	SERVINGS
5 MINT	17 *mint*	10

Feta Oregano Bread

NUTRITION Calories: 114 , Fat: 7g , Carb: 8g , Protein: 9g

INGREDIENTS

- *Almond flour, one cup*
- *Crumbled feta cheese, one cup*
- *Half cup of warm water*
- *Oregano dried, one teaspoon*
- *Baking powder, two-thirds of a teaspoon*
- *Extra virgin olive oil, a teaspoon*
- *Salt, half a teaspoon*
- *Swerve sweetener, one teaspoon*
- *Garlic powder, a quarter teaspoon*
- *Dried active yeast, one teaspoon*

DIRECTION

- Using a mixing container, combine the almond flour, swerve sweetener, dried oregano, baking powder, ground garlic, and salt.
- In another mixing container, combine the extra virgin olive oil and warm water.
- As per the instructions on the manual of your machine, pour the ingredients in the bread pan, taking care to follow how to mix in the yeast.
- Set the bread pan in the machine, and select the sweet bread setting, together with the bread size and crust type, if available, then press start once you have closed the lid of the machine.
- When the bread is ready, using oven mitts, remove the bread pan from the machine. Use a stainless spatula to extract the bread from the pan and turn the pan upside down on a metallic rack where the bread will cool off before slicing it.

PREPARATION	COOKING TIME	SERVINGS
5 MINT	15 *mint*	10

Low Carb Microwave Hamburger Bread

NUTRITION Cal: 90, Carbs: 4g/, Net Carbs: 2.5 g, Fiber: 4.5 g, , Fat: 8 g, Protein: 8g, Sugars: 3 g.

INGREDIENTS

- *Bagels*
- *¾ cup (68 g) almond flour*
- *1 teaspoon thickener*
- *1 huge egg*
- *1 ½ cups ground mozzarella*
- *tablespoons cream cheddar*
- *1 tablespoon spread, dissolved*
- *Sesame seeds to taste*
- *Fillings*
- *tablespoons pesto*
- *tablespoons cream cheddar*
- *1 cup arugula leaves*
- *cuts flame-broiled streaky bacon*

DIRECTION

- Preheat stove to 390°F.
- In a bowl combine the almond flour and thickener. At that point gather the egg and blend into a single unit until all around consolidated. Put in a safe spot. It will resemble a sticky ball.
- In a pot over medium-low warmth gradually dissolve the cream cheddar and mozzarella together and expel from heat once liquefied. This should be possible in the microwave also.
- Add your dissolved cheddar blend to the almond flour blend and ply until very much consolidated. The Mozzarella combine will stick in somewhat of a ball yet don't stress, endure with it. It will all, in the end, consolidate well. It's critical to get the Xanthan gum fused through the cheddar blend. On the off chance that the mixture gets too intense to even think about working, place in microwave for 10-20 seconds to warm and rehash until you have something that takes after batter.
- Split your batter into 3 pieces and fold into round logs. On the off chance that you have a doughnut dish place your logs into the container. If not, make hovers with each log and consolidate and place it on a heating plate. Attempt to ensure you have decent circles. The other method to do this is to make a ball and straighten somewhat on the heating plate and cut a hover out of the center on the off chance that you have a little cutout.
- Melt your spread and brush over the highest point of your bagels and sprinkle sesame seeds or your fixing of decision. The spread should enable the seeds to stick. Garlic and onion powder or cheddar causes decent increases in the event that you to have them for flavorful bagels.
- Place bagels in the stove for around 18 minutes. Watch out for them. The tops ought to go brilliant dark-colored.
- Take the bagels out of the stove and permit cooling.
- If you like your bagels toasted, cut them down the middle longwise and place back in the stove until marginally brilliant and toasty.
- Spread bagel with creamy cheddar, spread in pesto, include a couple of arugula leaves and top with your fresh bacon (or your filling of decision.)

PREPARATION	COOKING TIME	SERVINGS
7 MINT	15 *mint*	8

Keto Zucchini Bread with Walnuts

NUTRITION Cal: 100, Carbs: 4g/, Net Carbs: 2.5 g, Fiber: 4.5 g, Fat: 8 g, Protein: 9g, Sug-

INGREDIENTS

- *1 huge egg*
- *1 tablespoon almond flour*
- *1 tablespoon psyllium husk powder*
- *¼ teaspoon preparing powder*
- *¼ teaspoon cream of tartar*
- *1 tablespoon chicken soup*
- *1 tablespoon dissolved spread*

DIRECTION

- Crack an egg into a mug and pour in the dissolved spread. Mix together well until eggs are lighter in shading.
- Add the remainder of the fixings and blend well. You should wind up with a somewhat raw substance.
- Microwave for 60-75 seconds, contingent upon wattage of microwave (it will puff up in the mug, and lessen incredibly in size on you take it out).
- Slice down the middle and sauté in spread.

PREPARATION	COOKING TIME	SERVINGS
11 MINT	30 *mint*	12

Bacon Breakfast Bagels Bread

NUTRITION Cal: 90, Carbs: 4g/Net Carbs: 2.5 g, Fiber: 4.5 g, Fat: 8 g, Protein: 8g, Sugars: 3 g.

INGREDIENTS

- *Bagels*
- *¾ cup (68 g) almond flour*
- *1 teaspoon thickener*
- *1 huge egg*
- *1 ½ cups ground mozzarella*
- *tablespoons cream cheddar*
- *1 tablespoon spread, softened*
- *Sesame seeds to taste*
- *Fillings*
- *tablespoons pesto*
- *tablespoons cream cheddar*
- *1 cup arugula leaves*
- *cuts flame-broiled streaky bacon*

DIRECTION

- Preheat stove to 390°F.
- In a bowl combine the almond flour and thickener. At that point gather the egg and blend into a single unit until very much consolidated. Put in a safe spot. It will resemble a raw ball.
- In a pot over medium-low warmth gradually liquefy the cream cheddar and mozzarella together and expel from heat once softened. This should be possible in the microwave also.
- Add your softened cheddar blend to the almond flour blend and ply until all around consolidated. The Mozzarella combine will stick in somewhat of a ball yet don't stress, endure with it. It will all, in the long run, join well. It's imperative to get the Xanthan gum fused through the cheddar blend. On the off chance that the mixture gets too extreme to even think about working, place in microwave for 10-20 seconds to warm and rehash until you have something that looks like batter.
- Split your mixture into 3 pieces and fold into round logs. On the off chance that you have a doughnut skillet place your logs into the container. If not, make hovers with each log and consolidate and place it on a preparing plate. Attempt to ensure you have decent circles. The other method to do this is to make a ball and level marginally on the heating plate and cut a hover out of the center in the event that you have a little cutout.
- Melt your margarine and brush over the highest point of your bagels and sprinkle sesame seeds or your garnish of decision. The margarine should enable the seeds to stick. Garlic and onion powder or cheddar causes decent increments on the off chance that you to have them for flavorful bagels.
- Place bagels in the stove for around 18 minutes. Watch out for them. The tops ought to go brilliant dark-colored.
- Take the bagels out of the stove and permit cooling.
- If you like your bagels toasted, cut them down the middle the long way and spot back in the stove until somewhat brilliant and toasty.
- Spread bagel with creamy cheddar, spread in pesto, include a couple of arugula leaves and top with your fresh bacon (or your filling of decision.)

PREPARATION	COOKING TIME	SERVINGS
7 MINT	15 *mint*	8

Jalapeno Cornbread Mini Loaves

NUTRITION Cal: 230, Carbs: 4g/Net Carbs: 1.5 g, Fiber: 9.5 g, Fat: 10 g, Protein: 5g, Sug-

INGREDIENTS

- *Dry Ingredients:*
- *1 ½ cup almond flour*
- *½ cup brilliant flaxseed feast*
- *teaspoons heating powder*
- *1 teaspoon salt*
- *Wet Ingredients:*
- *½ cup full-fat harsh cream*
- *tablespoons softened spread*
- *enormous eggs*
- *drops fluid stevia*
- *1 teaspoon Amoretti sweet corn separate*
- *Include Ins*
- *½ cup ground sharp cheddar*
- *new jalapenos, seeded and films removed**

DIRECTION

- Preheat the stove to 375°F degrees. Set up a smaller than expected portion dish (8 portions) by splashing with cooking shower or lubing with margarine to forestall staying.
- In a huge bowl whisk together the dry fixings including the almond flour, brilliant flaxseed feast, preparing powder and salt.
- In a different medium estimated bowl whisk together the wet fixings. Blend the wet and dry fixings together at that point overlap the diced pepper and ground cheddar into the hitter.
- Spoon the hitter equally into the readied portion pan. Top each portion with a pepper ring to decorate.
- Bake for 20-22 minutes or until the portions begin to turn brilliant darker.
- Cool the portions in the search for gold 5 minutes and afterward evacuate to a wire rack to wrap up.

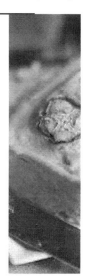

PREPARATION	COOKING TIME	SERVINGS
16 MINT	21 *mint*	5

Collagen Keto Bread

NUTRITION Cal: 20, Carbs: 8g/Net Carbs: 2.5 g, Fiber: 4.5 g, Fat: 6 g, Protein: 8g, Sugars: 3 g.

INGREDIENTS

- *1/2 cup Unflavored Grass-Fed Collagen Protein*
- *tablespoons almond flour (see formula notes beneath for without nut substitute)*
- *fed eggs, isolated*
- *1 tablespoon unflavored fluid coconut oil*
- *1 teaspoon sans aluminum preparing powder*
- *1 teaspoon thickener (see formula notes for substitute)*
- *Pinch Himalayan pink salt*
- *Optional: a spot of stevia*

DIRECTION

- Preheat broiler to 325 degrees F.
- Generously oil just the base piece of a standard size (1.5 quarts) glass or clay portion dish with coconut oil (or spread or ghee). Or on the other hand, you may utilize a bit of material paper cut to fit the base of your dish. Not oiling or covering the sides of your dish will enable the bread to append to the sides and remain lifted while it cools.
- In a huge bowl, beat the egg whites until firm pinnacles structure. Put in a safe spot.
- In a little bowl, whisk the dry fixings together and put them in a safe spot. Include the discretionary spot of stevia in case you're not an enthusiast of eggs. It'll help counterbalance the flavor without adding sweetness to your portion.
- In a little bowl, whisk together the wet fixings - egg yolks and fluid coconut oil and put in a safe spot.
- Add the dry and the wet fixings to the egg whites and blend until all-around fused. Your hitter will be thick and somewhat gooey.
- Pour the hitter into the oiled or lined dish and spot in the stove.
- Bake for 40 minutes. The bread will rise essentially in the stove.
- Remove from the stove and let it cool totally around 1 to 2 hours. The bread will sink a few and that is OK. When the bread is cooled, run the sharp edge of a blade around the edges of the dish to discharge the portion. Cut into 12 even cuts.

PREPARATION	COOKING TIME	SERVINGS
5 MINT	15 *mint*	8

Keto Breadticks

NUTRITION Cal: 60, Carbs: 4g/Net Carbs: 2.5 g, Fiber: 4.5 g, Fat: 6 g, Protein: 4g, Sug-

INGREDIENTS

- Bread Stick Base
- Cups Mozzarella Cheese (~8 oz.)
- 3/4 cup Almond Flour
- 1 tbsp. Psyllium Husk Powder
- 1 tbsp. Cream Cheese (~1.5 oz.)
- 1 huge Egg
- 1 tsp. Preparing Powder
- Italian Style
- tbsp. Italian Seasoning
- 1 tsp. Salt
- 1 tsp. Pepper
- Extra Cheesy
- 1 tsp. Garlic Powder
- 1 tsp. Onion Powder
- oz. Cheddar Cheese
- 1/4 cup Parmesan Cheese
- Cinnamon Sugar
- tbsp. Spread
- tbsp. Swerve Sweetener
- tbsp. Cinnamon

DIRECTION

- Pre-heat stove to 400F. Combine egg and cream cheddar until somewhat joined. In another bowl, consolidate all the dry fixings.
- Measure out the mozzarella cheddar and microwave in 20-second interims until sizzling.
- Add the egg, cream cheddar, and dry fixings into the mozzarella cheddar and combine.
- Using your hands, massage the batter together and press level on a Silpat.
- Transfer the batter to some thwart so you can utilize a pizza shaper on it, at that point season the mixture with the flavorings you like.
- Bake 13-15 minutes on top rack until fresh.
- Serve while warm!

PREPARATION	COOKING TIME	SERVINGS
6 MINT	30 mint	8

Almond Flour Keto Bread

NUTRITION Cal: 210, Carbs: 9g/Net Carbs: 2.5 g, Fiber: 5 g, Fat: 10 g, Protein: 9g, Sugars: 3 g.

INGREDIENTS

- 1 1/2 Cup Almond Flour
- Large eggs Separated
- 1/4 cup butter softened
- tsp. heating powder
- 1/4 tsp. Cream of Tartar It's alright on the off chance that you don't have this
- 1 squeeze Pink Himalayan Salt
- drops Liquid Stevia discretionary

DIRECTION

- Preheat broiler to 37
- Separate the egg whites from the yolks. Add Cream of Tartar to the whites and beat until delicate pinnacles are accomplished.
- In a nourishment, processor consolidate the egg yolks, 1/3 of the beaten egg whites, dissolved margarine, almond flour, preparing powder and salt (Adding ~6 drops of fluid stevia to the hitter can help lessen the mellow egg taste). Blend until consolidated. This will be an uneven thick batter until the whites are included.
- Add the staying 2/3 of the egg whites and tender procedure until completely fused. Be mindful so as not to over mix as this is the thing that gives the bread its volume!
- Pour blend into a buttered 8x4 portion dish. Prepare for 30 minutes. Check with a toothpick to guarantee the bread is cooked through. Appreciate! 1 portion makes 20 cuts.

PREPARATION	COOKING TIME	SERVINGS
7 MINT	15 mint	7

Paleo Coconut Bread

NUTRITION *Cal: 40, Carbs: 4g/Net Carbs: 2.5 g, Fiber: 7.5 g, Fat: 12 g, Protein: 6g, Sug-*

INGREDIENTS

- 1/2 cup coconut flour
- 1/4 teaspoon salt
- 1/4 teaspoon heating pop
- eggs
- ¼ cup coconut oil, liquefied
- ¼ unsweetened almond milk

DIRECTION

- Preheat broiler to 350°F.
- Line an 8×4 inch portion container with material paper.
- In a bowl consolidate the coconut flour, preparing pop and salt.
- In another bowl consolidate the eggs, milk, and oil.
- Slowly include the wet fixings into the dry fixings and blend until consolidated.
- Pour the blend into the readied portion container.
- Bake for 40-50 minutes, or until a toothpick, embedded in the center tells the truth.

PREPARATION	COOKING TIME	SERVINGS
12MINT	22 mint	8

Macadamia Nut Bread

NUTRITION *Cal: 40, Carbs: 4g, Net Carbs: 3.5 g, Fiber: 8.5 g, Fat: 14 g, Protein: 10g, Sugars: 3 g, Sugars: 3 g.*

INGREDIENTS

- oz. macadamia nuts I utilized the Royal Hawaiian brand
- enormous eggs
- 1/4 cup coconut flour (28 g)
- 1/2 teaspoon heating pop
- 1/2 teaspoon apple juice vinegar

DIRECTION

- Preheat broiler to 350F.
- To a blender or nourishment processor, include macadamia nuts and heartbeat until it becomes nut margarine. On the off chance that your blender doesn't work superbly without fluid, include eggs each in turn until the consistency is that of a nut margarine.
- Scrape drawbacks of blender or nourishment processor, and include remaining eggs. Mix until well-fused.
- Add in coconut flour, heating pop, and apple juice vinegar and heartbeat until consolidated.
- Grease a standard-size bread dish and include hitter. Smooth surface of hitter and spot-on a base rack of the broiler for 30-40 minutes, or until the top is brilliant dark-colored.
- Remove from stove and permit to cool in prospect 20 minutes before evacuating.
- Will store in a water/air proof compartment at room temperature for 3-4 days at room temperature or for multi-week in the refrigerator

PREPARATION	COOKING TIME	SERVINGS
5MINT	21 mint	6

Easy Cloud Bread

NUTRITION Cal: 300, Carbs: 4g/Net Carbs: 2.5 g, Fiber: 4.5 g, Fat: 8 g, Protein: 8g, Sugars: 3 g.

INGREDIENTS

- eggs
- teaspoon of coconut cream spoon from a refrigerated container of full-fat coconut milk
- 1/2 teaspoon preparing powder - discretionary fixings: ocean salt dark pepper and rosemary or whatever seasonings you like!

DIRECTION

- Firstly, prep everything. When you start going, you'll have to move rapidly so have everything convenient. Preheat the stove to 325f degrees and orchestrate a rack in the center. Line a heating sheet with material paper and put it in a safe spot. Get your devices: hand blender (you can utilize a stand blender, yet I see it as better for whipping egg whites so I can remain in charge), all fixings, any extra seasonings, two blending bowls (the bigger one ought to be utilized for egg whites), a huge spoon to scoop and drop the bread with.
- Using a full-fat jar of coconut milk that has been refrigerated medium-term or a few hours, spoon out the top coconut cream and add to the littler bowl.
- Separate eggs into the two dishes, adding the yolk to the bowl with the cream and be mindful so as not to let the yolk get into the whites in the bigger bowl.
- Using a hand blender, beat the yolk and cream together first until pleasant and smooth, ensure there are no clusters of coconut left.
- Wash your whisks well and dry them.
- Add the preparing powder into the whites and start beating on medium with the hand blender for a couple of moments, moving around and you'll see it get firmer. Prop up for a couple of moments, you need to get it as thick as you can with firm pinnacles. The thicker the better. Simply don't over-do it. When you can stop and dunk the speeds in deserting tops, you're prepared.
- Quickly and cautiously include the yolk-coconut blend into the whites, collapsing with a spatula, cautious not to empty excessively. Prop up until everything is very much consolidated yet soft.
- Now you can get your spoon and start dropping your hitter down on the heating sheet. Prop up as fast and cautiously as you can, or it will begin to dissolve. They should look cushiony.
- Steadily add your heating sheet to the center rack in the stove and prepare for approx. 20-25 minutes. You ought to have the option to scoop them up with your spatula and see a soft top and a level base. Store in the ice chest for about a week or freeze.

PREPARATION	COOKING TIME	SERVINGS
5 MINT	18 *mint*	7

Buttery & Soft Skillet Flatbread

NUTRITION Cal: 50, Carbs: 10g/ Net Carbs: 6g, Fiber: 4.5 g, Fat: 8 g, Protein: 9g, Sugars: 3 g.

INGREDIENTS

- 1 cup Almond Flour
- teaspoon Coconut Flour
- teaspoon Xanthan Gum
- 1/2 teaspoon heating Powder
- 1/2 teaspoon Falk Salt
- 1 Whole Egg + 1 Egg White
- 1 teaspoon Water
- 1 teaspoon Oil for searing
- 1 teaspoon liquefied Butter-for slathering

DIRECTION

- Whisk together the dry fixings (flours, thickener, preparing powder, salt) until very much consolidated.
- Add the egg and egg white and beat tenderly into the flour to fuse. The mixture will start to frame.
- Add the tablespoon of water and start to work the batter to permit the flour and thickener to retain the dampness.
- Cut the batter in 4 equivalent parts and press each area out with stick wrap. Watch the video for directions!
- Heat a huge skillet over medium warmth and include oil.
- Fry every flatbread for around 1 min on each side.
- Brush with margarine (while hot) and embellish with salt and cleaved parsley.

PREPARATION	COOKING TIME	SERVINGS
9 MINT	22 *mint*	8

Cranberry Jalapeño "Cornbread" Muffins

NUTRITION Cal: 10, Carbs: 4g/Net Carbs: 2.5 g, Fiber: 4.5 g, Fat: 8 g, Protein: 8g, Sugars: 10 g.

PREPARATION	COOKING TIME	SERVINGS
6 MINT	19 mins	8

DIRECTION

- Preheat stove to 325F and oil a biscuit tin well or line with paper liners.
- In a medium bowl, whisk together coconut flour, sugar, heating powder, and salt. Separate any clusters with the rear of a fork.
- Stir in eggs softened spread and almond milk and mix energetically. Mix in vanilla concentrate and keep on mixing until blend is smooth and very much joined. Mix in slashed cranberries and jalapeños.
- Divide player equally among arranged biscuit cups and spot one cut of jalapeño over each.
- Bake 25 to 30 minutes or until tops are set and an analyzer embedded in the middle confesses all. Give cool 10 minutes access dish; at that point move to a wire rack to cool totally.

INGREDIENTS

- 1 cup coconut flour
- 1/3 cup Swerve Sweetener or other erythritol
- 1 teaspoon heating powder
- 1/2 teaspoon salt
- enormous eggs, softly beaten
- 1 cup unsweetened almond milk
- 1/2 cup margarine, softened OR avocado oil
- 1/2 teaspoon vanilla
- 1 cup crisp cranberries cut down the middle
- teaspoon minced jalapeño peppers
- 1 jalapeño, seeds evacuated, cut into 12 cuts, for decorate

Keto Pumpkin Bread

NUTRITION Cal: 50, Carbs: 12g/ Net Carbs: 2.5 g Fiber: 4.5 g, Fat: 15 g, Protein: 8g, Sugars: 1 g.

PREPARATION	COOKING TIME	SERVINGS
6 MINT	21 mins	10

DIRECTION

- Preheat the stove to 350°F. Oil a 9"x5" portion skillet, and line with material paper.
- In a huge blending bowl, cream the margarine and sugar together until light and soft.
- Add the eggs, each in turn, and blend well to consolidate.
- Add the pumpkin puree and vanilla, and blend well to consolidate.
- In a different bowl, mix together the almond flour, coconut flour, preparing powder, cinnamon, nutmeg, ginger, and cloves, salt. Separate any pieces of almond flour or coconut flour.
- Add the dry fixings to the wet fixings, and mix to consolidate. (Alternatively, indicate 1/2 cup of blend in as cleaved nuts or chocolate chips.)
- Pour the hitter into the readied portion dish. Prepare for 45 - 55 minutes, or until a toothpick embedded into the focal point of the portion confesses all.
- If the bread is sautéing too rapidly, you can cover the skillet with a bit of aluminum foil.

INGREDIENTS

- 1/2 cup spread, relaxed
- 2/3 cup erythritol sugar, similar to Swerve
- eggs huge
- 3/4 cup pumpkin puree, canned (see notes for new)
- 1 teaspoon vanilla concentrate
- 1 1/2 cup almond flour
- 1/2 cup coconut flour
- 1 teaspoon preparing powder
- 1 teaspoon cinnamon
- 1/2 teaspoon nutmeg
- 1/4 teaspoon ginger
- 1/8 teaspoon cloves
- 1/2 teaspoon salt

Keto Bagels Bread

NUTRITION Cal: 10, Carbs: 1g/ Net Carbs: 1.5 g, Fiber: 2.5 g, Fat: 8 g, Protein: 9g, Sugars: 3 g.

PREPARATION	COOKING TIME	SERVINGS
5 MINT	17 mins	6

DIRECTION

- Preheat the stove to 320°F (160°C).
- Combine the almond flour, coconut flour, psyllium husk powder, preparing powder, garlic powder and salt in a bowl.
- In a different bowl, whisk the eggs and vinegar together. Gradually shower in the dissolved ghee (which ought not to be steaming hot) and speed in well.
- Add the wet blend to the dry blend and utilize a wooden spoon to join well. Leave to sit for 2-3 minutes.
- Divide the blend into 4 equivalent measured bits. Utilizing your hands, shape the blend into a round shape and spot onto a plate fixed with material paper. Utilize a little spoon or apple corer to make the middle gap.
- Brush the tops with olive oil and dissipate over the sesame seeds. Prepare in the broiler for 20-25 minutes until cooked through. Permit to cool marginally before getting a charge out of!

INGREDIENTS

- 1 cup (120 g) of almond flour
- 1/4 cup (28 g) of coconut flour
- 1 Tablespoon (7 g) of psyllium husk powder
- 1 teaspoon (2 g) of preparing powder
- 1 teaspoon (3 g) of garlic powder
- Pinch salt
- medium eggs (88 g)
- teaspoons (10 ml) of white wine vinegar
- 1/2 Tablespoons (38 ml) of ghee, dissolved
- 1 Tablespoon (15 ml) of olive oil
- 1 teaspoon (5 g) of sesame seeds

Low-Carb Blueberry English muffin Bread Loaf

NUTRITION Cal: 50, Carbs: 4g/ Net Carbs: 2.5 g, Fiber: 4.5 g, Fat: 7 g, Protein: 6g, Sugars: 7 g.

PREPARATION	COOKING TIME	SERVINGS
4 MINT	14 mins	5

DIRECTION

- Preheat stove to 350 degrees F.
- In a microwavable bowl dissolve nut margarine and spread together for 30 seconds, mix until joined well.
- In a huge bowl, whisk almond flour, salt, and heating powder together. Empty the nut spread blend into the huge bowl and mix to consolidate.
- Whisk the almond milk and eggs together at that point fill the bowl and mix well.
- Drop-in new blueberries or break separated solidified blueberries and tenderly mix into the hitter.
- Line a portion dish with material paper and daintily oil the material paper also.
- Pour the hitter into the portion dish and prepare 45 minutes or until a toothpick in focus confesses all.
- Cool for around 30 minutes at that point expel from container.
- Slice and toast each cut before serving.

INGREDIENTS

- 1/2 cup almond spread or cashew or nutty spread
- 1/4 cup spread ghee or coconut oil
- 1/2 cup almond flour
- 1/2 tsp. salt
- tsp. preparing powder
- 1/2 cup almond milk unsweetened
- eggs beaten
- 1/2 cup blueberries

Cinnamon Almond Flour Bread

NUTRITION Cal: 200, Carbs: 4g/ Net Carbs: 10.5 g, Fiber: 4.5 g, Fat: 8 g, Protein: 8g, Sugars: 3 g

PREPARATION	COOKING TIME	SERVINGS
7 MINT	18 mins	9

INGREDIENTS

- cups fine whitened almond flour (I utilize Bob's, Red Mill)
- teaspoon coconut flour
- 1/2 teaspoon ocean salt
- 1 teaspoon heating pop
- 1/4 cup Flaxseed supper or chia dinner (ground chia or flaxseed; see notes for how to make your own)
- Eggs and 1 egg white whisked together
- teaspoon Apple juice vinegar or lemon juice
- teaspoon maple syrup or nectar
- 2–3 teaspoon of explained spread (dissolved) or Coconut oil; separated. Vegetarian margarine likewise works
- 1 teaspoon cinnamon in addition to extra for fixing
- Optional chia seed to sprinkle on the top before preparing

DIRECTION

- Preheat stove to 350F. Line an 8×4 bread dish with material paper at the base and oil the sides.
- In a huge bowl, combine your almond flour, coconut flour, salt, preparing pop, flaxseed feast or chia supper, and 1/2 tablespoon of cinnamon.
- In another little bowl, whisk together your eggs and egg white. At that point include your maple syrup (or nectar), apple juice vinegar, and dissolved margarine (1.5 to 2 teaspoon).
- Mix wet fixings into dry. Make certain to expel any bunches that may have happened from the almond flour or coconut flour.
- Pour hitter into your lubed portion container.
- Bake at 350° for 30-35 minutes, until a toothpick embedded into the focal point of portion, tells the truth. Mine too around 35 minutes yet I am at elevation.
- Expel from and broiler.
- Next, whisk together the other 1 to 2 teaspoon of softened margarine (or oil) and blend it in with 1/2 teaspoon of cinnamon. Brush this over your cinnamon almond flour bread.
- Cool and serve or store for some other time.

Keto Banana Almond Bread

NUTRITION Calories: 147 Calories from fat: 90 Total Fat: 10 g Total Carbohydrates: 13 g Net Carbohydrates: 12 g Protein: 2 g

PREPARATION	COOKING TIME	SERVINGS
20 MINT	2 mins	12 slices

DIRECTION

- Prepare all the ingredients.
- Ensure all ingredients are at room temperature. Place the butter, eggs, milk, and mashed bananas in the bread bucket.
- In a mixing bowl, combine all the dry ingredients and mix well.
- Pour the dry ingredients in the bread bucket.
- Set the bread machine in QUICK BREAD then close the lid and let it cook until the machine beeps.
- Cool the bread before slicing and serving.

INGREDIENTS

- large eggs
- 1/3 cup butter, unsalted
- 1/8 cup almond milk, unsweetened
- medium mashed bananas
- 1 1/3 cup almond flour
- 0.63 tsp. Stevia extract sugar
- 1 ¼ tsps. Baking powder
- ½ tsp. baking soda
- ½ tsp. salt
- ½ cup chopped nuts

Keto Chocolate Zucchini Bread

NUTRITION *Cal: 300, Carbs: 7g/ Net Carbs: 11.5 g, Fiber: 4.5 g, Fat: 13 g, Protein: 1g, Sugars: 3 g.*

PREPARATION	COOKING TIME	SERVINGS
5 MINT	20 mins	8

INGREDIENTS

- 1 1/2 cup almond flour (170g)
- 1/4 cup unsweetened cocoa powder (25g)
- 1 1/2 teaspoon heating pop
- teaspoons ground cinnamon
- 1/4 teaspoon ocean salt
- 1/2 cup sugar-free precious stone sugar (Monk natural product or erythritol) (100g) or coconut sugar whenever refined sugar-free
- Wet Ingredients:
- 1 cup zucchini, finely ground measure pressed, dispose of juice/fluid if there is a few – around 2 little zucchini
- 1 enormous egg
- 1/4 cup + 2 tablespoon canned coconut cream 100ml
- 1/4 cup additional virgin coconut oil, softened, 60ml
- 1 teaspoon vanilla concentrate
- 1 teaspoon apple juice vinegar
- Filling - discretionary
- 1/2 cup sugar-free chocolate chips
- 1/2 cup cleaved pecans or nuts you like

DIRECTION

- Preheat broiler to 180C (375F). Line a heating portion skillet (9 inches x 5 inches) with material paper. Put in a safe spot.
- Remove the two furthest points of the zucchinis, keep the skin on.
- Finely mash the zucchini utilizing a vegetable grater. Measure the sum required in an estimation cup. Ensure you press/pack them solidly for an exact measure and to crush out any fluid from the ground zucchini, I, as a rule, don't have anyl in the event that you do, dispose of the fluid or keep for another formula.
- In an enormous blending bowl, mix all the dry fixings together: almond flour, unsweetened cocoa powder, sugar-free precious stone sugar, cinnamon, ocean salt, and heating pop. Put in a safe spot. Include all the wet fixings into the dry ingredients: ground zucchini, coconut oil, coconut cream, vanilla, egg, apple juice vinegar.
- Stir to join every one of the fixings together.
- Stir in the cleaved nuts and sugar-free chocolate chips.
- Transfer the chocolate bread player into the readied portion container.
- Bake 50 - 55 minutes, you might need to cover the bread portion with a bit of foil following 40 moments to maintain a strategic distance from the top to obscure excessively, up to you.
- The bread will remain somewhat wet in the center and solidify after completely chill off.

Microwave Mug Bread

NUTRITION *Cal: 20, Carbs: 4g/ Net Carbs: 2.5 g, Fiber: 4.5 g, Fat: 6 g, Protein: 7g, Sugars: 3 g.*

PREPARATION	COOKING TIME	SERVINGS
8 MINT	10 mins	10

DIRECTION

- Crack your egg into a microwave-safe ramekin or glass mug and beat it with a fork.
- Add 1 tbsp. of coconut flour and 1/4 tsp. of preparing powder to the egg, at that point microwave around 1 tbsp. of margarine in a different microwave-safe dish and add it to the blend. At that point blend it well with the fork. The blend ought to be genuinely thick.
- Pop the dish into the microwave for 90 seconds and be cautious when evacuating it as it will be hot. In the event that the bread doesn't fall directly out when you flip your dish over, pull the sides away with a fork or margarine blade and your bread should come directly out. Cut it down the middle and trim the sides if fundamental.

INGREDIENTS

- 1 egg
- 1 teaspoon coconut flour
- 1/4 teaspoon preparing powder
- 1 teaspoon spread

Microwave Flax Bread

NUTRITION Cal: 30, Carbs: 4g/ Net Carbs: 2.5 g, Fiber: 4.5 g, Fat: 3 g, Protein: 1g, Sugars: 4 g.

PREPARATION	COOKING TIME	SERVINGS
7 MINT	25 mins	13

INGREDIENTS

- 1 teaspoon spread
- 1 huge egg
- teaspoon ground flax-seed
- 1/2 teaspoon preparing powder

DIRECTION

- Add 1 tbsp. of spread to a microwave-safe ramekin and liquefy it in the microwave (10-20 seconds). Split your egg into the dish with the margarine and beat it with a fork.
- Add 4 tbsp. of ground flaxseed, 1/2 tsp. of preparing powder, and a spot of salt. At that point blend it well with the fork. The blend ought to be thick, so shake the dish around a piece to even it out.
- Pop the dish into the microwave for 2 minutes and be cautious when evacuating it as it will be hot. On the off chance that the bread doesn't fall directly out when you flip your dish over, pull the sides away with a fork or margarine blade and your bread should come directly out. Cool it on a rack and cut it down the middle.

Keto Ciabatta Bread

NUTRITION Calories: 286 Calories from fat: 171 Total Fat: 19 g Total Carbohydrates: 9 g Net Carbohydrates: 5 g Protein: 21

PREPARATION	COOKING TIME	SERVINGS
120 MINT	40 mins	6

DIRECTION

- 1   In a bowl, combine ½-cup warm water, sugar and yeast. Cover and let it sit for 10 minutes or until frothy.
- 2   In your bread machine bucket, add the yeast mixture, the remaining ½ cup and 2 tbsps. water and olive oil. Add flour, flax seed, salt, and baking powder. Place the bread bucket back in the bread machine and close the lid.
- 3   Set the bread machine to DOUGH cycle, close the lid then press the START button. After 10 minutes, stop the bread machine. You will have a very sticky dough.
- 4   Pour the dough on a floured surface and divide into half before rolling into tube like shape (about 2.5 x 7 inches). Place the cut dough on a greased cookie sheet.
- 5   Preheat your oven for 2 to 3 minutes at 110 degrees F. Turn the oven off and place the dough inside to rise for 1 hour. After 1 hour, you should have about 3.5 x 8 inches raised dough.
- 6   Preheat your oven at 350 degrees F to start baking.
- 7   Brush your raised dough with melted butter, then bake for 15 minutes. Take out of the oven and brush once more with butter before returning inside the oven for another 10 to 15 minutes until the dough's internal temperature reaches 200 degrees F.
- 8   Once done, let the loaf cool for 1 hour before slicing.
- 9   Serve with scrambled egg or your favorite jam.

INGREDIENTS

- 1 cup + 2 tbsps. warm water, divided
- 1 tsp. sugar
- ¼ tsp. dry active yeast
- 1 cup vital wheat gluten
- 1 cup super fine almond flour
- ¼ cup flax seed meal
- ¾ tsp. salt
- 1 ½ tsp. baking powder
- tbsps. extra virgin olive oil
- 1 tbsp. melted butter

Keto Milk and Honey Breakfast Loaf

NUTRITION Calories: 39 Calories from fat: 27 Total Fat: 3 g Total Carbohydrates: 3 g
Net Carbohydrates: 3 g Protein: 1 g

PREPARATION	COOKING TIME	SERVINGS
2 MINT	10 mins	18 slices

DIRECTION

- Put all ingredients in the bread bucket as listed in the ingredient list.
- Select the BASIC cycle on your bread machine setting, close the lid then press START.
- Once the loaf is ready, remove from the machine and place in a cooling rack.
- Slice and serve with your favorite spread.

INGREDIENTS

- 1 cup + 1 tbsp. almond milk, unsweetened
- tbsps. honey
- tbsps. melted butter
- 1 ½ tsp. salts
- cups almond flour
- 1 tsps. active dry yeast

Protein Keto Bread

NUTRITION Calories 165 Total Fat 14 g Saturated Fat 7 g Cholesterol 632 mg Sodium 497 mg Total Carbs 6 g Fiber 3 g Sugar 1 g Protein 5 g

PREPARATION	COOKING TIME	SERVINGS
10 MINT	40 mins	12

DIRECTION

- Start by preheating the oven to 325 degrees F.
- Grease a ceramic loaf dish with coconut oil and layer it with parchment paper.
- Add egg whites to a bowl and beat well until it forms peaks.
- In a separate bowl, mix the dry ingredients together.
- Mix wet ingredients in another bowl and beat well.
- Fold in dry mixture and mix well until smooth.
- Fold in the egg whites and mix evenly.
- Spread the bread batter in the prepared loaf pan.
- Bake the bread for 40 minutes or until it's done.
- Slice into 12 slices and serve.

INGREDIENTS

- 1/2 cup unflavored protein powder
- tbsp. almond flour
- pastured eggs, separated
- 1 tbsp. coconut oil
- 1 tsp. baking powder
- 1 tsp. xanthan gum
- 1 pinch Himalayan pink salt
- 1 pinch stevia (optional)

Super Seed Bread

NUTRITION *Cal: 70, Carbs: 4g/Net Carbs: 2.5 g, Fiber: 4.5 g,Fat: 8 g, Protein: 8g, Sugars: 3 g.*

PREPARATION	COOKING TIME	SERVINGS
5 MINT	22 *mins*	7

DIRECTION

- In a huge blending bowl, include every single dry fixing and blend well. You can make your own ground sesame seeds by mixing them until they're a fine powder.
- Melt the coconut oil in the microwave (around 30 seconds), add it to the dry blend and mix well. At that point include 1/4 cups fluid egg whites and 1/2 cup unsweetened almond milk. Blend well and let the blend represent 10-15 minutes while you preheat your stove to 325° F.
- Wet some material paper under warm water and shake it off, at that point press it into a 9" x 5" bread tin. Include your blend and press it into the edges of the tin. You can likewise add some additional seeds to the highest point of the blend here. Trim the abundance material paper and put it in the stove for 70 minutes.
- Slice the whole portion and let cool on a drying rack. This bread can empty if not cut at the earliest opportunity and left to cool on a rack.

INGREDIENTS

- 2/3 cup entire psyllium husk
- 1/4 cup chia seeds
- 1/4 cup pumpkin seeds
- 1/4 cup hemp or sunflower seeds
- Teaspoon ground sesame seeds or ground flaxseeds 1 teaspoon preparing powder
- 1/4 teaspoon salt
- Teaspoon coconut oil
- 1 1/4 cups fluid egg
- 1/2 cup unsweetened almond milk

Great flavor cheese bread with the added kick of pimento olives.

NUTRITION *124 Calories, 4 g total fat (2 g sat. fat), 9 mg chol., 299 mg sodium, 19 g carb. 1 fiber, 5 g protein*

PREPARATION	COOKING TIME	SERVINGS
5 MINT	3 *hour*	1 loaf

DIRECTION

- Add all ingredients except olives to machine pan.
- Select basic bread setting.
- At prompt before second knead, mix in olives.

INGREDIENTS

- 1 cup water room temperature
- tsp. sugar
- 3/4 tsp. salt
- 1 ¼ cups shredded sharp cheddar cheese
- cups bread flour
- tsp. active dry yeast
- 3/4 cup pimiento olives, drained and sliced

Pumpkin Pecan Bread

NUTRITION 159 Calories, 6 g total fat (1 g sat. fat), 14 mg chol., 126 mg sodium, 23 g carb. 1 fiber, 4 g protein

PREPARATION	COOKING TIME	SERVINGS
10 MINT	3 hour	1 loaf, 16 servings

DIRECTION

- Add all ingredients to machine pan.
- Select basic cycle.

INGREDIENTS

- 1/2 cup milk
- 1/2 cup canned pumpkin
- 1 egg
- tablespoons margarine or butter, cut up
- cups bread flour
- tablespoons packed brown sugar
- 3/4 tsp. salt
- 1/4 tsp. ground nutmeg
- 1/4 tsp. ground ginger
- 1/8 tsp. ground cloves
- 1 tsp. active dry yeast or bread machine yeast
- 3/4 cup coarsely chopped pecans

Ricotta Chive Bread

NUTRITION 92 Calories, 0 g total fat (0 g sat. fat), 2 mg chol., 207 mg sodium, 17 g carb. 1 fiber, 3 g

PREPARATION	COOKING TIME	SERVINGS
5 MINT	3 hour	1 loaf

DIRECTION

- Add ingredients to bread machine pan except dried fruit.
- Choose basic bread setting and light/medium crust.

INGREDIENTS

- 1 cup lukewarm water
- 1/3 cup whole or part-skim ricotta cheese
- 1 ½ tsp. salt
- 1 tablespoon granulated sugar
- cups bread flour
- 1/2 cup chopped chives
- ½ tsp. instant yeast

Red Hot Cinnamon Bread

NUTRITION 207 Calories, 6.9 g total fat (4.1 g sat. fat), 28 mg chol., 317 mg sodium, 30 g carb. 1 fiber, 4.6 g protein ,62. Cheddar Olive Loaf

PREPARATION	COOKING TIME	SERVINGS
5 MINT	3 *hour*	1 loaf

INGREDIENTS

- 1/4 cup lukewarm water
- 1/2 cup lukewarm milk
- 1/4 cup softened butter
- ¼ tsp. instant yeast
- 1 ¼ tsp. salt
- 1/4 cup sugar
- 1 tsp. vanilla
- 1 large egg, lightly beaten
- cups all-purpose flour
- 1/2 cup Cinnamon Red Hot candies

DIRECTION

- Add ingredients to bread machine pan except candy.
- Choose dough setting.
- After cycle is over, turn dough out into bowl and cover, let rise for 45 minutes to one hour.
- Gently punch down dough and shape into a rectangle.
- Knead in the cinnamon candies in 1/3 at a t time.
- Shape the dough into a loaf and place in a greased or parchment lined loaf pan.
- Tent the pan loosely with lightly greased plastic wrap, and allow a second rise for 40-50 minutes.
- Preheat oven 350 degrees.
- Bake 30-40 minutes.
- Remove and cool on wire rack before slicing.

Cheese Cauliflower Broccoli Bread

NUTRITION 156 Calories, 7.4 g total fat (2.2 g sat. fat), 8 mg chol., 56 mg sodium, 17 g carb. 0 fiber, 4.9 g protein

PREPARATION	COOKING TIME	SERVINGS
10 MINT	3 *hour*	1 loaf

DIRECTION

- Add all ingredients to machine pan.
- Select basic bread setting.

INGREDIENTS

- 1/4 cup water
- tablespoons oil
- 1 egg white
- 1 tsp. lemon juice
- 2/3 cup grated cheddar cheese
- Tablespoons green onion
- 1/2 cup broccoli, chopped
- 1/2 cup cauliflower, chopped
- 1/2 tsp. lemon-pepper seasoning
- cup bread flour
- 1 tsp. regular or quick-rising yeast

Wild Rice Cranberry Bread

NUTRITION *225 Calories, 7.8 g total fat (1.2 g sat. fat), 5 mg chol., 182 mg sodium, 33 g carb. 1 fiber, 6g protein*

PREPARATION	COOKING TIME	SERVINGS
5 MINT	3 hour	1 loaf

DIRECTION

- Add all ingredients to machine pan except the cranberries.
- Place pan into the oven chamber.
- Select basic bread setting.
- At the signal to add ingredients, add in the cranberries.

INGREDIENTS

- 1 ¼ cup water
- ¼ cup skim milk powder
- 1 ¼ tsp. salt
- tablespoon liquid honey
- 1 tablespoon extra-virgin olive oil
- cup all-purpose flour
- 3/4 cup cooked wild rice
- ¼ cup pine nuts
- 3/4 tsp. celery seeds
- 1/8 tsp. freshly ground black pepper
- 1 tsp. bread machine or instant yeast
- 2/3 cup dried cranberries

Orange Cappuccino Bread

NUTRITION *155 Calories, 2 g total fat (1 g sat. fat), 5 mg chol., 270 mg sodium, 31 g carb. 1 fiber, 4 g protein*

PREPARATION	COOKING TIME	SERVINGS
10 MINT	3 hour	1 loaf

DIRECTION

- Add all ingredients to machine pan.
- Select basic bread setting.

INGREDIENTS

- 1 cup water
- 1 tablespoon instant coffee granules
- tablespoons butter or margarine, softened
- 1 tsp. grated orange peel
- cups Bread flour
- tablespoons dry milk
- 1/4 cup sugar
- 1 ¼ tsp. salt
- ¼ tsp. bread machine or quick active dry yeast

Celery Bread

NUTRITION 73 Calories, 3.6 g total fat (0 g sat. fat), 55 mg chol., 186 mg sodium, 8 g carb. 0 fiber, 2.6 g protein

PREPARATION	COOKING TIME	SERVINGS
10 MINT	3 hour	1 loaf

DIRECTION

- Add all ingredients to machine pan.
- Select basic bread setting.

INGREDIENTS

- 1 (10 oz.) can cream of celery soup
- tablespoons low-fat milk, heated
- 1 tablespoon vegetable oil
- 1 ¼ tsp. celery, garlic, or onion salt
- 3/4 cup celery, fresh/slice thin
- 1 tablespoon celery leaves, fresh, chopped -optional
- 1 egg
- cups bread flour
- 1/4 tsp. sugar
- 1/4 tsp. ginger
- 1/2 cup quick-cooking oats
- tablespoons gluten
- tsp. celery seeds
- 1 package active dry yeast

Cottage Cheese Bread

NUTRITION 171 Calories, 3.6 g total fat (1 g sat. fat), 18 mg chol., 234 mg sodium, 26 g carb. 1 fiber, 7.3 g protein

PREPARATION	COOKING TIME	SERVINGS
10 MINT	3 hour	1 loaf

DIRECTION

- Add all ingredients to machine pan. Use the order suggested by manufacturer.
- Select basic bread setting.
- Tip: If dough is too sticky, add up to ½ cup more flour.

INGREDIENTS

- 1/2 cup water
- 1 cup cottage cheese
- tablespoons margarine
- 1 egg
- 1 tablespoon white sugar
- 1/4 tsp. baking soda
- 1 tsp. salt
- cups bread flour
- ½ tsp. active dry yeast

Anise Almond Bread

PREPARATION	COOKING TIME	SERVINGS
10 MINT	3 *hour*	*1 loaf*

DIRECTION

- Add all ingredients to machine pan except almonds.
- Select basic bread setting.
- After prompt, add almonds.

INGREDIENTS

- 3/4 cup water
- 1 or 1⁄4 cup egg substitute
- 1/4 cup butter or margarine, softened
- 1/4 cup sugar
- 1/2 tsp. salt
- cup bread flour
- 1 tsp. anise seed
- tsp. active dry yeast
- 1/2 cup almonds, chopped small

The Best Corn Bread You'll Ever Eat

NUTRITION *Calories: 328 Total Fat: 15.9 g Cholesterol: 39 mg Sodium: 772 mg Total Carbohydrate: 40.8 g Protein: 6.4 g*

PREPARATION	COOKING TIME	SERVINGS
5 MINT	30 *mins*	8

DIRECTION

- Heat oven to 425 degrees F (220 degrees C). Grease a 9 inch iron skillet.
- In a large bowl, beat the egg. Add milk, oil, sour cream, cream corn, and cornmeal mix; stir until cornmeal is just dampened. Pour batter into greased skillet.
- Bake for 25 to 30 minutes, or until knife inserted in center comes out clean.

INGREDIENTS

- 1 egg
- 1 1/3 cups milk
- 1/4 cup vegetable oil
- cups self-rising corn meal mix
- 1 (8 ounce) can cream-style corn
- 1 cup sour cream

Three Ingredient Buttermilk Cornbread

NUTRITION Calories: 157 Total Fat: 2.6 g Cholesterol: 2 mg Sodium: 50 mg Total Carbohydrate: 28.6 g

PREPARATION	COOKING TIME	SERVINGS
10 MINT	20 mins	8

INGREDIENTS

- vegetable oil as needed
- 1 1/2 cups buttermilk
- 1 1/2 cups cornmeal
- 1/2 cup all-purpose flour

DIRECTION

- Preheat oven to 450 degrees F (230 degrees C). Pour enough oil into a skillet to coat the bottom; place into oven.
- Mix buttermilk, cornmeal, and flour together in a bowl until smooth. Remove skillet from oven; pour in buttermilk mixture.
- Bake in the preheated oven until cornbread is golden brown, 20 to 25 minutes.

Easy Keto Bread

NUTRITION Cal: 220, Carbs: 4gNet Carbs: 2.5 g, Fiber: 4 g, Fat: 12 g, Protein: 8g, Sugars: 3 g.

PREPARATION	COOKING TIME	SERVINGS
9 MINT	21 mins	5

INGREDIENTS

- enormous eggs
- 2/3 cup almond flour or almond supper
- 1/3 cup coconut flour
  3 teaspoon coconut oil
- 1/2 cup unsalted margarine
  teaspoon heating powder
- 1 teaspoon salt margarine or an olive oil shower

DIRECTION

- Crack 6 enormous eggs into a nourishment processor or blending bowl and mix well. At that point include the almond flour or almond supper and the coconut flour.
- Melt the coconut oil and margarine in the microwave and add it to the blend. At that point include the salt and heating powder and blend or mix everything completely. Let represent 10-15 minutes so the blend thickens while you preheat your broiler to 350° F.
- Coat a 9" x 5" heating tin with margarine or an olive oil shower and add your thickened blend to the tin. Pop the tin into the broiler and heat for 40 minutes. Haul the bread out when it turns a brilliant dark colored on top and let it cool on a rack.

Fantastic Bread

NUTRITION Cal: 40, Carbs: 4g/Net Carbs: 2.5 g, Fiber: 5.5 g, Fat: 9 g, Protein: 6g, Sugars: 3 g.

PREPARATION	COOKING TIME	SERVINGS
5 MINT	20 *mins*	6

DIRECTION

- Add the dry fixings in a huge blending bowl and mix. The nuts are discretionary or can be fill in for different kinds of nuts on the off chance that you like.
- Crack 6 huge eggs into a different blending bowl, include one cup full-fat yogurt, and blend well in with a hand blender. Include the dry blend and blend completely with a hand blender. Let represent 10-15 minutes while you preheat your broiler to 350° F.
- Rinse material paper under warm water and shake it off before crushing it into your preparing tin, at that point add your blend to the tin and press it into the sides. You can include nuts like almonds, sesame seeds, and pumpkin seeds to the highest point of the portion and pop it into the stove for 55 minutes. Haul the bread out when completed and let it cool on a rack.

INGREDIENTS

- 1 cup almond flour or almond supper
- tbsp. entire psyllium husk 2 teaspoon of preparing powder
- 1/2 teaspoon of salt (discretionary) little bunch almond fragments (discretionary) little bunch squashed pecans
- huge eggs
- 1 cup full-fat yogurt

Almond Keto Bread

NUTRITION Calories 107 Total Fat 9.3 g Saturated Fat 4.8 g Cholesterol 77 mg , Sodium 135 mg , Total, Carbs 2.6 g , Fiber 0.8 g , Sugar 9.9 g , Protein 3.9 g

PREPARATION	COOKING TIME	SERVINGS
10 MINT	30 *mins*	10

DIRECTION

- Start by preheating your oven to 375 degrees F.
- Now, separate the egg yolks from their whites.
- Beat the whites with cream of tartar in a mixing bowl until it's foamy and creamy.
- Blend egg yolks with butter, almond flour, salt, baking powder, stevia, and 1/3 of the egg white mixture in a food processor.
- Once blended well, fold in the remaining egg whites then transfer the batter to a greased 8x4 loaf pan.
- Bake the bread for 30 minutes or until it's done.
- Slice into 20 slices and serve fresh.

INGREDIENTS

- 1 1/2 cup almond flour
- large eggs, separated
- 1/4 cup butter, melted
- tsp. baking powder
- 1/4 tsp. cream of tartar
- 1 pinch pink Himalayan salt
- drops liquid stevia

Keto Breakfast Bread

NUTRITION Calories: 234 ,Fat: 23g ,Carb: 1g , Protein: 7g

PREPARATION	COOKING TIME	SERVINGS
15 MINT	40 mins	16 slices

INGREDIENTS

- ½ tsp. xanthan gum
- ½ tsp. salt
- Tbsp. coconut oil
- ½ cup butter, melted
- 1 tsp. baking powder
- cups of almond flour
- eggs

DIRECTION

- Preheat the oven to 355F.
- Beat eggs in a bowl on high for 2 minutes.
- Add coconut oil and butter to the eggs and continue to beat.
- Line a loaf pan with baking paper and pour the beaten eggs.
- Pour in the rest of the ingredients and mix until it becomes thick.
- Bake until a toothpick comes out dry, about 40 to 45 minutes.

Keto Sweet Challah Bread

NUTRITION Calories: 158 , Calories from fat: 117, Total Fat: 13 g, Total Carbohydrates: 2 g , Net Carbohydrates: 2 g, Protein: 9 g

PREPARATION	COOKING TIME	SERVINGS
20 MINT	3 hour	20 slices

DIRECTION

- Place all ingredients on the bread machine pan except for lemon zest and cranberries.
- Select the SWEET BREAD cycle (or WHITE BREAD cycle) on the bread machine setting and light on the CRUST COLOR setting. Close the lid and press START.
- Just before the final rise, pause the bread machine and transfer the dough on a floured surface. Spread the dough and hand press the cranberries and lemon zest.
- Divide the dough into three equal parts. Roll each part of the dough to a 10-inch long rope. Lay all three ropes parallel to each other and braid together gently. Tuck the ends to form an oblong loaf. Brush the dough with egg white.
- Remove the kneading paddle of the bread machine before placing the dough back in the pan. Press START button again to resume the cycle.
- Once the cycle is finished, you can remove the challah and transfer it on a cooling rack.
- Slice and serve.

INGREDIENTS

- eggs
- 50 g sukrin plus
- 345 g cream cheese
- 60 g butter
- 60 g heavy cream
- 50 g vegetable oil
- 100 g unflavored whey protein
- 85 g protein whey vanilla
- ½ tsp. salt
- g baking soda
- g. baking powder
- g xanthan
- ½ small lemon zest
- 30 g dried cranberries

Keto Blueberry-Banana Loaf

NUTRITION Calories: 119 , Calories from fat: 90, Total Fat: 9 g, Total Carbohydrates: 9 g , Net Carbohydrates: 7 g, Protein: 2 g

PREPARATION	COOKING TIME	SERVINGS
10 MINT	2 hour	12 slices

DIRECTION

- Prepare the ingredients. Beat the eggs and mash the bananas. Soften the butter in the microwave for 30 seconds. Mix the water and the milk.
- Put the bananas, eggs, butter, water and milk in the bread bucket.
- Add in all the dry ingredients except blueberries.
- Start the bread machine by selecting QUICK BREAD then close the lid. After the first kneading, open the lid and add in the blueberries. Close the lid and let the cycle continue until the end.
- Once cooked, remove the bread from the bucket and let it cool in a cooling rack before slicing.
- Serve.

INGREDIENTS

- ½ cup warm water
- 1 tbsp. almond milk, unsweetened
- eggs, small
- 2 tbsps. Butter, melted and unsalted
- medium sized mashed bananas
- 0.75 tsp. stevia extract
- cups almond flour
- ½ tsp. salt
- 1 tsps. Baking powder
- 1 tsp. baking soda
- 1 cup frozen blueberries

Keto English Muffin Loaf

NUTRITION Calories: 22 , Calories from fat: 9, Total Fat: 1 g , Total Carbohydrates: 3 g , Net Carbohydrates: 3 g, Protein: 2 g

PREPARATION	COOKING TIME	SERVINGS
10 MINT	3 hour	1-pound loaf of 8 slices

DIRECTION

- Measure all the ingredients in the bread machine pan in the order listed above.
- Turn on bread machine and process. Select BASIC cycle; choose normal CRUST COLOR setting. Close the lid and press START button.
- Once cooked, place bread in cooling rack.
- Slice, then toast and serve.

INGREDIENTS

- 1 cup warm water (80 degrees F)
- tbsps. Sugar
- tbsps. Non-fat dry milk
- 1 tsp. salt
- ¼ tsp. baking soda
- ½ cups almond flour
- 1 tbsp. vital wheat gluten
- 1 ¾ tsp. dry active yeast

Keto Breakfast Meat Lovers Pizza

NUTRITION Calories: 470 , Calories from fat: 333, Total Fat: 37 g, Total Carbohydrates: 4 g , Net Carbohydrates: 3 g, Protein: 28 g

PREPARATION	COOKING TIME	SERVINGS
90 MINT	30 mins	8

DIRECTION

- To start the crust, combine and melt the mozzarella and cream cheese in the microwave for 30 seconds.
- Pour the cheese melt in the bread bucket then add the eggs and almond flour. Place the bread bucket inside the bread machine.
- Turn the bread machine on by selecting DOUGH cycle, close the lid then press start and wait for the cycle to finish in about 90 minutes.
- While waiting for the dough, prepare the cheese sauce by combining whip cream, cream cheese, and butter in a saucepan over medium heat until melted.
- Whisk in the mustard and pepper.
- Remove from heat and whisk in the cheddar and gruyere until it turns creamy.
- Preheat your oven at 425 degrees F before you start shaping the dough. Prepare a pizza pan and spray with non-stick baking spray. Set aside.
- Roll your dough into a 12-inch diameter circle between 2 sheets of parchment paper.
- Bake for 10 minutes until golden brown.
- To do the sauce and toppings, whisk six eggs and cream in a bowl until combined.
- Heat butter over medium fire in a large skillet. Add the egg mixture and scramble the egg until it turns soft fluffy and slightly wet appearance.
- Spread ½ cup of the cheese sauce onto the pizza crust, then topped with the scrambled egg, bacon, and sausage. Sprinkle the grated cheddar on top.
- Return to the over for another 5 minutes.
- Remove from the oven and sprinkle green onions on top.
- Slice and serve.
- Notes:
- Cheese sauce recipe yields 2 ½ cups and you only need ½ cup for the pizza. You can store the remaining sauce in an air tight lidded jar.
- Recipe nutrition info includes the ½-cup cheese sauce.

INGREDIENTS

- Crust
- cups mozzarella cheese, shredded
- tbsps. Cream cheese
- 1 egg
- ¾ cup almond flour
- Toppings:
- eggs
- tbsps. Heavy cream
- 1 tbsp. butter
- ½ cup crumbled bacon
- ½ cup cooked crumbled breakfast sausage
- ½ cup cheese sauce
- ¼ cup cheddar, shredded
- tbsps. Green onions, chopped
- Cheese Sauce:
- 1 ¼ cup heavy whipping cream
- oz. cream cheese
- tbsps. Butter
- ½ tsp. ground mustard
- ½ tsp. pepper
- oz. grated cheddar
- oz. grated gruyere

Coconut Cloud Bread

NUTRITION Calories 158 , Total Fat 15.2 g , Saturated Fat 5.2 g , Cholesterol 269 mg , Sodium 178 mg ,Total Carbs 7.4 g , Sugar 1.1 g , Fiber 3.5 g , Protein 5.5 g

PREPARATION	COOKING TIME	SERVINGS
10 MINT	25 mins	4

DIRECTION

- First, separate the egg yolks and egg whites.
- Beat egg yolks in a bowl.
- Stir in cream and continue beating with a hand mixer until creamy and smooth.
- Beat the egg whites with baking powder in another bowl until it forms peaks.
- Quickly add yolk mixture to the whites and mix well until fluffy.
- Spread ¼ of the batter on to a baking sheet separately to make 4 circles.
- Bake the batter for 25 minutes approximately at 350 degrees F.
- Serve.

INGREDIENTS

- eggs
- tbsp. coconut cream
- 1/2 tsp. baking powder
- Optional toppings:
- sea salt
- black pepper
- rosemary

Keto Kalamata Olive Loaf

NUTRITION Calories: 161, Calories from fat: 130, Total Fat: 14 g, Total Carbohydrates: 8 g, Net Carbohydrates: 5 g, Protein: 5 g

PREPARATION	COOKING TIME	SERVINGS
2 HOUR	10 mins	10 slices

INGREDIENTS

- ½ cup brine from olives
- 1 cup warm water
- tbsps. olive oil
- 1 ½ tsp. salt
- tbsps. sugar
- cups almond flour
- 1 2/3 cup almond meal
- 1 ½ tsp. dried basil leaves
- 1 tsps. active dry yeast
- ½ cup olives finely chopped

DIRECTION

- Combine the brine and warm water.
- Using the bread bucket, put all ingredients except olives in the order of their appearance on the ingredient list starting with the brine mixture.
- Select the WHEAT BREAD cycle on your machine. If there is no WHEAT BREAD cycle, you can select BASIC cycle. Close the cover and press START.
- With the first beep of the machine, open the lid and add in the olives. Close the lid and let the cycle continue.
- When the cycle ends, you can take the loaf out and let it cool in a cooling rack.
- Slice before serving.

Rosemary and Garlic Bread

NUTRITION Calories 214 ,Total Fat 19 g ,Saturated Fat 5.8 g ,Cholesterol 15 mg ,Sodium 123 mg ,Total,Carbs 6.5 g ,Sugar 1.9 g ,Fiber 2.1 g ,Protein 6.5 g

PREPARATION	COOKING TIME	SERVINGS
10 MINT	50 mins	8

DIRECTION

- Start by whisking rosemary, salt, garlic, onion, baking powder, and coconut flour in a bowl.
- Beat eggs in a mixing bowl until creamy.
- Now, put butter in a large bowl and melt it in the microwave.
- Slowly stir in the whisked eggs and continue beating with a hand mixer.
- Now, whisk in the dry mixture and mix well until well incorporated.
- Spread the batter in an 8x4 inch loaf pan and bake it for 50 minutes approximately at 350 degrees F.
- Slice and serve with butter on top

INGREDIENTS

- 1/2 cup coconut flour
- 1 stick butter (8 tbsp.)
- large eggs
- 1 tsp. baking powder
- tsp. dried rosemary
- 1/2-1 tsp. garlic powder
- 1/2 tsp. onion powder
- 1/4 tsp. pink Himalayan salt

Psyllium Husk Bread

NUTRITION Calories 220 ,Total Fat 20.1 g ,Saturated Fat 7.4 g ,Cholesterol 132 mg ,Sodium 157 mg ,Total, Carbs 63 g ,Sugar 0.4 g ,Fiber 2.4 g ,Protein 6.1 g

PREPARATION   **COOKING TIME**   **SERVINGS**

10 MINT   35 mins   10

INGREDIENTS

- 1/2 cup coconut flour
- tbsp. psyllium husk powder
- 1/2 tsp. baking powder
- 1/4 tsp. pink Himalayan salt
- 3/4 cup water
- large eggs
- tbsp. butter

DIRECTION

- Start by whisking the husk powder, salt, baking powder, and coconut flour in a bowl.
- Beat eggs with water and melted butter in a mixer until its smooth.
- Slowly stir in the dry mixture and mix well until smooth.
- Make 10 dinner rolls out of this bread dough and place the dough on a baking sheet.
- Bake them for 35 minutes, approximately, at 350 degrees F until all done.
- Slice and serve.

Garlic Focaccia Bread

NUTRITION Calories 301 ,Total Fat 26.3 g ,Saturated Fat 14.8 g ,Cholesterol 322 mg ,Sodium 597 mg ,Total Carbs 2.6 g Fiber 0.6 g Sugar 1.9 g , Protein 12 g

PREPARATION   **COOKING TIME**   **SERVINGS**

10 MINT   20 mins   4

DIRECTION

- Start by preheating the oven to 350 degrees F.
- Layer a baking sheet with parchment paper.
- Now, whisk all the dry ingredients in a bowl.
- Beat lemon juice, oil, and egg in a bowl until well incorporated.
- Whisk in dry ingredients and mix well until it forms a dough.
- Spread the dough on a baking sheet and cover it with aluminum foil.
- Bake for 10 minutes approximately then remove the foil.
- Drizzle olive oil on top and bake for another 10 minutes uncovered.
- Garnish with basil and Italian seasoning.
- Serve.

INGREDIENTS

- 1 cup almond flour
- ¼ cup coconut flour
- ½ tsp. xanthan gum
- 1 tsp. garlic powder
- 1 tsp. flaky salt
- ½ tsp. baking soda
- ½ tsp. baking powder

Parsley Cheddar Bread

NUTRITION Calories 113 ,Total Fat 8.4 g ,Saturated Fat 12.1 g ,Cholesterol 27 mg ,Sodium 39 mg ,Total Carbs 9.2 g ,Sugar 3.1 g ,Fiber 4.6 g ,Protein 8.1 g

PREPARATION	COOKING TIME	SERVINGS
10 MINT	4 mins	2

INGREDIENTS

- 1 tbsp. butter
- tbsp. coconut flour
- 1 large egg
- 1 tbsp. heavy whipping cream
- tbsp. water
- 1/4 cup cheddar cheese
- 1/8 tsp. garlic powder
- 1/8 tsp. onion powder
- 1/8 tsp. dried parsley
- 1/8 tsp. pink Himalayan salt
- 1/8 tsp. black pepper
- 1/4 tsp. baking powder

DIRECTION

- Melt the butter by heating it in a coffee mug for 20 seconds.
- Slowly stir in seasonings, baking powder, and coconut flour. Mix well using a fork until smooth.
- Whisk in cream, cheese, water, and egg.
- Beat well until smooth then bake for 3 minutes in the microwave.
- Allow the bread to cool then serve.

Keto Yeast Loaf Bread

NUTRITION Calories: 99 ,Calories from fat: 45,Total Fat: 5 g,Total Carbohydrates: 7 g ,Net Carbohydrates: 5 g, Protein: 9 g

PREPARATION	COOKING TIME	SERVINGS
5 MINT	4 mins	16 slices

DIRECTION

- Mix the sugar, water and yeast in the bread bucket to proof the yeast. If the yeast does not bubble, toss and replace it.
- Combine all the dry ingredients in a bowl and mix thoroughly. Pour over the wet ingredients in the bread bucket.
- Set the bread machine and select BASIC cycle to bake the loaf. Close the lid. This takes 3 to 4 hours.
- When the cycle ends, remove the bread from the bread machine.
- Cool on a rack before slicing.
- Serve with butter or light jam.

INGREDIENTS

- 1 package dry yeast
- ½ tsp. sugar
- 1 1/8 cup warm water about 90-100 degrees F
- tbsps. Olive oil or avocado oil
- 1 cup vital wheat gluten flour
- ¼ cup oat flour
- ¾ cup soy flour
- ¼ cup flax meal
- ¼ cup wheat bran course, unprocessed
- 1 tbsp. sugar
- 1 ½ tsp. baking powder
- 1 tsp. salt

Buttery Flatbread

NUTRITION Calories 216 , Total Fat 20.9 g , Saturated Fat 8.1 g ,Cholesterol 241 mg , Total Carbs 8.3 g , Sugar 1.8 g , Fiber 3.8 g , Sodium 8 mg , Protein 6.4 g

PREPARATION	COOKING TIME	SERVINGS
10 MINT	8 mins	4

DIRECTION

- Start by whisking baking powder, salt, flours, and xanthan gum in a bowl.
- Beat egg whites and egg in a bowl until creamy.
- Fold in flour mixture and mix until well incorporated.
- Add a tablespoon of water to the dough and cut it into 4 equal parts.
- Spread each part out into a flatbread and cook each for 1 minute per side in a skillet with oil.
- Garnish with butter, parsley, and salt.
- Serve.

INGREDIENTS

- 1 cup almond flour
- tbsp. coconut flour
- tsp. xanthan gum
- 1/2 tsp. baking powder
- 1/2 tsp. flaky salt
- 1 whole egg + 1 egg white
- 1 tbsp. water
- 1 tbsp. oil, for frying
- 1 tbsp. melted butter, for slathering

German Pumpernickel Bread

NUTRITION Calories 119, Carbohydrates 22.4 g, Total Fat 2.3 g, Cholesterol 0mg, Protein 3 g, Sodium 295 mg

PREPARATION	COOKING TIME	SERVINGS
2 HOUR	1 10 hour mint	1 loaf

DIRECTION

- Put everything in your bread machine.
- Select the primary cycle.
- Hit the start button.
- Transfer bread to a rack for cooling once done.

INGREDIENTS

- 1 1/2 tablespoon vegetable oil
- 1 1/8 cups warm water
- Three tablespoons cocoa
- 1/3 cup molasses
- 1 ½ teaspoons salt
- One tablespoon caraway seeds
- 1 cup rye flour
- 1 ½ cups of bread flour
- 1 ½ tablespoon wheat gluten
- 1 cup whole wheat flour
- 2 ½ teaspoons bread machine yeast

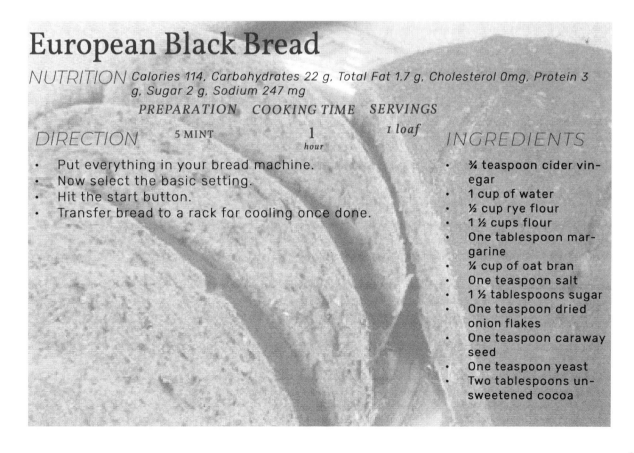

Chapter 24.
International Bread

European Black Bread

NUTRITION *Calories 114, Carbohydrates 22 g, Total Fat 1.7 g, Cholesterol 0mg, Protein 3 g, Sugar 2 g, Sodium 247 mg*

PREPARATION   COOKING TIME   SERVINGS

DIRECTION   5 MINT   1   1 loaf
                                      hour

- Put everything in your bread machine.
- Now select the basic setting.
- Hit the start button.
- Transfer bread to a rack for cooling once done.

INGREDIENTS

- ¾ teaspoon cider vinegar
- 1 cup of water
- ½ cup rye flour
- 1 ½ cups flour
- One tablespoon margarine
- ¼ cup of oat bran
- One teaspoon salt
- 1 ½ tablespoons sugar
- One teaspoon dried onion flakes
- One teaspoon caraway seed
- One teaspoon yeast
- Two tablespoons unsweetened cocoa

French Baguettes

NUTRITION Calories 201, Carbohydrates 42 g, Total Fat 0.6 g, Cholesterol 0 mg, Protein 6 g, Fiber 1.7 g, Sugar 0.1 g, Sodium 293 mg

PREPARATION	COOKING TIME	SERVINGS
25 MINT	15 mins	2 loaves

INGREDIENTS

- One ¼ cups warm water
- 3 ½ cups bread flour
- One teaspoon salt
- One package active dry yeast

DIRECTION

- Place ingredients in the bread machine. Select the dough cycle. Hit the start button.
- When the dough cycle is finished, remove it with floured hands and cut in half on a well-floured.
- Take each half of dough and roll it to make a loaf about 12 inches long in the shape of French bread.
- Place on a greased baking sheet and cover with a towel.
- Let rise until doubled, about 1 hour.
- Preheat oven to 450 F (220 ° C).
- Bake until golden brown, turning the pan around once halfway during baking.
- Transfer the loaves to a rack.

Portuguese Sweet Bread

NUTRITION Calories 139, Carbohydrates 24 g, Total Fat 8.3 g, Cholesterol 14 mg, Protein 3 g, Fiber 0g, Sugar 4 g, Sodium 147 mg

PREPARATION	COOKING TIME		SERVINGS
2 HOURS	1 hour	5 mins	1 loaf

DIRECTION

- Place everything into your bread machine.
- Select the sweet bread setting. Hit the start button.
- Transfer the loaves to a rack for cooling once done.

INGREDIENTS

- One egg, beaten
- 1 cup milk
- 1/3 cup sugar
- Two tablespoons margarine
- 3 cups bread flour
- ¾ teaspoon salt
- 2 ½ teaspoons active dry yeast

Italian Bread

NUTRITION Calories 105, Carbohydrates 20.6 g, Total Fat 0.9 g, Cholesterol 9 mg, Protein 3.1 g, Fiber 1 g, Sugar 1g, Sodium 179 mg, Potassium 39 mg

PREPARATION	COOKING TIME	SERVINGS
2 HOUR	1 hour 10 mins	2 loaves

INGREDIENTS

- One tablespoon of light brown sugar
- 4 cups all-purpose flour, unbleached
- 1 ½ teaspoon of salt
- One 1/3 cups + 1 tablespoon warm water
- One package active dry yeast
- 1 ½ teaspoon of olive oil
- One egg
- Two tablespoons cornmeal

DIRECTION

- Place flour, brown sugar, 1/3 cup warm water, salt, olive oil, and yeast in your bread machine. Select the dough cycle. Hit the start button.
- Deflate your dough. Turn it on a floured surface.
- Form two loaves from the dough.
- Keep them on your cutting board. The seam side should be down. Sprinkle some cornmeal on your board.
- Place a damp cloth on your loaves to cover them.
- Wait for 40 minutes. The volume should double.
- In the meantime, preheat your oven to 190 °C.
- Beat 1 tablespoon of water and an egg in a bowl.
- Brush this mixture on your loaves.
- Make an extended cut at the center of your loaves with a knife.
- Shake your cutting board gently, making sure that the loaves do not stick.
- Now slide your loaves on a baking sheet.
- Bake in your oven for about 35 minutes.

Pita Bread

NUTRITION Calories 191, Carbohydrates 37g, Total Fat 3g, Cholesterol 0mg, Protein 5g, Fiber 1g, Sugar 1g, Sodium 293mg, Potassium 66mg

PREPARATION	COOKING TIME	SERVINGS
35 MINT	20 mins	8

DIRECTION

- Place all the ingredients in your bread pan.
- Select the dough setting. Hit the start button.
- The machine beeps after the dough rises adequately.
- Turn the dough on a floured surface.
- Roll and stretch the dough gently into a 12-inch rope.
- Cut into eight pieces with a knife.
- Now roll each piece into a ball. It should be smooth.
- Roll each ball into a 7-inch circle. Keep covered with a towel on a floured top for 30 minutes for the pita to rise. It should get puffy slightly.
- Preheat your oven to 260 degrees C.
- Keep the pitas on your wire cake rack. Transfer to the oven rack directly.
- Bake the pitas for 5 minutes. They should be puffed. The top should start to brown.
- Take out from the oven. Keep the pitas immediately in a sealed paper bag. You can also cover using a damp kitchen towel.
- Split the top edge or cut into half once the pitas are soft. You can also have the whole pitas if you want.

INGREDIENTS

- 3 cups of all-purpose flour
- 1 1/8 cups warm water
- One tablespoon of vegetable oil
- One teaspoon salt
- 1 ½ teaspoon active dry yeast
- One active teaspoon white sugar

Syrian Bread

NUTRITION Calories 204, Carbohydrates 36g, Total Fat 5g, Cholesterol 0mg, Protein 5g, Fiber 1g, Sugar 0g, Sodium 438mg, Potassium 66mg

PREPARATION	COOKING TIME	SERVINGS
20 MINT	20 mins	8

INGREDIENTS

- Two tablespoons vegetable oil
- 1 cup of water
- 1 ½ teaspoons salt
- ½ teaspoon white sugar
- 1 ½ teaspoon active dry yeast
- 3 cups all-purpose flour

DIRECTION

- Put everything in your bread machine pan.
- Select the dough cycle. Hit the start button.
- Preheat your oven to 475 degrees F.
- Turn to dough on a lightly floured surface once done.
- Divide it into eight equal pieces. Form them into rounds.
- Take a damp cloth and cover the rounds with it.
- Now roll the dough into flat thin circles. They should have a diameter of around 8 inches.
- Cook in your preheated baking sheets until they are golden brown and puffed.

Ethiopian Milk and Honey Bread

NUTRITION Calories 129, Carbohydrates 20 g, Total Fat 3.8 g, Cholesterol 0 mg, Protein 2.4 g, Fiber 0.6 g, Sugars 3.3 g, Sodium 78 mg

PREPARATION	COOKING TIME	SERVINGS
2 HOUR	1 hour 15 mins	1 loaf

DIRECTION

- Add everything to the pan of your bread
- Select the white bread or basic setting and the medium crust setting.
- Hit the start button.
- Take out your hot loaf once it is done.
- Keep on your wire rack for cooling.
- Slice your bread once it is cold and serve.

INGREDIENTS

- Three tablespoons honey
- 1 cup + 1 tablespoon milk
- 3 cups bread flour
- Three tablespoons melted butter
- Two teaspoons active dry yeast
- 1 ½ teaspoons salt

Swedish Cardamom Bread

NUTRITION Calories 135, Carbohydrates 22g, Total Fat 7g, Cholesterol 20mg, Protein 3g, Fiber 1g, Sugar 3g, Sodium 100mg

PREPARATION
35 MINT

COOKING TIME
15
mins

SERVINGS
1 loaf

INGREDIENTS

- ¼ cup of sugar
- ¾ cup of warm milk
- ¾ teaspoon cardamom
- ½ teaspoon salt
- ¼ cup of softened butter
- One egg
- Two ¼ teaspoons bread machine yeast
- 3 cups all-purpose flour
- Five tablespoons milk for brushing
- Two tablespoons sugar for sprinkling

DIRECTION

- Put everything (except milk for brushing and sugar for sprinkling) in the pan of your bread machine.
- Select the dough cycle. Hit the start button. You should have an elastic and smooth dough once the process is complete. It should be double in size.
- Transfer to a lightly floured surface.
- Now divide into three balls. Set aside for 10 minutes.
- Roll all the balls into long ropes of around 14 inches.
- Braid the shapes. Pinch ends under securely and keeps on a cookie sheet. You can also divide your dough into two balls. Smooth them and keep on your bread pan.
- Brush milk over the braid. Sprinkle sugar lightly.
- Now bake in your oven for 25 minutes at 375 degrees F (190 degrees C).
- Take a foil and cover for the final 10 minutes. It's prevents over-browning.
- Transfer to your cooling rack.

Fiji Sweet Potato Bread

NUTRITION Calories: 168 Cal, Carbohydrates: 28 g, Fat: 5g, Cholesterol: 0 mg, Protein: 4 g, Fiber: 1g, Sugar 3 g, Sodium: 292 mg

PREPARATION
2 HOUR

COOKING TIME
1 hour 10 mins

SERVINGS
1 loaf

DIRECTION

- Add everything in the pan of your bread.
- Select the white bread and the crust you want.
- Hit the start button.
- Set aside on wire racks for cooling before slicing.

INGREDIENTS

- One teaspoon vanilla extract
- ½ cup of warm water
- 4 cups flour
- 1 cup sweet mashed potatoes
- Two tablespoons softened butter
- ½ teaspoon cinnamon
- 1 ½ teaspoons salt
- 1/3 cup brown sugar
- Two tablespoons powdered milk
- Two teaspoons yeast

Chapter 25.
Fruit and Vegetable Bread

Orange and Walnut Bread

NUTRITION *Calories: 121   Fiber: 1.1 g   Fat: 1.9 g   Carbs: 2.9g   Protein: 3.9 g.*

INGREDIENTS

- 1 1/3 cups warm water
- 1 ½ tablespoon olive oil
- 1 ½ teaspoons salt
- Two tablespoons sugar
- 4 cups all-purpose flour; or bread flour
- Two teaspoons yeast

DIRECTION

- Put the warm water in your bread machine first.
- Next, put in the olive oil, then the salt, and finally the sugar. Make sure to follow that exact order. Then put in the flour. Make sure to cover the liquid ingredients.
- In the center of the flour, make a small indentation. Make sure the indentation doesn't go down far enough to touch the liquid. Put the yeast in the indentation.
- Set the bread machine to the French Bread Cycle.
- After 5 minutes of kneading, check on the dough. If the dough is stiff and dry, add ½ - 1 tablespoon of water until the dough becomes a softball.
- If the dough is too damp, add one tablespoon of flour until the right consistency is reached. Allow the bread cool for about 10 minutes, then cut it.

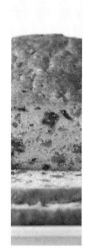

PREPARATION	COOKING TIME	SERVINGS
2 30 mins	30 mints	14

Banana Bread

NUTRITION Calories: 310 calories ,Total Carbohydrate: 40 g ,Fat: 13 g , Protein: 3 g

INGREDIENTS

- ONE TEASPOON BAKING POW-
DER
- 1/2 TEASPOON BAKING SODA
- TWO BANANAS, PEELED AND
HALVED LENGTHWISE
- 2 CUPS ALL-PURPOSE FLOUR
- TWO EGGS
- THREE TABLESPOON VEGETA-
BLE OIL
- 3/4 CUP WHITE SUGAR

DIRECTION

- Put all the ingredients in the bread pan—select dough setting. Start and mix for about 3-5 minutes.
- After 3-5 minutes, press stop. Do not continue to mix. Smooth out the top of the dough
- Using the spatula and then select bake, start and bake for about 50 minutes. After 50 minutes, insert a toothpick into the top center to test doneness.
- Test the loaf again. When the bread is completely baked, remove the pan from the machine and let the bread remain in the pan for10 minutes. Remove bread and cool in a wire rack.

PREPARATION	COOKING TIME	SERVINGS
1 hour,40 Mint	40-45 mins	1 loaf

Apple with Pumpkin Bread

NUTRITION Calories: 228 calories; Total Carbohydrate: 30 g , Total Fat: 4

INGREDIENTS

- 1/3 cup dried apples, chopped
- 1 1/2 teaspoon bread machine yeast
- 4 cups bread flour
- 1/3 cup ground pecans
- 1/4 teaspoon ground nutmeg
- 1/4 teaspoon ground ginger
- 1/4 teaspoon allspice
- 1/2 teaspoon ground cinnamon
- 1 1/4 teaspoon salt
- Two tablespoons unsalted butter, cubed
- 1/3 cup dry skim milk powder
- 1/4 cup honey
- Two large eggs, at room temperature
- 2/3 cup pumpkin puree
- 2/3 cup water, with a temperature of 80 to 90 degrees F (26 to 32 degrees C)

DIRECTION

- Put all ingredients, except the dried apples, in the bread pan in this order: water, pumpkin puree, eggs, honey, skim milk, butter, salt, allspice, cinnamon, pecans, nutmeg, ginger, flour, and yeast.
- Secure the pan in the machine and lock the lid.
- Place the dried apples in the fruit and nut dispenser.
- Turn on the machine. Choose the sweet setting and your desired colour of the crust.
- Carefully unmold the baked bread once done and allow it to cool for 20 minutes before slicing.

PREPARATION	COOKING TIME	SERVINGS
2 HOURS 50 MINT	45 mints	2 loaves

Peaches and Cream Bread

NUTRITION Calories: 153 calories, Total Carbohydrate: 27 g , Total Fat: 4 g , Protein: 5 g ,

INGREDIENTS

- ½ cup canned peaches, drained and chopped
- ¼ cup heavy whipping cream, at 80°F to 90°F
- One egg, at room temperature
- ¾ tablespoon melted butter cooled
- 1½ tablespoons sugar
- ¾ teaspoon salt
- ¼ teaspoon ground cinnamon
- 1/8 teaspoon ground nutmeg
- ¼ cup whole-wheat flour
- 1¾ cups white bread flour
- ¾ teaspoons bread machine or instant yeast

DIRECTION

- Put all ingredients as recommended by your bread machine manufacturer.
- Set the machine for Basic White bread, select medium crust, then press Start.
- When the loaf is finished, remove the bucket from the machine.
- Let it cool for five minutes.
- Shake the bucket gently to remove the loaf, then turn it out onto a rack to cool.

PREPARATION	COOKING TIME	SERVINGS
2 HOUR	15 *mints*	8

Pure Peach Bread

NUTRITION Calories: 51 calories, Total Carbohydrate: 12 g , Cholesterol: 0 g , Total Fat: 0.3 g , Protein: 1.20 g , Fiber: 2 g

INGREDIENTS

- ¾ cup peaches, chopped
- 1/3 cup heavy whipping cream
- One egg
- One tablespoon butter, melted at room temperature
- 1/3 teaspoon ground cinnamon
- 1/8 teaspoon ground nutmeg
- Two ¼ tablespoons sugar
- One 1/8 teaspoons salt
- 1/3 cup whole-wheat flour
- Two 2/3 cups white bread flour
- One 1/8 teaspoon instant or bread machine yeast

DIRECTION

- Take 1 ½ pound size loaf pan and add the liquid ingredients and then add the dry ingredients.
- Place the loaf pan in the machine and close its top lid.
- For selecting a bread cycle, press "Basic Bread/White Bread/Regular Bread," and for choosing a crust type, press "Light" or "Medium."
- Start the machine, and it will start preparing the bread.
- After the bread loaf is completed, open the lid and take out the loaf pan.
- Allow the pan to cool down for 10-15 minutes on a wire rack. Gently shake the pan and remove the bread loaf.
- Make slices and serve.

PREPARATION	COOKING TIME	SERVINGS
2 *hour*	15 *mints*	12

Warm Spiced Pumpkin Bread

NUTRITION Calories: 251 calories, Total Carbohydrate: 43 g , Total Fat: 7 g , Protein: 5 g ,

INGREDIENTS

- BUTTER FOR GREASING THE BUCKET
- 1½ CUPS PUMPKIN PURÉE
- THREE EGGS, AT ROOM TEMPERATURE
- 1/3 CUP MELTED BUTTER COOLED
- 1 CUP OF SUGAR
- 3 CUPS ALL-PURPOSE FLOUR
- 1½ TEASPOONS BAKING POWDER
- ¾ TEASPOON GROUND CINNAMON
- ½ TEASPOON BAKING SODA
- ¼ TEASPOON GROUND NUTMEG
- ¼ TEASPOON GROUND GINGER
- ¼ TEASPOON SALT
- PINCH GROUND CLOVES

DIRECTION

- Lightly grease the bread bucket with butter.
- Add the pumpkin, eggs, butter, and sugar.
- Program the machine for Quick/Rapid setting and press Start.
- Let the wet ingredients be mixed by the paddles until the first fast mixing cycle is finished, about 10 minutes into the process.
- Stir according to the order. Flour, baking powder, cinnamon, baking soda, nutmeg, ginger, salt, and cloves until well blended.
- Add the dry ingredients to the bucket when the second fast mixing cycle starts.
- When the loaf is finished, remove the bucket from the machine.
- Cool the loaf for five minutes.
- Gently shake the bucket, then remove the loaf and turn it out onto a rack to cool.

PREPARATION	COOKING TIME	SERVINGS
2 hours	**15** mins	*12-16*

Date Delight Bread

NUTRITION Calories: 220 Cal, Carbohydrates: 52 g, Cholesterol: 0 g, Fat 5 g

INGREDIENTS

- ¾ cup water, lukewarm
- ½ cup milk, lukewarm
- Two tablespoons butter, melted at room temperature
- ¼ cup honey
- Three tablespoons molasses
- One tablespoon sugar
- Two ¼ cups whole-wheat flour
- One ¼ cups white bread flour
- Two tablespoons skim milk powder
- One teaspoon salt
- One tablespoon unsweetened cocoa powder
- 1 ½ teaspoon instant or bread machine yeast
- ¾ cup chopped dates

DIRECTION

- Take 1 ½ pound size loaf pan and add the liquid ingredients and then add the dry ingredients. (Do not add the dates as of now.)
- Place the loaf pan in the machine and close its top lid.
- Plug the bread machine into the power socket. For selecting a bread cycle, press "Basic Bread/White Bread/Regular Bread" or "Fruit/Nut Bread," and for choosing a crust type, press "Light" or "Medium."
- Start the machine, and it will start preparing the bread. When the machine beeps or signals, add the dates.
- After the bread loaf is completed, open the lid and take out the loaf pan.
- Allow the pan to cool down for 10-15 minutes on a wire rack. Gently shake the pan and remove the bread loaf.
- Make slices and serve

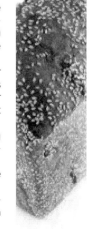

PREPARATION	COOKING	SERVINGS
2 HOURS	15 mints	*12*

Sun Vegetable Bread

NUTRITION Calories 253, Total Fat 2.6g, Saturated Fat 0.5g; Cholesterol 0g;, Sodium 444mg, Total, Carbohydrate 49.6g, Dietary Fiber 2.6g, Total Sugars 0.6g, Protein 7.2g

INGREDIENTS

- 2 cups (250 g) wheat flour
- 2 cups (250 g) whole-wheat flour
- 2 teaspoons panifarin
- 2 teaspoons yeast
- 1½ teaspoons salt
- 1 tablespoon sugar
- 1 tablespoon paprika dried slices
- 2 tablespoons dried beets
- 1 tablespoon dried garlic
- 1½ cups water
- 1 tablespoon vegetable oil

DIRECTION

- Set baking program, which should be 4 hours; crust color is Medium.
- Be sure to look at the kneading phase of the dough, to get a smooth and soft bun.

PREPARATION	COOKING TIME	SERVINGS
15 MINT	3 hour 50 mints	8 slices

Tomato Bread

NUTRITION Calories 281, Total Fat 3.3g, Saturated Fat 0.6g, Cholesterol 0g, Sodium 590mg, Total Carbohydrate 54.3g, Dietary Fiber 2.4g, Total Sugars 1.9g, Protein 7.6g

INGREDIENTS

- 3 tablespoons tomato paste
- 1½ cups (340 ml) water
- 4 1/3 cups (560 g) flour
- 1½ tablespoon vegetable oil
- 2 teaspoons sugar
- 2 teaspoons salt
- 1 ½ teaspoons dry yeast
- ½ teaspoon oregano, dried
- ½ teaspoon ground sweet paprika

DIRECTION

- Dilute the tomato paste in warm water. If you do not like the tomato flavor, reduce the amount of tomato paste, but putting less than 1 tablespoon does not make sense, because the color will fade.
- Prepare the spices. I added a little more oregano as well as Provencal herbs to the oregano and paprika (this bread also begs for spices).
- Sieve the flour to enrich it with oxygen. Add the spices to the flour and mix well.
- Pour the vegetable oil into the bread maker container. Add the tomato/water mixture, sugar, salt, and then the flour with spices, and then the yeast.
- Turn on the bread maker (the Basic program – I have the WHITE BREAD – the crust Medium).
- After the end of the baking cycle, turn off the bread maker. Remove the bread container and take out the hot bread. Place it on the grate for cooling for 1 hour.

PREPARATION	COOKING TIME	SERVINGS
5 MINT	3 hour 30 mints	8 slices

Tomato Onion Bread

NUTRITION Calories 241, Total Fat 6.4g, Saturated Fat 1.1g, Cholesterol 1g, Sodium 305mg, Total Carbohydrate 40g, Dietary Fiber 3.5g, Total Sugars 6.8g, Protein 6.7g

INGREDIENTS

- 2 CUPS ALL-PURPOSE FLOUR
- 1 CUP WHOLE MEAL FLOUR
- ½ CUP WARM WATER
- 4 3/4 OUNCES (140 ML) MILK
- 3 TABLESPOONS OLIVE OIL
- 2 TABLESPOONS SUGAR
- 1 TEASPOON SALT
- 2 TEASPOONS DRY YEAST
- ½ TEASPOON BAKING POWDER
- 5 SUN-DRIED TOMATOES
- 1 ONION
- ¼ TEASPOON BLACK PEPPER

DIRECTION

- Prepare all the necessary products. Finely chop the onion and sauté in a frying pan. Cut up the sun-dried tomatoes (10 halves).
- Pour all liquid ingredients into the bowl; then cover with flour and put in the tomatoes and onions. Pour in the yeast and baking powder, without touching the liquid.
- Select the baking mode and start. You can choose the Bread with Additives program, and then the bread maker will knead the dough at low speeds.

PREPARATION	COOKING TIME	SERVINGS
15 MINT	3 hour 50 mints	12 slices

Curd Onion Bread with Sesame Seeds

NUTRITION Calories 277, Total Fat 4.7g, Saturated Fat 2.3g, Cholesterol 9g, Sodium 547mg, Total Carbohydrate 48.4g, Dietary Fiber 1.9g, Total Sugars 3.3g, Protein 9.4g

INGREDIENTS

- 3/4 cup water
- 3 2/3 cups wheat flour
- 3/4 cup cottage cheese
- 2 tablespoons softened butter
- 2 tablespoon sugar
- 1 ½ teaspoons salt
- 1 ½ tablespoon sesame seeds
- 2 tablespoons dried onions
- 1 ¼ teaspoons dry yeast

DIRECTION

- Put the products in the bread maker according to its instructions. I have this order, presented with the ingredients.
- Bake on the BASIC program.

PREPARATION	COOKING TIME	SERVINGS
10 MINT	3 hour 50 mints	8 slices

Squash Carrot Bread

NUTRITION Calories 220, Total Fat 4.3g, Saturated Fat 0.8g, Cholesterol 0g, Sodium 313mg, Total Carbohydrate 39.1g, Dietary Fiber 4.1g, Total Sugars 2.7g, Protein 6.6g

INGREDIENTS

- 1 small zucchini
- 1 baby carrot
- 1 cup whey
- 1 ½ cups (180 g) white wheat flour
- 3/4 cup (100 g) whole wheat flour
- 3/4 cup (100 g) rye flour
- 2 tablespoons vegetable oil
- 1 teaspoon yeast, fresh
- 1 teaspoon salt
- ½ teaspoon sugar

DIRECTION

- Cut/dice carrots and zucchini to about 8-10 mm (1/2 inch) in size.
- In a frying pan, warm the vegetable oil and fry the vegetables over medium heat until soft. If desired, season the vegetables with salt and pepper.
- Transfer the vegetables to a flat plate so that they cool down more quickly. While still hot, they cannot be added to the dough.
- Now dissolve the yeast in the serum.
- Send all kinds of flour, serum with yeast, as well as salt and sugar to the bakery.
- Knead the dough in the Dough for the Rolls program.
- At the very end of the batch, add the vegetables to the dough.
- After adding vegetables, the dough will become moister. After fermentation process, which will last about an hour before the doubling of the volume of the dough, shift it onto a thickly floured surface.
- Turn into a loaf and put it in an oiled form.
- Conceal the form using a food film and leave for 1 to 1 1/3 hours.
- Preheat oven to 450°F and put bread in it.
- Bake the bread for 15 minutes, and then gently remove it from the mold. Lay it on the grate and bake for 15-20 minutes more

PREPARATION	COOKING TIME	SERVINGS
15 MINT	3 45 hour mints	8 slices

Strawberry Shortcake Bread

NUTRITION Calories 277, Cholesterol 9g, Carbohydrate 48.4g, Dietary Fiber 1.9g, Sugars 3.3g, Protein 9.4g

INGREDIENTS

- 1/2 cups milk, at 80°F to 90°F
- Three tablespoons melted butter, cooled
- Three tablespoons sugar
- 1½ teaspoons salt
- ¾ cup sliced fresh strawberries
- 1 cup quick oats
- 2¼ cups white bread flour
- 1½ teaspoons bread machine or instant yeast

DIRECTION

- Preparing the Ingredients. Place the ingredients in your Hamilton Beach bread machine.
- Select the Bake cycle. Program the machine for Whitbread, choose light or medium crust, and press Start.
- If the loaf is done, remove the bucket from the machine.
- Let the loaf cool for 5 minutes. Moderately shake the can to remove the loaf and turn it out onto a rack to cool.

PREPARATION	COOKING TIME	SERVINGS
10 mins	25 mints	8

Fragrant Orange Bread

NUTRITION Calories 277, Cholesterol 9g, Carbohydrate 48.4g, Dietary Fiber 1.9g, Sugars

INGREDIENTS

- 1 CUP MILK,
- THREE TABLESPOONS FRESH-LY CLASPED ORANGE JUICE
- THREE TABLESPOONS SUGAR
- ONE TABLESPOON MELTED BUTTER COOLED
- ONE TEASPOON SALT
- 3 CUPS WHITE BREAD FLOUR
- ZEST OF 1 ORANGE
- 1¼ TEASPOONS BREAD MA-CHINE OR INSTANT YEAST

DIRECTION

- Preparing the Ingredients. Place the ingredients in your Hamilton Beach bread machine.
- Select the Bake cycle. Program the machine for Whitbread, choose the light or medium crust, and press Start. If the loaf is done, remove the bucket from the machine. Allow the loaf to cool for 5 minutes
- Moderately shake the pan to eliminate the loaf and turn it out onto a rack to cool.

PREPARATION	COOKING TIME	SERVINGS
15 mint	25 mins	8

Blueberry Bread

NUTRITION Calories: 180 calories , Total Carbohydrate: 250 g , Fat: 3 g , Protein: 9 g

INGREDIENTS

- 1 1/8 to 1¼ cups Water
-
- 2 teaspoons Salt
- 4½ cups Bread flour
- 1½ teaspoons Grated lemon peel
- teaspoons Cardamom
- tablespoons Nonfat dry milk
- 2½ teaspoons Red star brand active dry yeast
- 2/3 cup dried blueberries
- ounces Cream cheese, softened
- tablespoons Butter or margarine
- ¼ cup Sugar

DIRECTION

- Place all Ingredients except dried blueberries in bread pan, using the least amount of liquid listed in the recipe. Select light crust setting and the raisin / nut cycle. Press the start button.
- Watch the dough as you knead. After 5 to 10 minutes, if it is dry and hard or if the machine seems to strain to knead it, add more liquid 1 tablespoon at a time until the dough forms a ball that is soft, tender, and slightly sticky to the touch.
- When stimulated, add dried cranberries.
- After the bake cycle is complete, remove the bread from the pan, place on the cake and allow to cool.

PREPARATION		COOKING TIME	SERVINGS
3 HOUR	15 MINT	45-50 mints	*8 slices*

Pineapple Coconut Bread

NUTRITION Calories 277, Cholesterol 9g, Carbohydrate 48.4g, Dietary Fiber 1.9g, Sugars 3.3g, Protein 9.4g

PREPARATION	COOKING TIME	SERVINGS
10 MINT	15 *mins*	8

DIRECTION

- Preparing the Ingredients. Place the butter, eggs, coconut milk, pineapple juice, sugar, and coconut extract in your Hamilton Beach bread machine.
- Select the Bake cycle. Program the machine for Rapid bread and press Start. While the wet ingredients are mingling, stir together the flour, coconut, baking powder, and salt in a small bowl. After the first mixing is done and the machine motions, add the dry ingredients. When the loaf is done, eliminate the bucket from the machine. Let the loaf cool for 5 minutes. Slightly shake the pot to remove the loaf and turn it out onto a rack to cool.

INGREDIENTS

- Six tablespoons butter, at room temperature
- Two eggs, at room temperature
- ½ cup coconut milk, at room temperature
- ½ cup pineapple juice, at room temperature
- 1 cup of sugar
- 1½ teaspoons coconut extract
- 2 cups all-purpose flour
- ¾ cup shredded sweetened coconut
- One teaspoon baking powder
- ½ teaspoon salt

Lemon-Lime Blueberry Bread

NUTRITION Calories 277, Cholesterol 9g, Carbohydrate 48.4g, Dietary Fiber 1.9g, Sugars 3.3g, Protein 9.4g

PREPARATION	COOKING TIME	SERVINGS
10 MINTS	30 *mins*	8

DIRECTION

- Preparing the Ingredients. Place the ingredients in your Hamilton Beach bread machine.
- Select the Bake cycle. Program the machine for White bread, choose light or medium crust, then press Start.
- Remove the bucket from the machine.
- Let the loaf cool for 5 minutes.
- Gently shake the pan to remove the loaf and turn it out onto a rack to cool.

INGREDIENTS

- ¾ cup plain yogurt, at room temperature
- ½ cup of water
- Three tablespoons honey
- One tablespoon melted butter cooled
- 1½ teaspoons salt
- ½ teaspoon lemon extract
- One teaspoon lime zest
- 1 cup dried blueberries
- 3 cups white bread flour
- 2¼ teaspoons bread machine or instant yeast

Fruit Syrup Bread

NUTRITION *Calories 277, Cholesterol 9g, Carbohydrate 48.4g, Dietary Fiber 1.9g, Sugars 3.3g, Protein 9.4g*

PREPARATION	COOKING TIME	SERVINGS
10 MINT	25 mins	8

DIRECTION

- Preparing the Ingredients. Combine the syrup and 1/2 cup water. Heat until lukewarm. Add more water to precisely 1 cup of water.
- Place all the ingredients, except for the rolled oats and butter, in a liquid-dry-yeast layering.
- Put the pan in the Hamilton Beach bread machine.
- Load the rolled oats in the automatic dispenser.
- Select the Bake cycle. Choose whole-wheat loaf.
- Press start and wait until the loaf is cooked.
- Brush the top with butter once cooked.
- The machine will start the keep warm mode after the bread is complete.
- Let it remain in that mode for about 10 minutes before unplugging.
- Remove the pan and let it cool down for about 10 minutes.

INGREDIENTS

- 3 2/3 cups whole wheat flour
- 1 1/2 tsp. instant yeast
- 1/4 cup unsalted butter, melted
- 1 cup lukewarm water
- 2 tbsp. sugar
- 1/4 cup rolled oats
- 1/2 tsp. salt
- 1/2 cup of syrup from preserved fruit

Cranberry Yogurt Bread

NUTRITION *Calories 277, Cholesterol 9g, Carbohydrate 48.4g, Dietary Fiber 1.9g, Sugars 3.3g, Protein 9.4g*

PREPARATION	COOKING TIME	SERVINGS
10 MINTS	25 mints	8

DIRECTION

- Preparing the Ingredients. Place all ingredients, except cranberries and raisins, in the bread pan in the liquid-dry-yeast layering.
- Put the pan in the Hamilton Beach bread machine.
- Load the fruits in the automatic dispenser.
- Select the Bake cycle. Choose White bread.
- Press start and wait until the loaf is cooked.
- The machine will start the keep warm mode after the bread is complete.
- Allow it to stay in that mode for at least 10 minutes before unplugging.
- Remove the pan and let it cool down for about 10 minutes.

INGREDIENTS

- 3 cups + 2 tbsp. bread or all-purpose flour
- 1/2 cup lukewarm water
- 1 tbsp. olive or coconut oil
- 1 tbsp. orange or lemon essential oil
- 3 tbsp. sugar
- 3/4 cup yogurt
- 2 tsp. instant yeast
- 1 cup dried cried cranberries
- 1/2 cup raisins

Peaches and butter cream Bread

NUTRITION Calories 277, Cholesterol 9g, Carbohydrate 48.4g, Dietary Fiber 1.9g, Sugars
3.3g, Protein 9.4g

PREPARATION	COOKING TIME	SERVINGS
10 MINT	25 mins	8

DIRECTION

- Preparing the Ingredients. Place the ingredients in your Hamilton Beach bread machine.
- Select the Bake cycle. Program the machine for Whit-bread, select light or medium crust, and press Start.
- When the loaf is done, eliminate the bucket from the machine.
- Let the loaf cool for 5 minutes.
- Shake the bucket to eliminate the loaf, and place it out onto a rack to cool.

INGREDIENTS

- 3/4 cup canned peaches, drained and chopped
- 1/3 cup heavy whipping cream, at 80°F to 90°F
- One egg, at room temperature
- One tablespoon melted butter cooled
- Two 1/4 tablespoons sugar
- 1 1/8 teaspoons salt
- 1/3 teaspoon ground cinnamon
- 1/8 teaspoon ground nutmeg
- 1/3 cup whole-wheat flour
- 2 2/3 cups white bread flour
- 1 1/6 teaspoons bread machine or instant yeast

Zucchini and Berries Loaf

NUTRITION Calories 277, Cholesterol 9g, Carbohydrate 48.4g, Dietary Fiber 1.9g,
Sugars 3.3g, Protein 9.4g

PREPARATION	COOKING TIME	SERVINGS
1 HOUR	25 mints	8

DIRECTION

- Preparing the Ingredients. Blend the dry and wet ingredients in two different bowls.
- Place all ingredients, except the berries, in the bread pan in the liquid-dry-yeast-zucchini layering.
- Put the pan in the Hamilton Beach bread machine.
- Load the berries in the automatic dispenser.
- Select the Bake cycle. Set to Rapid White bake for 1 hour. Press Start.
- Five minutes into the cycle, add the berries.
- Wait until the loaf is cooked.
- The machine will start the keep warm mode after the bread is complete.
- Let it stay in that mode for 10 minutes before unplugging.
- Remove the pan and let it cool down for about 10 minutes.

INGREDIENTS

- 2 1/4 cups flour
- Three eggs whisked lightly
- 1 2/3 cups sugar
- 2 tsp. vanilla
- 3/4 cup vegetable oil
- 3/4 tsp. baking powder
- pinch of baking soda
- 1/4 tsp. salt
- 2 tsp. cinnamon
- 1 1/2 cup blueberries
- 1 1/2 cup shredded zucchini

Cinnamon and Raisin Pumpernickel Bread

NUTRITION Calories 277, Cholesterol 9g, Carbohydrate 48.4g, Dietary Fiber 1.9g, Sugars 3.3g, Protein 9.4g

PREPARATION **COOKING TIME** **SERVINGS**

DIRECTION   10 HOURS   225 hrs   8   INGREDIENTS

- 1. Preparing the Ingredients. In a bowl, combine the water, molasses, salt, and oil. Stir until incorporated.
- 2. Place all ingredients, except raisins, in the bread pan in the liquid-dry-yeast layering.
- 3. Put the pan in the Hamilton Beach bread machine.
- 4. Load the raisins in the automatic dispenser
- 5. Select the Bake cycle. Choose Whole Wheat loaf.
- 6. Press start and wait until the loaf is cooked.
- 7. The machine will start the keep warm mode after the bread is complete.
- 8. Make it stay in that mode for about 10 minutes before unplugging.
- 9. Remove the pan and let it cool down for about 10 minutes

- 1 cup bread flour
- 1/3 cup rye flour
- 3/4 cup wheat flour
- 5/6 cup lukewarm water
- 2 tbsp. cocoa powder
- 6 tbsp. oil or melted shortening
- 1/2 tbsp. salt
- 1 tbsp. instant yeast
- 1/2 cup molasses
- 1/4 cup honey
- 1 1/2 tbsp. cinnamon
- 1 cup raisins

Yeasted Carrot Bread

NUTRITION Calories 277, Cholesterol 9g, Carbohydrate 48.4g, Dietary Fiber 1.9g, Sugars 3.3g, Protein 9.4g

PREPARATION **COOKING TIME** **SERVINGS**

DIRECTION   10 MINTS   25 mints   8   INGREDIENTS

- Preparing the Ingredients. Place the ingredients in your Hamilton Beach bread machine.
- Select the Bake cycle. Program the machine for Rapid bread and press Start.
- If the loaf is done, remove the bucket from the machine.
- Let the loaf cool for 5 minutes.
- Mildly shake the bucket to remove the loaf and try it out onto a rack to cool.

- 1 lb. whole-wheat pizza dough
- 3 tbsps. garlic-flavoured olive oil
- 2 cups thinly sliced cooked collard greens
- 1 cup shredded Cheddar cheese
- ¼ cup crumbled cooked bacon

Zucchini Rye Bread

NUTRITION *Calories 277, Cholesterol 9g, Carbohydrate 48.4g, Dietary Fiber 1.9g, Sugars 3.3g, Protein 9.4g*

PREPARATION	COOKING TIME	SERVINGS
20 HOUR	125 hours	8

DIRECTION

- Preparing the Ingredients. Dry the shredded zucchini but placing it in a towel and wringing it to remove excess moisture.
- Place all the ingredients in the liquid-zucchini-flour-yeast layering.
- Put the pan in the Hamilton Beach bread machine.
- Select the Bake cycle. Choose White bread and medium crust.
- Press start and wait until the loaf is cooked.
- The machine will start the keep warm mode after the bread is complete.
- Let it stay in that mode for nearly 10 minutes before unplugging.
- Remove the pan and let it cool down for about 10 minutes

INGREDIENTS

- 2 cups all-purpose or bread flour
- 2 3/4 cup rye flour
- 2 tbsp. cocoa powder
- 1/2 cup cornmeal
- 1 tbsp. instant yeast
- 1/4 cup olive oil
- 3 tbsp. molasses or honey
- 1 1/2 cup lukewarm water
- 1 tsp. salt
- 1 1/2 cup zucchini, shredded

Chapter 26. White Bread

Savory Onion Bread

NUTRITION

PREPARATION   **COOKING TIME**   **SERVINGS**

DIRECTION

10 MINT   25 mins   8

- Cut the sausage into small cubes.
- Grate the cheese on a grater
- Chop the garlic.
- Add all ingredients to the machine according to the instructions.
- Turn on the baking program, and let it do the work

INGREDIENTS

- 1 cup water, at 80°F to 90°F
- Three tablespoons melted butter, cooled
- 1 1/2 tablespoons sugar
- 11/8 teaspoons salt
- Three tablespoons dried minced onion
- 1 1/2 tablespoons chopped fresh chives
- 3 cups white bread flour
- One teaspoon bread machine or instant yeast

Basic White Bread

NUTRITION Carbs: 18 g , Fat: 1 g , Protein: 3 g , Calories: 95

PREPARATION   **COOKING TIME**   **SERVINGS**

DIRECTION

5 MINTS   3 hour   16

- Add each ingredient to the bread machine in the order and at the temperature recommended by your bread machine manufacturer.
- Close the lid, select the basic or white bread, low crust setting on your bread machine, and press start.
- When the bread machine has finished baking, remove the bread and put it on a cooling rack.

INGREDIENTS

- 1 cup warm water (about 110°F/45°C)
- 2 Tablespoon sugar
- 2¼ teaspoon (.25-ounce package) bread machine yeast
- ¼ cup rice bran oil
- 3 cups bread flour
- 1 teaspoon salt

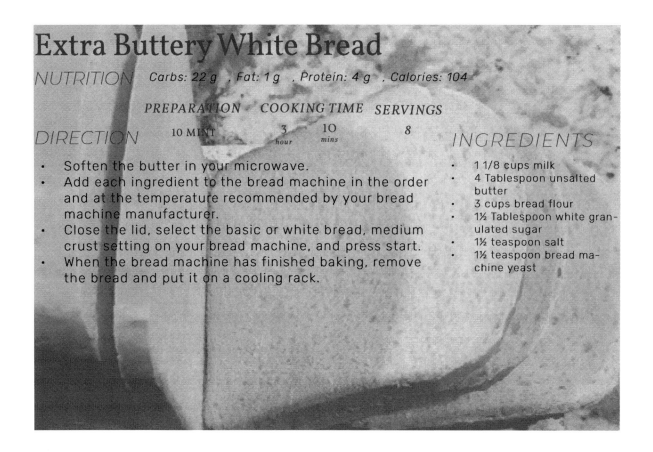

Extra Buttery White Bread

NUTRITION   Carbs: 22 g , Fat: 1 g , Protein: 4 g , Calories: 104

	PREPARATION	COOKING TIME	SERVINGS
DIRECTION	10 MINT	3 hour 10 mins	8

- Soften the butter in your microwave.
- Add each ingredient to the bread machine in the order and at the temperature recommended by your bread machine manufacturer.
- Close the lid, select the basic or white bread, medium crust setting on your bread machine, and press start.
- When the bread machine has finished baking, remove the bread and put it on a cooling rack.

INGREDIENTS

- 1 1/8 cups milk
- 4 Tablespoon unsalted butter
- 3 cups bread flour
- 1½ Tablespoon white granulated sugar
- 1½ teaspoon salt
- 1½ teaspoon bread machine yeast

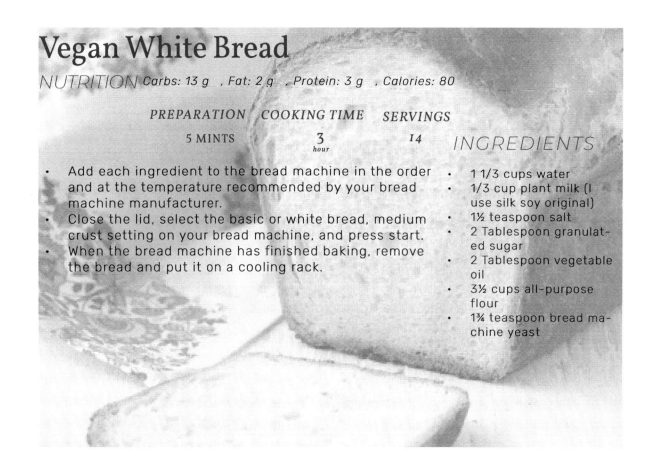

Vegan White Bread

NUTRITION Carbs: 13 g , Fat: 2 g , Protein: 3 g , Calories: 80

	PREPARATION	COOKING TIME	SERVINGS
	5 MINTS	3 hour	14

- Add each ingredient to the bread machine in the order and at the temperature recommended by your bread machine manufacturer.
- Close the lid, select the basic or white bread, medium crust setting on your bread machine, and press start.
- When the bread machine has finished baking, remove the bread and put it on a cooling rack.

INGREDIENTS

- 1 1/3 cups water
- 1/3 cup plant milk (I use silk soy original)
- 1½ teaspoon salt
- 2 Tablespoon granulated sugar
- 2 Tablespoon vegetable oil
- 3½ cups all-purpose flour
- 1¾ teaspoon bread machine yeast

Mom's White Bread

NUTRITION Carbs: 1 g , Fat: 3 g , Protein: 90 g , Calories: 74

PREPARATION	COOKING TIME	SERVINGS
5 MINT	3 *houe*	16

DIRECTION

- Add each ingredient to the bread machine in the order and at the temperature recommended by your bread machine manufacturer.
- Close the lid, select the basic or white bread, medium crust setting on your bread machine, and press start.
- When the bread machine has finished baking, remove the bread and put it on a cooling rack.

INGREDIENTS

- 1 cup and 3 Table-spoon water
- 2 Tablespoon vegeta-ble oil
- 1½ teaspoon salt
- 2 Tablespoon sugar
- 3¼ cups white bread flour
- 2 teaspoon active dry yeast

Rice Flour Rice Bread

NUTRITION Carbs: 24 g , Fat: 1 g , Protein: 2 g , Calories: 95

PREPARATION	COOKING TIME	SERVINGS
10 MINTS	3 *hour*	16

DIRECTION

- In a medium-size bowl, add the oil, water, eggs, and vinegar.
- In a large dish, add the yeast, salt, xanthan gum, dry milk powder, rice flour, and sugar. Mix with a whisk until incorporated.
- Add each ingredient to the bread machine in the order and at the temperature recommended by your bread machine manufacturer.
- Close the lid, select the whole wheat, medium crust setting on your bread machine, and press start.
- When the bread machine has finished baking, remove the bread and put it on a cooling rack.

INGREDIENTS

- 3 eggs
- 1½ cups water
- 3 Tablespoon vegeta-ble oil
- 1 teaspoon apple ci-der vinegar
- 2¼ teaspoon active dry yeast
- 3¼ cups white rice flour
- 2½ teaspoon xanthan gum
- 1½ teaspoon salt
- ½ cup dry milk pow-der
- 3 Tablespoon white sugar

Italian White Bread

NUTRITION Carbs: 11 g , Fat: 1 g , Protein: 2 g , Calories: 78

INGREDIENTS

- ¾ cup cold water
- 2 cups bread flour
- 1 Tablespoon sugar
- 1 teaspoon salt
- 1 Tablespoon olive oil
- 1 teaspoon active dry yeast

DIRECTION

- Add each ingredient to the bread machine in the order and at the temperature recommended by your bread machine manufacturer.
- Close the lid, select the Italian or basic bread, low crust setting on your bread machine, and press start.
- When the bread machine has finished baking, remove the bread and put it on a cooling rack.

PREPARATION	COOKING TIME	SERVINGS
5 *mins*	3 *hour*	*14*

Anadama White Bread

NUTRITION Carbs: 19 g , Fat: 1 g , Protein: 2 g , Calories: 76

INGREDIENTS

- 1 1/8 cups water (110°F/43°C)
- 1/3 cup molasses
- 1½ Tablespoon butter at room temperature
- 1 teaspoon salt
- 1/3 cup yellow cornmeal
- 3½ cups bread flour
- 2½ teaspoon bread machine yeast

DIRECTION

- Add each ingredient to the bread machine in the order and at the temperature recommended by your bread machine manufacturer.
- Close the lid, select the basic bread, low crust setting on your bread machine, and press start.
- When the bread machine has finished baking, remove the bread and put it on a cooling rack.

PREPARATION	COOKING TIME	SERVINGS
10 *mins*	25 *mints*	8

Soft White Bread

NUTRITION Carbs: 18 g , Fat: 1 g , Protein: 4 g , Calories: 74

INGREDIENTS

- 2 cups water
- 4 teaspoon yeast
- 6 Tablespoon sugar
- ½ cup vegetable oil
- 2 teaspoon salt
- 3 cups strong white flour

DIRECTION

- Add each ingredient to the bread machine in the order and at the temperature recommended by your bread machine manufacturer.
- Close the lid, select the basic bread, low crust setting on your bread machine, and press start.
- When the bread machine has finished baking, remove the bread and put it on a cooling rack.

PREPARATION	COOKING TIME	SERVINGS
5 mins	3 hour	14

Chapter 27.
Special Bread Recipes

Gluten-Free Simple Sandwich Bread

NUTRITION Calories: 137, Sodium: 85 mg, Dietary Fiber: 2.7 g, Fat: 4.6 g, Carbs: 22.1 g,

INGREDIENTS

- 1 1/2 cups sorghum flour
- 1 cup tapioca starch or potato starch
- 1/3 cup gluten-free millet flour or gluten-free oat flour
- Two teaspoons xanthan gum
- 1 1/4 teaspoons fine sea salt
- 2 1/2 teaspoons gluten-free yeast for bread machines
- 1 1/4 cups warm water
- Three tablespoons extra virgin olive oil
- One tablespoon honey or raw agave nectar
- 1/2 teaspoon mild rice vinegar or lemon juice
- Two organic free-range eggs, beaten

DIRECTION

- Blend the dry ingredients except for the yeast and set aside.
- Add the liquid ingredients to the bread maker pan first, then gently pour the mixed dry ingredients on top of the liquid.
- Make a well in the center part of the dry ingredients and add the yeast.
- Set for Rapid 1 hour 20 minutes, medium crust color, and press Start.
- In the end, put it on a cooling rack for 15 minutes before slicing to serve.

PREPARATION	COOKING TIME	SERVINGS
15	60	12
mins	mins	

Grain-Free Chia Bread

NUTRITION Calories: 375, Sodium: 462 mg, Dietary Fiber: 22.3 g, Fat: 18.3 g, Carbs: 42 g, Protein: 12.2 g

INGREDIENTS

- 1 cup of warm water
- Three large organic eggs, room temperature
- 1/4 cup olive oil
- One tablespoon apple cider vinegar
- 1 cup gluten-free chia seeds, ground to flour
- 1 cup almond meal flour
- 1/2 cup potato starch
- 1/4 cup coconut flour
- 3/4 cup millet flour
- One tablespoon xanthan gum
- 1 1/2 teaspoons salt
- Two tablespoons sugar
- Three tablespoons nonfat dry milk
- Six teaspoons instant yeast

DIRECTION

- Whisk wet ingredients together and place it in the bread maker pan.
- Whisk dry ingredients, except yeast, together, and add on top of wet ingredients.
- Make a well in the dry ingredients and add yeast.
- Select the Whole Wheat cycle, light crust color, and press Start.
- Allow cooling completely before serving.

PREPARATION	COOKING TIME	SERVINGS
5	3	12
mins	hours	

Gluten-Free Brown Bread

NUTRITION Calories: 201, Sodium: 390 mg, Dietary Fiber: 10.6 g, Fat: 5.7 g, Carbs: 35.5 g, Protein: 5.1 g

INGREDIENTS

- Two large eggs, lightly beaten
- 1 3/4 cups warm water
- Three tablespoons canola oil
- 1 cup brown rice flour
- 3/4 cup oat flour
- 1/4 cup tapioca starch
- 1 1/4 cups potato starch
- 1 1/2 teaspoons salt
- Two tablespoons brown sugar
- Two tablespoons gluten-free flaxseed meal
- 1/2 cup nonfat dry milk powder
- 2 1/2 teaspoons xanthan gum
- Three tablespoons psyllium, whole husks
- 2 1/2 teaspoons gluten-free yeast for bread machines

DIRECTION

- Add the eggs, water, and canola oil to the bread maker pan and stir until combined.
- Whisk all of the dry ingredients except the yeast together in a large mixing bowl.
- Add the dry ingredients on topmost of the wet ingredients.
- Create a well in the center of the dry ingredients and add the yeast.
- Set Gluten-Free cycle, medium crust color, and then press Start.
- When the bread is done, lay the pan on its side to cool before slicing to serve.

PREPARATION	COOKING TIME	SERVINGS
5	3	12
mins	*hour*	

Easy Gluten-Free, Dairy-Free Bread

NUTRITION Calories: 241, Sodium: 164 mg, Dietary Fiber: 5.6 g, Fat: 6.8 g, Carbs: 41 g, Protein: 4.5 g

INGREDIENTS

- 1 1/2 cups warm water
- Two teaspoons active dry yeast
- Two teaspoons sugar
- Two eggs, room temperature
- One egg white, room temperature
- 1 1/2 tablespoons apple cider vinegar
- 4 1/2 tablespoons olive oil
- 3 1/3 cups multi-purpose gluten-free flour

DIRECTION

- Start with adding the yeast and sugar to the water, then stir to mix in a large mixing bowl; set aside until foamy, about 8 to 10 minutes.
- Whisk the two eggs and one egg white together in a separate mixing bowl and add to the bread maker's baking pan.
- Pour apple cider vinegar and oil into baking pan.
- Add foamy yeast/water mixture to baking pan.
- Add the multi-purpose gluten-free flour on top.
- Set for Gluten-Free bread setting and Start.
- Remove and invert the pan onto a cooling rack to remove the bread from the baking pan. Allow cooling completely before slicing to serve.

PREPARATION	COOKING TIME	SERVINGS
15	2	12
mins	*hours*	

Gluten-Free Sourdough Bread

NUTRITION Calories: 299, Sodium: 327 mg, Dietary Fiber: 1.0 g, Fat: 7.3 g, Carbs: 46 g, Protein: 5.2 g

INGREDIENTS

- 1 cup of water
- Three eggs
- 3/4 cup ricotta cheese
- 1/4 cup honey
- 1/4 cup vegetable oil
- One teaspoon cider vinegar
- 3/4 cup gluten-free sourdough starter
- 2 cups white rice flour
- 2/3 cup potato starch
- 1/3 cup tapioca flour
- 1/2 cup dry milk powder
- 3 1/2 teaspoons xanthan gum
- 1 1/2 teaspoons salt

DIRECTION

- Combine wet ingredients and pour into bread maker pan.
- Mix dry ingredients in a large mixing bowl, and add on top of the wet ingredients.
- Select the Gluten-Free cycle and press Start.
- Remove the pan from the machine and allow the bread to remain in the pan for approximately 10 minutes.
- Transfer to a cooling rack before slicing.

PREPARATION	COOKING TIME	SERVINGS
5	3	14
mins	*hour*	

Gluten-Free Crusty Boule Bread

NUTRITION Calories: 480, Sodium: 490 mg, Dietary Fiber: 67.9 g, Fat: 3.2 g, Carbs: 103.9 g, Protein: 2.4 g

INGREDIENTS

- 3 1/4 cups gluten-free flour mix
- One tablespoon active dry yeast
- 1 1/2 teaspoons kosher salt
- One tablespoon guar gum
- 1 1/3 cups warm water
- Two large eggs, room temperature
- Two tablespoons, plus two teaspoons olive oil
- One tablespoon honey

DIRECTION

- Combine all of the dry ingredients, do not include the yeast, in a large mixing bowl; set aside.
- Mix the water, eggs, oil, and honey in a separate mixing bowl.
- Pour the wet ingredients into the bread maker.
- I am adding the dry ingredients on top of the wet ingredients.
- Form a well in the center part of the dry ingredients and add the yeast.
- Set to Gluten-Free setting and press Start.
- Remove baked bread and allow it to cool completely. Hollow out and fill with soup or dip to use as a boule or slice for serving.

PREPARATION	COOKING TIME	SERVINGS
15	3	12
mins	*mins*	

Gluten-Free Potato Bread

NUTRITION Calories: 232, Sodium: 173 mg, Dietary Fiber: 6.3 g, Fat: 13.2 g, Carbs: 17.4 g, Protein: 10.4 g

INGREDIENTS

- One medium russet potato, baked, or mashed leftovers
- Two packets gluten-free quick yeast
- Three tablespoons honey
- 3/4 cup warm almond milk
- Two eggs, one egg white
- 3 2/3 cups almond flour
- 3/4 cup tapioca flour
- One teaspoon sea salt
- One teaspoon dried chive
- One tablespoon apple cider vinegar
- 1/4 cup olive oil

DIRECTION

- Combine the entire dry ingredients, except the yeast, in a large mixing bowl; set aside.
- Whisk together the milk, eggs, oil, apple cider, and honey in a separate mixing bowl.
- Pour the wet ingredients into the bread maker.
- Add the dry ingredients on top of the wet ingredients.
- Produce a well in the dry ingredients and add the yeast.
- Set to Gluten-Free bread setting, light crust color, and press Start.
- Allow cooling completely before slicing.

PREPARATION	COOKING TIME	SERVINGS
5	3	12
mins	*hour*	

Sorghum Bread

NUTRITION Calories: 169, Sodium: 151 mg, Dietary Fiber: 2.5 g, Fat: 6.3 g, Carbs: 25.8 g, Protein: 3.3 g

INGREDIENTS

- 1 1/2 cups sorghum flour
- 1/2 cup tapioca starch
- 1/2 cup brown rice flour
- One teaspoon xanthan gum
- One teaspoon guar gum
- 1/3 teaspoon salt
- Three tablespoons sugar
- 2 1/4 teaspoons instant yeast
- Three eggs (room temperature, lightly beaten)
- 1/4 cup oil
- 1 1/2 teaspoons vinegar
- 3/4-1 cup milk (105 - 115°F)

DIRECTION

- Blend the dry ingredients in a bowl, not including the yeast.
- Add the wet ingredients to the bread maker pan, then add the dry ingredients on top.
- Next is making a well in the center of the dry ingredients and add the yeast.
- Set to Basic bread cycle, light crust color, and press Start.
- Remove and lay on its side to cool on a wire rack before serving.

PREPARATION	COOKING TIME	SERVINGS
5	3	12
mins	*hours*	

Paleo Coconut Bread

NUTRITION Calories: 190, Sodium: 243 mg, Dietary Fiber: 5.2 g, Fat: 10.3 g, Carbs: 20.4 g, Protein: 4.5 g

INGREDIENTS

- Four tablespoons chia seeds
- One tablespoon flax meal
- 3/4 cup, plus one tablespoon water
- 1/4 cup coconut oil
- Three eggs, room temperature
- 1/2 cup almond milk
- One tablespoon honey
- 2 cups almond flour
- 1 1/4 cups tapioca flour
- 1/3 cup coconut flour
- One teaspoon salt
- 1/4 cup flax meal
- Two teaspoons cream of tartar
- One teaspoon baking soda
- Two teaspoons active dry yeast

DIRECTION

- Combine the chia seeds plus a tablespoon of flax meal in a mixing bowl; stir in the water, and set aside.
- Dissolve the coconut oil in a dish, and let it cool down to lukewarm.
- Whisk in the eggs, almond milk, and honey.
- Whisk in the chia seeds and flax meal gel and pour it into the bread maker pan.
- Stir the almond flour, tapioca flour, coconut flour, salt, and 1/4 cup of flax meal.
- Whisk the cream of tartar and baking soda in a separate bowl and combine it with the other dry ingredients.
- Put the dry ingredients into the bread machine.
- Make a little well on top and add the yeast.
- Start the machine on the Wheat cycle, light or medium crust color, and press Start.
- Remove to cool completely before slicing to serve.

PREPARATION	COOKING TIME	SERVINGS
10	3	16
mins	hour	

Gluten-Free Oat and Honey Bread

NUTRITION Calories: 151, Sodium: 265 mg, Dietary Fiber: 4.3 g, Fat: 4.5 g, Carbs: 27.2 g, Protein: 3.5 g

INGREDIENTS

- 1 1/4 cups warm water
- Three tablespoons honey
- Two eggs
- Three tablespoons butter, melted
- 1 1/4 cups gluten-free oats
- 1 1/4 cups brown rice flour
- 1/2 cup potato starch
- Two teaspoons xanthan gum
- 1 1/2 teaspoons sugar
- 3/4 teaspoon salt
- 1 1/2 tablespoons active dry yeast

DIRECTION

- Add ingredients in the order listed above, except for the yeast.
- Then form a well in the center of the dry ingredients and add the yeast.
- Select the Gluten-Free cycle, light crust color, and press Start.
- Remove bread and allow the bread to cool on its side on a cooling rack for 20 minutes before slicing to serve.

PREPARATION	COOKING TIME	SERVINGS
15	3	12
mins	hours	

Gluten-Free Cinnamon Raisin Bread

NUTRITION Calories: 192, Sodium: 173 mg, Dietary Fiber: 4.4 g, Fat: 4.7 g, Carbs: 38.2 g, Protein: 2.7 g

INGREDIENTS

- 3/4 cup almond milk
- Two tablespoons flax meal
- Six tablespoons warm water
- 1 1/2 teaspoons apple cider vinegar
- Two tablespoons butter
- 1 1/2 tablespoons honey
- 1 2/3 cups brown rice flour
- 1/4 cup corn starch
- Two tablespoons potato starch
- 1 1/2 teaspoons xanthan gum
- One tablespoon cinnamon
- 1/2 teaspoon salt
- One teaspoon active dry yeast
- 1/2 cup raisins

DIRECTION

- Mix flax and water and let the mixture stand for 5 minutes.
- Combine dry ingredients in a separate bowl, except for the yeast.
- Add wet ingredients to the bread machine.
- Add the dry mixture on top and make a well in the middle of the dry mix.
- Add the yeast to the well.
- Set to Gluten-Free, light crust color, and press Start.
- After the first kneading and rise cycle, add raisins.
- Remove to a cooling rack when baked and let cool for 15 minutes before slicing.

PREPARATION	COOKING TIME	SERVINGS
5	3	12
mins	hour	

Gluten-Free White Bread

NUTRITION Calories: 151, Sodium: 265 mg, Dietary Fiber: 4.3 g, Fat: 4.5 g, Carbs: 27.2 g, Protein: 3.5 g

INGREDIENTS

- 2 cups white rice flour
- 1 cup potato starch
- 1/2 cup soy flour
- 1/2 cup cornstarch
- 1 tsp. vinegar
- 1 tsp. xanthan gum
- 1 tsp. instant yeast (bread yeast should be gluten-free, but always check)
- 1 1/4 cup buttermilk
- Three eggs
- 1/4 cup sugar or honey
- 1/4 cup coconut or olive oil

DIRECTION

- Place all ingredients in the Cuisinart bread pan in the liquid-dry-yeast layering.
- Put the pan in the Cuisinart bread machine.
- Select the Bake cycle. Choose Gluten Free. Press Start.
- Five minutes into the kneading process, pause the machine and check the firmness of the dough. Add more flour if necessary.
- Resume and wait until the loaf are cooked.
- The machine will start the keep warm mode after the bread is complete.
- Allow it to stay in that mode for about 10 minutes before unplugging.
- Remove the pan and let it cool down for about 10 minutes.

PREPARATION	COOKING TIME	SERVINGS
15	25	8
mins	mints	

Brown Rice Bread

NUTRITION Calories: 151, Sodium: 265 mg, Dietary Fiber: 4.3 g, Fat: 4.5 g, Carbs: 27.2 g, Protein: 3.5 g

INGREDIENTS

- brown rice flour
- Two eggs
- 1 1/4 cup almond milk
- 1 tsp. vinegar
- 1/2 cup coconut oil
- 2 tbsp. sugar
- 1/2 tsp. salt
- 2 1/4 tsp. instant yeast

DIRECTION

- Place all ingredients in the Cuisinart bread pan in the liquid-dry-yeast layering.
- Put the pan in the Cuisinart bread machine.
- Select the Bake cycle. Choose Gluten-free. Press Start.
- Five minutes into the kneading process, pause the machine, and check the consistency of the dough. Add more flour if necessary.
- Resume and wait until the loaf are cooked.
- The machine will start the keep warm mode after the bread is complete.
- Make it stay in that mode for about 10 minutes before unplugging.
- Remove the pan and let it cool down for about 10 minutes.

PREPARATION	COOKING TIME	SERVINGS
10	25	8
mins	mins	

Brown Rice and Cranberry Bread

NUTRITION Calories: 151, Sodium: 265 mg, Dietary Fiber: 4.3 g, Fat: 4.5 g, Carbs: 27.2 g, Protein: 3.5 g

INGREDIENTS

- Three eggs, beaten
- 1 tsp. white vinegar
- 3 tbsp. gluten-free oil
- 1 1/2 cup lukewarm water
- 3 cups brown rice flour
- 1 tbsp. xanthan gum
- 1/4 cup flaxseed meal
- 1 tsp. salt
- 1/4 cup sugar
- 1/2 cup powdered milk
- 2/3 cup cranberries, dried and cut into bits
- 2 1/4 tsp. instant yeast (bread yeast should be gluten-free, but always check)

DIRECTION

- Preparing the Ingredients. Mix all the wet and the dry ingredients, except the yeast and cranberries, separately.
- Place all ingredients in the Cuisinart bread pan in the liquid-dry-yeast layering.
- Put the pan in the Cuisinart bread machine.
- Load the cranberries in the automatic dispenser.
- Select the Bake cycle. Choose Gluten-free. Press start and wait until the loaf is cooked.
- The machine will start the keep warm mode after the bread is complete.
- Let it stay in that mode for around 10 minutes before unplugging.
- Remove the pan and let it cool down for about 10 minutes. Layer them in the bread machine, in the liquid-dry-yeast layering. Do not add the cranberries.

PREPARATION	COOKING TIME	SERVINGS
10	25	8
mins	mints	

Gluten-Free Peasant Bread

NUTRITION Calories: 151, Sodium: 265 mg, Dietary Fiber: 4.3 g, Fat: 4.5 g, Carbs: 27.2 g, Protein: 3.5 g

INGREDIENTS

- 2 cups brown rice flour
- 1 cup potato starch
- 1 tbsp. xanthan gum
- 2 tbsp. sugar
- 2 tbsp. yeast (bread yeast should be gluten-free, but always check)
- 3 tbsp. vegetable oil
- Five eggs
- 1 tsp. white vinegar

DIRECTION

- Preparing the Ingredients. Bloom the yeast in water with the sugar for five minutes.
- Place all ingredients in the Cuisinart bread pan in the yeast-liquid-dry layering.
- Put the pan in the Cuisinart bread machine.
- Select the Bake cycle. Choose Gluten Free. Press start and stand by until the loaf is cooked.
- The machine will start the keep warm mode after the bread is complete.
- Let it stay in that mode for approximately 10 minutes before unplugging.
- Remove the pan and let it cool down for about 10 minutes.

PREPARATION	COOKING TIME	SERVINGS
10	25	8
mins	*mins*	

Gluten-Free Hawaiian Loaf

NUTRITION Calories: 151, Sodium: 265 mg, Dietary Fiber: 4.3 g, Fat: 4.5 g, Carbs: 27.2 g, Protein: 3.5 g

INGREDIENTS

- 4 cups gluten-free four
- 1 tsp. xanthan gum
- 2 1/2 tsp. (bread yeast should be gluten-free, but always check)
- 1/4 cup white sugar
- 1/2 cup softened butter
- One egg, beaten
- 1 cup fresh pineapple juice, warm
- 1/2 tsp. salt
- 1 tsp. vanilla extract

DIRECTION

- Place all ingredients in the Cuisinart bread pan in the liquid-dry-yeast layering.
- Put the pan in the Cuisinart bread machine.
- Select the Bake cycle. Choose Gluten Free. Press open and wait until the loaf is cooked.
- The machine will start the keep warm mode after the bread is complete.
- Let it stay in that mode for 10 minutes before unplugging.
- Remove the pan and let it cool down for about 10 minutes.

PREPARATION	COOKING TIME	SERVINGS
10	25	8
mins	*mints*	

Vegan Gluten-Free Bread

NUTRITION Calories: 151, Sodium: 265 mg, Dietary Fiber: 4.3 g, Fat: 4.5 g, Carbs: 27.2 g,

INGREDIENTS

- 1 cup almond flour
- 1 cup brown or white rice flour
- 2 tbsp. potato flour
- 4 tsp. baking powder
- 1/4 tsp. baking soda
- 1 cup almond milk
- 1 tbsp. white vinegar

DIRECTION

- Place all ingredients in the Cuisinart bread pan in the liquid-dry-yeast layering.
- Put the pan in the Cuisinart bread machine.
- Select the Bake cycle. Choose Gluten Free.
- Press start and wait until the loaf is cooked.
- The machine will start the keep warm mode after the bread is complete.
- Let it stay in that mode for at least 10 minutes before unplugging.
- Remove the pan and let it cool down for about 10 minutes.

PREPARATION	COOKING TIME	SERVINGS
10	25	8
mins	mins	

Oat Sourdough Loaf

NUTRITION Calories: 151, Sodium: 265 mg, Dietary Fiber: 4.3 g, Fat: 4.5 g, Carbs: 27.2 g, Protein: 3.5 g

INGREDIENTS

- 3 cups whole wheat or bread flour
- 250g starter (see Sourdough Starter recipe)
- 1/2 cup water
- 3 tbsp. honey
- 1 tbsp. dark brown sugar or honey
- One stick butter, melted
- 1 tbsp. instant yeast
- 1 tsp. salt
- 3/4 quick-cooking oatmeal

DIRECTION

- Preparing the Ingredients. Grind the oatmeal through the food processor. Next is by merging it with the rest of the dry ingredients, except yeast, in a bowl.
- Place all the liquid ingredients in the bread pan. Add the starter, dry mix, then the yeast.
- Put the pan in the Cuisinart bread machine.
- Select the Bake cycle. Choose Artisan Dough. Press start and stand by until the loaf is cooked.
- The machine will start the keep warm mode after the bread is complete.
- Allow it to remain in that mode for about 10 minutes before unplugging.
- Remove the pan and let it cool down for about 10 minutes.

PREPARATION	COOKING TIME	SERVINGS
10	25	8
mins	mints	

Basic Sourdough Loaf

NUTRITION Calories: 151, Sodium: 265 mg, Dietary Fiber: 4.3 g, Fat: 4.5 g, Carbs: 27.2 g, Protein: 3.5 g

INGREDIENTS

- 3 cups bread flour
- 225g starter (see Sourdough Starter recipe)
- 1/2 cup warm water
- 1 tsp. salt
- 1 1/2 tsp. sugar
- 1 tbsp. oil

DIRECTION

- Preparing the Ingredients. Add the water and the starter to the bread pan. Add the oil, sugar, flour, and salt.
- Put all ingredients in the bread pan in the liquid-dry-yeast layering.
- Put the pan in the Cuisinart bread machine.
- Select the Bake cycle. Choose Artisan Dough. Press start and wait until the loaf is cooked.
- The machine will start the keep warm mode after the bread is complete.
- Allow it to stay in that mode for 10 minutes before unplugging.
- Remove the pan and let it cool down for about 10 minutes.

PREPARATION	COOKING TIME	SERVINGS
10	25	8
mins	*mins*	

Multigrain Sourdough Loaf

NUTRITION Calories: 151, Sodium: 265 mg, Dietary Fiber: 4.3 g, Fat: 4.5 g, Carbs: 27.2 g, Protein: 3.5 g

INGREDIENTS

- 2/3 cup water, at 80°F to 90°F
- ¾ cup Simple Sourdough Starter (See Sourdough Starter recipe), fed, active, and at room temperature
- Two tablespoons melted butter, cooled
- 2½ tablespoons sugar
- ¾ teaspoon salt
- ¾ cup multigrain cereal (Bob's Red Mill or equivalent)
- 2 2/3 cups white bread flour
- 1½ teaspoons bread machine or instant yeast

DIRECTION

- Preparing the Ingredients. Place the ingredients in your Cuisinart bread machine.
- Select the Bake cycle. Program the machine for Whole-Grain bread, select light or medium crust, and press Start.
- When the loaf is finished, remove the bucket from the machine.
- Let the loaf cool for 5 minutes.
- Gently shake the bucket to get the loaf.
- Turn it out onto a cooling rack.

PREPARATION	COOKING TIME	SERVINGS
10	25	8
mins	*mints*	

Sweet Potato Rolls

NUTRITION Carbs – 28 G, Fat – 3 G, Protein – 6 G , Calories – 160

INGREDIENTS

- Two meshed medium sweet potatoes
- 1 cup milk
- 3.2 tablespoons melted butter
- 1 large beaten egg
- 4 cups all-purpose flour
- 4 tablespoons sugar
- 1 teaspoon salt
- 2.5 teaspoons active dry yeast

DIRECTION

- Peel potatoes and cut in cubes
- Boil salted water
- Add potato to water and reduce the heat. Cover the pan and cook for about 22 minutes
- Drain and mash
- Cool and measure 1 cup
- Add Ingredients to the bread machine according to manufacturer's recommendations
- Use the basic dough cycle
- When it finishes, tear pieces to make balls, place in a baking pan
- Cover rolls through a cloth and let rise for about 40 minutes
- Preheat oven to 370 F
- Bake until nicely browned
- Brush the tops with melted or softened butter

PREPARATION	COOKING TIME	SERVINGS
25	40	8
mins	*mints*	

Cinnamon Rolls

NUTRITION Carbs – 28 G, Fat – 3 G, Protein – 6 G , Calories – 160

INGREDIENTS

- 1 cup milk
- 1 large egg
- tablespoons butter
- cups bread flour
- tablespoons sugar
- 0.5 teaspoon salt
- teaspoons active dry yeast
- 0.5 cup butter
- 0.5 cup sugar
- teaspoons cinnamon
- 0.5 teaspoon nutmeg
- 0.3 cup nuts
- 1 cup of powdered sugar
- tablespoons milk
- 0.5 teaspoon vanilla

DIRECTION

- Cinnamon Rolls:
- Add ingredients for the cinnamon rolls to bread machine according to manufacturer's recommendations
- Use dough cycle
- Place dough onto a floured surface when the cycle is done
- Knead the dough for one minute, let it rest for 15 minutes
- Preheat oven to 370 F
- Roll the dough out in a rectangle
- Spread melted butter over the dough
- Sprinkle sugar, cinnamon, nutmeg, chopped nuts
- Roll the dough up on the side
- Press edges and form into evenly shaped roll
- Cut the entire roll into one-inch pieces
- Place rolls into a baking pan
- Cover and let the dough and wait for it to rise until double in size
- This part will take 30 to 45 minutes
- Bake the rolls until golden brown
- Cool in pan for 15 minutes, drizzle with powdered sugar icing
- 1. Combine powdered sugar, milk, vanilla
- 2. Blend until smooth

PREPARATION	COOKING TIME	SERVINGS
5	25	8
mins	mins	

Blueberry Rolls

NUTRITION Carbs – 28 G, Fat – 3 G, Protein – 6 G , Calories – 160

INGREDIENTS

- 1 cup milk
- 1 large egg
- 2 teaspoons vanilla extract
- 3 cups all-purpose flour
- 0.3 cup sugar
- 1.2 teaspoon salt
- 2 tablespoons butter
- 1 tablespoon active dry yeast
- 1.2 cup blueberries
- 1.2 teaspoon cinnamon
- 1 tablespoon water
- 1 large egg yolk
- For the Vanilla Icing:
- 4 cups confectioners' sugar
- 1 tablespoon butter
- 1 teaspoon vanilla extract
- 2 tablespoons water

DIRECTION

- Whisk milk with egg and vanilla extract
- Add milk flour mixture, sugar, salt, butter and yeast to the bread machine pan according to manufacturer's recommendations
- Start on the dough cycle
- Add blueberries and ground cinnamon at beep
- Grease a baking pan
- Put dough onto a floured surface and punch it
- Knead, adding more flour, if needed
- Shape the dough into balls and place them in the prepared round pan
- Cover the pan with a kitchen towel and let the rolls rise for 40 minutes
- Heat the oven to 355 F
- Whisk water and egg yolk
- Brush the mixture over the rolls
- Bake for 25 minutes
- Remove to a rack and let cool
- Icing:
- Combine sugar with melted butter and vanilla extract
- Add hot water
- Transfer the rolls to a rack
- Drizzle the icing over the rolls

PREPARATION	COOKING TIME	SERVINGS
50	40	8
mins	mints	

Mini Maple Cinnamon Rolls

NUTRITION Carbs – 28 G, Fat – 3 G, Protein – 6 G , Calories – 160

INGREDIENTS

- 2 cup whole milk
- 1.2 cup maple syrup
- 1.2 cup butter
- 1 large egg
- 1 teaspoon salt
- 3 cups bread flour
- 0.5 ounces active dry yeast
- 0.5 cup packed brown sugar
- 2 tablespoons bread flour
- 4 teaspoons ground cinnamon
- 2 tablespoons cold butter

DIRECTION

- Select dough setting
- When the cycle completes, turn dough onto a floured surface
- Roll into two rectangles
- Combine brown sugar, flour, cinnamon
- Cut in butter
- Sprinkle half over rectangles
- Roll up, pinch seam to seal
- Cut each into 12 slices
- Place in a baking pan
- Cover and let rise for 20 minutes
- Bake at 370° F until golden brown
- Cool for 5 minutes
- Combine butter, confectioners' sugar, syrup and milk
- Spread over rolls

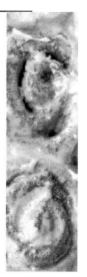

PREPARATION	COOKING TIME	SERVINGS
25 mins	25 mins	12

Golden Honey Pan Rolls

NUTRITION Carbs – 28 G, Fat – 3 G, Protein – 6 G , Calories – 160

INGREDIENTS

- 1.2 cup warm milk
- 1 large egg
- 1 large egg yolk
- 0.5 cup canola oil
- 2 tablespoons honey
- 1 teaspoons salt
- 3.5 cups bread flour
- 2.5 teaspoons active dry yeast

DIRECTION

- Place the first few ingredients in bread machine according to manufacturer's recommendations
- Select dough setting
- Punch down
- Cover and let rest for 12 minutes
- Divide into 24 pieces
- Shape them into balls
- Place in 2 greased baking pans
- Cover and let rise for 30 minutes
- Combine butter, sugar, honey, egg white
- Drizzle over dough
- Bake at 350°F for 20-25 minutes
- Brush with additional honey

PREPARATION	COOKING TIME	SERVINGS
25 mins	35 mints	24

Hawaiian Dinner Rolls

NUTRITION Carbs – 28 G, Fat – 3 G, Protein – 6 G , Calories – 160

INGREDIENTS

- 1 can crushed pineapple
- 0.5 cup pineapple juice
- 0.5 cup water
- 1 large egg
- 0.5 cup butter
- 0.5 cup nonfat milk powder
- 1 tablespoon sugar
- 1.5 teaspoons salt
- 3.5 cups bread flour
- 2.5 teaspoons active dry yeast
- 1 cup sweetened shredded coconut

DIRECTION

- In bread machine pan, place the first 10 Ingredients according to manufacturer's recommendations
- Select dough setting
- Add coconut just before final kneading
- Turn dough onto a lightly floured surface, when cycle is complete
- Cover, let rest for 10 minutes
- Divide into 15 portions
- Roll each portion into a ball. Place in a greased baking pan
- Cover and let rise in until doubled
- Bake at 370°F until golden brown

PREPARATION	COOKING TIME	SERVINGS
25	15	25
mins	mins	

Calzone Rolls

NUTRITION Carbs – 28 G, Fat – 3 G, Protein – 6 G , Calories – 160

INGREDIENTS

- 1.5 cups water
- 2 tablespoons nonfat milk powder
- 2.2 tablespoons sugar
- 2 tablespoons shortening
- 1.5 teaspoons salt
- 4.5 cups all-purpose flour
- 2.5 teaspoons active dry yeast
- 0.5 cup chopped onion
- 0.5 cup sliced fresh mushrooms
- 0.5 cup chopped green pepper
- 0.5 cup chopped sweet red pepper
- 1 tablespoon olive oil
- 1.5 cup pizza sauce
- 0.5 cup diced pepperoni
- 1 cup shredded pizza cheese blend
- 0.5 cup chopped ripe olives

DIRECTION

- In bread machine pan, put all the first 7 Ingredients according to manufacturer's recommendations
- Select dough setting
- Sauté the onion, mushrooms and peppers in oil in a skillet
- Cool
- Turn onto a floured surface
- Divide in half
- Rest for 5 minutes
- Roll each portion into rectangle and spread with pizza sauce
- Top with pepperoni, onion mixture, pizza cheese and olives
- Roll up each rectangle
- Cut each into 12 slices
- Place slices cut side down in 2 oiled skillets
- Sprinkle with Parmesan cheese
- Cover and let rise until doubled
- Bake at 370°F
- Serve warm

PREPARATION	COOKING TIME	SERVINGS
5	25	12
mins	mints	

Cheese Stuffed Garlic Rolls

NUTRITION Carbs – 28 G, Fat – 3 G, Protein – 6 G , Calories – 160

INGREDIENTS

- 3.2 cup bread flour
- 1.2 teaspoons salt
- 2 teaspoons granulated sugar
- 2.2 teaspoons olive oil
- 1 cup warm water
- 1 package active dry yeast
- 4 stick mozzarella string cheese sticks
- 0.5 stick melted butter
- 1 garlic salt

DIRECTION

- Heat the water
- Add yeast and stir
- Let sit for 10 minutes
- Pour yeast mixture in the bread pan
- Add sugar, flour, oil and salt
- Set machine to the dough cycle
- Let the cycle finish
- Remove from bread pan after the first rise
- Knead dough until no longer sticky on a floured surface
- Cut cheese sticks into 4 equal size pieces
- Pinch off dough pieces and place a cut piece of cheese into center
- Form ball around the cheese
- After cheese is secured, edges sealed, roll the ball to form a rounder ball
- Spray non-stick cooking spray on a pan
- Place each ball about an inch apart
- Cover, let rise until doubled
- Preheat oven to 345°F after dough has risen
- Bake for 15-20 minutes
- Mix melted butter and garlic
- Brush this mix over hot rolls
- Serve with pizza or spaghetti sauce

PREPARATION	COOKING TIME	SERVINGS
5 mins	25 mins	4

Whole Wheat Rolls

NUTRITION Carbs – 28 G, Fat – 3 G, Protein – 6 G , Calories – 160

INGREDIENTS

- 1 cup warm milk
- 0.5 cup room temperature butter
- 2 eggs
- 1 cup all-purpose flour
- 1.2 teaspoons salt
- 3.2 cup whole wheat flour
- 3.2 teaspoons instant yeast
- 0.5 cup warm milk

DIRECTION

- Place all Ingredients according to manufacturer's recommendations
- Start dough cycle
- When cycle is finished, remove from pan
- Shape dough pieces into balls
- Place on a greased baking sheet
- Let rolls rise for about 40 min. before baking
- Preheat oven to 345°F
- Bake rolls for 20 to 25
- Remove from oven and let cool
- Serve warm

PREPARATION	COOKING TIME	SERVINGS
50 mins	25 mints	8

Yeast Rolls

NUTRITION Carbs – 28 G, Fat – 3 G, Protein – 6 G , Calories – 160

INGREDIENTS

- 0.5 cup water
- 0.5 cup milk
- 1 egg
- 1.5 cup butter
- 1.5 cup sugar
- 1.2 teaspoons sall
- 3.5 cup all-purpose flour
- 2.5 teaspoons yeast
- 0.5 cup melted butter

DIRECTION

- Place all Ingredients: into bread maker as recorded. EXCLUDE THE MELTED BUTTER
- Hand-picked dough cycle
- When finished shape dough into balls
- Brush dough with 0.5 c. melted butter
- Conceal and let rise 1 hour or longer
- Bake 375° for 15 minutes

PREPARATION	COOKING TIME	SERVINGS
60	25	8
mins	*hour*	

Butter Rolls

NUTRITION Carbs – 28 G, Fat – 3 G, Protein – 6 G , Calories – 160

INGREDIENTS

- 1 cup warm milk
- 0.5 cup butter
- 0.5 cup sugar
- Two eggs
- 1.4 teaspoons salt
- 4 cup bread flour
- 2.5 teaspoons active dry yeast

DIRECTION

- In the bread machine, add butter, warm milk, softened eggs
- Set dough cycle
- Form into balls
- Put in greased pan
- Grease pan with butter and form the small balls per butter roll
- Cover and let rise until doubled.
- Bake at 350°F for 18 minutes
- Check at 15 minutes

PREPARATION	COOKING TIME	SERVINGS
5	25	8
mins	*mints*	

Beer Rolls

NUTRITION Calories: 159 calories;, Total Fat: 2.7 , Sodium: 56 , Total Carbohydrate: 27.9 , Cholesterol: 4 , Protein: 4.4

PREPARATION	COOKING TIME	SERVINGS
5	25 mins	8

DIRECTION

- Let a 10-12-oz beer sit for a couple of hours until it gets to room temperature and is no longer fizzy. The process will take about 3-4 hours.
- In the bread machine pan, put in the flattened beer, butter, cinnamon, salt, and honey. Set in the flour and yeast making sure that the yeast won't get in contact with the liquid. Choose the Dough cycle on the machine and press the Start button to run the machine.
- Take the dough out from the bread machine pan once it has expanded in size. Shape the dough into a long loaf, then cut the loaf into even pieces and shape each portion into dinner rolls. Put the rolls on a baking sheet enclosed with flour, cover the rolls, and let it rise in volume for about 45 minutes.
- Use a brush to coat the top of the rolls with melted butter.
- Put in the preheated 350°F (175°C) oven and bake for 30 minutes until it turns golden brown.

INGREDIENTS

- 4 cups bread flour
- Two tablespoons honey
- 1/4 teaspoon salt
- One tablespoon margarine
- 10 ounces dark beer
- 1 (.25 ounce) package active dry yeast
- One pinch of ground cinnamon
- Two tablespoons butter, melted

Bread Machine Rolls

NUTRITION Calories: 165 calories;, Sodium: 227 , Total Carbohydrate: 29.5 , Cholesterol: 6 , Protein: 5.6 , Total Fat: 2.5

PREPARATION	COOKING TIME	SERVINGS
5 MINTS	25 mins	8

DIRECTION

- In the bread machine, place the bread flour, sugar, salt, milk powder, water, butter, and yeast in this order or the order suggested by the manufacturer.
- Pick the Dough cycle on the machine and press the Start button.
- Take the risen dough from the bread machine and deflate it; put it on a clean surface that is a little bit floured. Separate the dough into 12 even portions and shape them into balls. On lightly greased baking sheets, put in the dough balls. Make use of a somewhat wet cloth to cover the dough rolls and allow it to rise in volume for about 40 minutes until it has doubled in size. While waiting for the preheat the oven to 350°F (175°C).
- Combine two tablespoons of water and egg white in a small bowl and use a brush to coat the rolls with it slightly. Put it in the warm-up oven and bake for 15 minutes until the rolls turn golden brown.

INGREDIENTS

- 3 cups bread flour
- Three tablespoons white sugar
- One teaspoon salt
- 1/4 cup dry milk powder
- 1 cup of warm water
- Two tablespoons butter softened
- 1 (.25 ounce) package active dry yeast
- One egg white
- Two tablespoons water

Honey Brown Rolls

NUTRITION Calories: 212 calories;, Total Fat: 3 , Sodium: 211 , Total Carbohydrate: 42.3 , Cholesterol: 5 , Protein: 6

PREPARATION	COOKING TIME	SERVINGS
5 MINT	25 mins	8

DIRECTION

- In the bread machine pan, place the water, butter, honey, sugar, whole wheat flour, bread flour, instant coffee granules, cocoa powder, vital wheat gluten, yeast, and salt in the order the manufacturer recommended. Select dough setting, then press Start and wait for the cycle to be completed.
- Transfer the pan with dough from the machine, and prepare warm water to put the pan in (about 32 degrees C, 90 degrees F). Cover the pan using a towel, and allow the bread to rise about 60 minutes until doubled.
- On a floured work surface, turn the dough out, and punch down. Separate into three portions for small loaves or 12 equal parts for rolls. Shape into balls. Prepare a parchment paper-lined baking sheet, and put rolls on. Spread sesame seeds. Wait for it rises in a warm environment, about half of an hour until doubled
- Prepare the oven to 175 degrees C (350 degrees F).
- Spray water inside the preheated oven, and put rolls into the oven right after. Bake for 15 to 20 minutes until light golden brown for rolls. With loaves, bake for 20 to 25 minutes, until they are brown and sound hollow when tapping.

INGREDIENTS

- 1 1/2 cups warm water
- One tablespoon white sugar
- Two tablespoons butter
- 1/2 cup honey
- 2 cups bread flour
- 1 2/3 cups whole wheat flour
- One tablespoon vital wheat gluten (optional)
- One tablespoon unsweetened cocoa powder
- Two teaspoons instant coffee granules
- One teaspoon salt
- 2 1/4 teaspoons bread machine yeast
- Two teaspoons sesame seeds for sprinkling (optional)

Hot Ube Pan desal (Filipino Purple Yam Bread Rolls)

NUTRITION Calories: 77 calories;, Sodium: 136 , Total Carbohydrate: 6.5 , Cholesterol: 27 , Protein: 2 , Total Fat: 4.8

PREPARATION	COOKING TIME	SERVINGS
5	25 mins	8

DIRECTION

- Into a microwave-safe bowl, pour the milk, and then heat for about 1 minute in the microwave until warm.
- Into a microwave-safe bowl, add the butter, and then heat for about 30 seconds in the microwave until melted.
- In a bowl, put the eggs and then cover with warm water for one minute. Drain the water and then crack into the bowl. Use a fork to beat lightly.
- Into the bread machine, add the following in this order; warm milk, melted butter, eggs, salt, bread flour, purple yam powder, and bread machine yeast. Then set the machine to the "Dough" cycle.
- Preheat the oven.
- Place the dough into a greased bowl. Then use your fist to deflate the dough. Chop into 24 oval pieces. Fold every piece to form a ball.
- Into a shallow plate, add bread crumbs, and fold the dough balls in the bread crumbs until coated. Transfer into an ungreased baking pan, placing close together and touching each other a bit.
- Bake for around 15 minutes using the oven or wait until the tops become golden brown.

INGREDIENTS

- 1 1/2 cups 2% milk
- 1/2 cup unsalted butter
- Two eggs
- One teaspoon salt
- 3 cups bread flour
- 1 (4 ounces) packet purple yam powder or more to taste
- 3 1/2 teaspoons bread machine yeast
- 1/2 cup unseasoned bread crumbs

Oatmeal Sourdough Rolls

NUTRITION Calories: 126 calories, Protein: 3 , Total Fat: 4.3 , Sodium: 173 , Total Carbo-hydrate: 18.9, Cholesterol: 8

PREPARATION	COOKING TIME	SERVINGS
5	25 mins	8

DIRECTION

- Into the bread machine pan, put the ingredients according to the order given by the manufacturer. Choose the Dough Cycle and then push the Start button.
- Once the cycle is complete, place the dough onto a lightly floured surface and separate into 24 rolls. Cover using a towel and allow the rolls to rise for about 1 hour until doubled.
- Preheat the oven, then coat a large baking sheet lightly with grease.
- Spread the rolls onto the baking sheet prepared and then bake for about 10 to 12 minutes until browned lightly.

INGREDIENTS

- 1 cup sourdough starter
- 1/2 cup warm water
- Three tablespoons honey
- One tablespoon molasses
- One egg, lightly beaten
- 1/2 cup margarine
- 1/2 cup quick-cooking oats
- 3 cups all-purpose flour
- One teaspoon salt
- 1/2 teaspoon baking soda
- Two teaspoons yeast

Potato Rosemary Rolls

NUTRITION Calories: 46 calories;, Total Fat: 2.8 , Sodium: 529 , Total Carbohydrate: 4.2 , Cholesterol: 18 , Protein: 1.4

PREPARATION	COOKING TIME	SERVINGS
5 MINTS	25 mins	8

DIRECTION

- Add and measure warm water, dry milk, olive oil, rosemary, potato flakes, bread flour, sugar, salt, and yeast in your bread machine pan in the order the manufacturer suggested. Set the machine to the Dough cycle and press Start.
- Separate dough into 12 pieces. To each sample, shape into a 10-inch rope; the rope comes up through the middle, coil rope and tuck in the end. On a baking sheet dusted with cornmeal, put 2 inches apart. Cover and allow to rise for 45 minutes.
- Spread with melted butter or egg glaze on the top and lightly sprinkle kosher salt—Bake for 15 to 20 minutes at 190 degrees C (375 degrees F).

INGREDIENTS

- 1 1/8 cups warm water
- Two tablespoons olive oil
- Two tablespoons nonfat dry milk powder
- 1/2 cup dry potato flakes
- One tablespoon white sugar
- One teaspoon dried rosemary, crushed
- One teaspoon salt
- 3 cups bread flour
- 1 1/2 teaspoons bread machine yeast
- One tablespoon cornmeal
- One egg, beaten
- Two teaspoons kosher salt

Pull-Apart Hot Cross Buns

NUTRITION Calories: 415 calories; , Total Carbohydrate: 76.9 , Cholesterol: 38 , Protein: 6.7 , Total Fat: 9.2, Sodium: 124

PREPARATION	COOKING TIME	SERVINGS
5 MINT	25 mins	8

DIRECTION

- Drizzle yeast atop the warm water and allow to sit for about 5 minutes until dissolved. Into a bread machine, add flour, salt, sugar, and cardamom, 1 1/4 cups of milk, butter, and egg. Then top with yeast mixture. Cover with the lid and use the Dough setting. In case you are using dried cranberries, dried cherries, or raisins, add them after the beep sound.
- Once the dough has completed, separate into 12 parts and then form into balls. Transfer them into a 9x13 inch baking dish that is greased. Use plastic wrap to cover and reserve to rise for about 45 minutes until doubled in volume.
- Preheat an oven to 175 degrees C (350 degrees F). Peel off the plastic wrap from rolls. Then bake for about 20 to 25 minutes in the oven until turned golden brown. Prepare the frosting by whisking almond extract, 1/4 cup of milk, and confectioners' sugar together until smooth. Once the buns cool, sprinkle frosting on top of them in a cross pattern.

INGREDIENTS

- 1 (.25 ounce) package active dry yeast
- 1/4 cup water
- 4 1/4 cups all-purpose flour
- 1/4 teaspoon salt
- 1/2 cup white sugar
- One teaspoon ground cardamom
- 1 1/4 cups lukewarm milk
- 1/2 cup butter, melted
- One egg
- 1/4 cup golden raisins (optional)
- 1/4 cup dried cherries (optional)
- 1/4 cup dried cranberries (optional)
- 2 1/2 cups confectioners' sugar
- 1/4 cup milk
- One teaspoon almond extract

Soft Onion Sandwich Rolls

NUTRITION Calories: 260 calories, Sodium: 487 , Total Carbohydrate: 45.9 , Cholesterol: 13 , Protein: 6.9 , Total Fat: 5.3

PREPARATION	COOKING TIME	SERVINGS
10 MINTS	25 mins	8

DIRECTION

- Into the bread machine pan, add the following in this order: milk, water, butter, salt, sugar, onion powder, three tablespoons of dried onion, potato flakes, flour, and yeast. Then use the Dough cycle and start the machine.
- After the cycle has ended, take out the dough from the machine and knead on a lightly floured surface. Chop into eight equal pieces and shape into balls. Then flatten the balls gently until they're four inches in diameter. In case the balls keep shrinking back, let them rest for 1 minute before flattening. Transfer onto a baking sheet and then use a towel to cover loosely. Place in a draft-free place to rise for about 40 minutes until doubled in volume.
- Preheat an oven to 175 degrees C (350 degrees F). In a cup, whisk together the water and egg white. Rub across the tops of the risen rolls and drizzle with the remaining minced onion.
- Bake for about 15 to 20 minutes until turning golden brown. Let to cool completely and then cut horizontally in half before serving.

INGREDIENTS

- 3/4 cup lukewarm milk
- Five tablespoons lukewarm water
- Three tablespoons butter softened
- 1 1/2 teaspoons salt
- Three tablespoons white sugar
- One teaspoon onion powder
- Three tablespoons dried minced onion
- 1/4 cup instant potato flakes
- 3 cups all-purpose flour
- 1 (.25 ounce) envelope active dry yeast
- One egg white
- One tablespoon water
- 1/4 cup dried minced onion

Fruit Bread

NUTRITION Carbohydrates 5 g . Fats 10.9 g . Protein 10.8 g . Calories 441

	PREPARATION	COOKING TIME	SERVINGS
DIRECTION	3	0 MINS	8

DIRECTION

- Put all of the ingredients to your bread machine, carefully following the instructions of the manufacturer (except fruits).
- Set the program of your bread machine to basic/sweet and set crust type to light or medium.
- Press starts.
- Once the machine beeps, add fruits.
- Wait until the cycle completes.
- Once the loaf is ready, take the bucket out and let the loaf cool for 5 minutes.
- Gently shake the bucket to remove loaf.
- Move it to a cooling rack, slice and serve.
- Enjoy!

INGREDIENTS

- 1 egg
- 1 cup milk
- tablespoons rum
- ¼ cup butter
- ¼ cup brown sugar
- cups almond flour
- 1 tablespoon instant yeast
- 1 teaspoon salt
- Fruits:
- ¼ cups dried apricots, coarsely chopped
- ¼ cups prunes, coarsely chopped
- ¼ cups candied cherry, pitted
- ½ cups seedless raisins
- ¼ cup almonds, chopped

Marzipan Cherry Bread

NUTRITION Carbohydrates 4.2 g , Fats 16.4 g , Protein 12.2 g , Calories 511

PREPARATION	COOKING TIME	SERVINGS
3	0 *houe*	8

DIRECTION

- Put all of the ingredients to your bread machine, carefully following the instructions of the manufacturer (except marzipan and cherry).
- Set the program of your bread machine to basic/sweet and set crust type to light or medium.
- Press starts.
- Once the machine beeps, add marzipan and cherry.
- Wait until the cycle completes.
- Once the loaf is ready, take the bucket out and let the loaf cool for 5 minutes.
- Gently shake the bucket to remove loaf.
- Move it to a cooling rack, slice and serve.
- Enjoy!

INGREDIENTS

- 1 egg
- ¾ cup milk
- 1 tablespoon almond liqueur
- tablespoons orange juice
- ½ cup ground almonds
- ¼ cup butter
- 1/3 cup sugar
- cups almond flour
- 1 tablespoon instant yeast
- 1 teaspoon salt
- ½ cup marzipan
- ½ cup dried cherries, pitted

Ginger Prune Bread

NUTRITION Carbohydrates 4 g , Fats 8.3 g , Protein 10.1 g , Calories 387

PREPARATION	COOKING TIME	SERVINGS
3	0 *hour*	8

DIRECTION

- Put all of the ingredients to your bread machine, carefully following the instructions of the manufacturer (except ginger and prunes).
- Set the program of your bread machine to basic/sweet and set crust type to light or medium.
- Press starts.
- Once the machine beeps, add ginger and prunes.
- Wait until the cycle completes.
- Once the loaf is ready, take the bucket out and let the loaf cool for 5 minutes.
- Gently shake the bucket to remove loaf.
- Move it to a cooling rack, slice and serve.
- Enjoy!

INGREDIENTS

- eggs
- 1 cup milk
- ¼ cup butter
- ¼ cup sugar
- cups almond flour
- 1 tablespoon instant yeast
- 1 teaspoon salt
- 1 cup prunes, coarsely chopped
- 1 tablespoon fresh ginger, grated

Lemon Fruit Bread

NUTRITION Carbohydrates 3.9 g, Fats 10.6 g, Protein 10 g , Calories 438 , Total fat 10.6 , Saturated fat 4.9 g, Cholesterol 38 mg

	PREPARATION	COOKING TIME	SERVINGS
DIRECTION	3	0 hour	8

INGREDIENTS

- Put all of the ingredients to your bread machine, carefully following the instructions of the manufacturer (except fruits, zest, and nuts).
- Set the program of your bread machine to basic/sweet and set crust type to light or medium.
- Press starts.
- Once the machine beeps, add fruits, zest, and nuts.
- Wait until the cycle completes.
- Once the loaf is ready, take the bucket out and let the loaf cool for 5 minutes.
- Gently shake the bucket to remove loaf.
- Move to a cooling rack, slice and serve.
- Enjoy!

- 1 egg
- 1 cup milk
- ¼ cup butter
- 1/3 cup sugar
- cups almond flour
- 1 tablespoon instant yeast
- 1 teaspoon salt
- ½ cup candied lemons
- 1½ teaspoon lemon zest, grated
- ½ cup raisins
- ½ cup cashew nuts

Homemade Omega-3 Bread

NUTRITION Carbohydrates 4.5 g, Fats 9 g , Protein 11.1 g , Calories 289

	PREPARATION	COOKING TIME	SERVINGS
DIRECTION	3.5	0 hour	8

INGREDIENTS

- Soak the flaxseeds in cool water for 30 minutes.
- Combine all the liquid ingredients in the bread pan, then add sifted almond flour, flaxseed flour, yeast, sugar, and salt.
- Set it to the basic program.
- After the signal sounds, add sesame seeds and strained flaxseeds.

- 3/5 cup milk
- ½ cup water
- eggs
- tablespoons rapeseed oil
- cups almond flour
- 1 cup flax flour
- teaspoons dry yeast
- teaspoons salt
- tablespoons cane sugar
- tablespoons flaxseeds
- 1 tablespoon sesame seeds

Ham & Cheese Rolls

NUTRITION Protein: 17 grams, Net carbs: 3 gram, Fat: 13 grams, Sugar: 1 gram,, Calories: 198

PREPARATION	COOKING TIME	SERVINGS
20	0 hour	6

DIRECTION

- Heat the stove to the temperature of 375° Fahrenheit. Prepare a flat sheet with a layer of baking lining.
- Blend the diced ham, eggs, mozzarella, and cheddar cheese in a glass dish until integrated well.
- Heat for approximately 18 minutes in the stove until they turn slightly golden.
- Enjoy immediately.

INGREDIENTS

- 0.5 cup cheddar cheese, shredded
- 1 cup deli ham, diced
- 0.75 cup mozzarella cheese, shredded
- large eggs
- 0.5 cup parmesan cheese, grated
- Standard sized flat sheet

Low Carb Carrot Bread

NUTRITION 128 calories, Fat 15g, Carbohydrates 5g, Protein 5g

PREPARATION	COOKING TIME	SERVINGS
4.5 HOURS	0 hour	1 loaf

DIRECTION

- Using a bread machine, add in the flour, baking powder, xanthan gum, baking soda, cinnamon, ginger, nutmeg, sweetener, almond milk, butter, vanilla extract, maple extract, vinegar, eggs, shredded carrots, and salt to taste in the order recommended by the machine manufacturer.
- Set the bread machine to basic bread, select the crust color and loaf size if desired then bake the carrot bread according to the instructions on the machine.
- Once baked, place the bread on a rack to cool for a few minutes, slice and serve.

INGREDIENTS

- Teaspoons of cinnamon.
- 1/2 teaspoon of ginger.
- 1/4 teaspoon of nutmeg.
- Tablespoons of granulated sweetener.
- 1/3 cup of unsweetened almond milk.
- 1/2 cup of melted butter.
- 1 teaspoon of vanilla extract.
- 1 teaspoon of maple extract.
- 1/2 teaspoon of apple

Raisin Bread Delis

NUTRITION Calories 132, Fat 6.58g, Carbohydrates 12.36g, Fiber 6.02g, Protein 6.28g.

PREPARATION	COOKING TIME	SERVINGS
1.5 HOURS	0 hour	15 slices

DIRECTION

- Using a bread machine, add in the coconut flour, almond flour, psyllium husk powder, chopped raisins, sweetener, baking powder, cinnamon, egg whites, butter, vinegar, and salt to taste in the order recommended by the machine manufacturer then set the machine to basic bread setting.
- Pick the crust color and loaf size if desired then bake the carrot bread according to the instructions on the machine.
- Once baked, place the bread on a rack to cool for a few minutes, slice and serve.

INGREDIENTS

- 1/2 cup of coconut flour.
- 1/2 cup of almond flour.
- Tablespoons of psyllium husk powder.
- 1/4 cup of chopped raisins.
- Tablespoons of swerve.
- 1 tablespoon of baking powder.
- 1/2 teaspoon of ground cinnamon.
- 1/4 teaspoon of salt to taste.
- Cups of egg whites.
- Tablespoons of melted butter.
- Tablespoons of apple cider vinegar

Amazing Buttery Dinner Buns

NUTRITION Calories: 135, Total Fat: 2g, Saturated Fat: 0g, Protein: 4g, Carbs: 26g, Fiber: 1g, Sugar: 10g

PREPARATION	COOKING TIME	SERVINGS
3.5 HOURS	0 hour	15-20 Buns

DIRECTION

- Put all of the ingredients to your Bread Machine (except melted butter).
- Set the program to "Dough" cycle and let the cycle run.
- Remove the dough (using lightly floured hands) and carefully place it on a floured surface.
- Cover with a light film/cling paper and let the dough rise for 10 minutes.
- Take a large cookie sheet and grease with butter.
- Cut the risen dough into 15-20 pieces and shape them into balls.
- Place the balls onto the sheet (2 inches apart) and cover.
- Place in a warm place and let them rise for 30-40 minutes until the dough doubles.
- Preheat your oven at 375 degrees F, transfer the cookie sheet to your oven and bake for 12-15 minutes.
- Brush the top with a bit of butter, enjoy!

INGREDIENTS

- 1 cup water
- tablespoons butter
- 1 whole egg
- and ¼ cups bread flour
- ¼ cup sugar
- 1 teaspoon salt
- teaspoon active dry yeast

Delicious Multigrain Buns

NUTRITION Calories: 145, Total Fat: 2g, Saturated Fat: 1g, Protein: 4g, Carbs: 27, Fiber: 1g, Sugar: 10g

PREPARATION	COOKING TIME	SERVINGS
3.5 HOURS	0 houe	15-20 Buns

DIRECTION

- Put all of the ingredients to your Bread Machine (except melted butter).
- Set the program to "Dough" cycle and let the cycle run.
- Remove the dough (using lightly floured hands) and carefully place it on a floured surface.
- Cover with a light film/cling paper and let the dough rise for 10 minutes.
- Take a large cookie sheet and grease with butter.
- Cut the risen dough into 15-20 pieces and shape them into balls.
- Place the balls onto the sheet (2 inches apart) and cover.
- Place in a warm place and let them rise for 30-40 minutes until the dough doubles.
- Brush the top with a bit of butter, enjoy!

INGREDIENTS

- Melted Butter for grease
- ½ tablespoons honey
- ½ teaspoon salt
- ½ cup multigrain flour
- 1 and ½ cups white bread flour
- 1 teaspoon active dry yeast

Lemon and Poppy Buns

NUTRITION Calories: 231, Total Fat: 11g, Saturated Fat: 1g, Protein: 4g, Carbs: 31g, Fiber: 1g, Sugar: 12g

PREPARATION	COOKING TIME	SERVINGS
3.5 HOURS	0 hour	10-20 Buns

DIRECTION

- Put all of the ingredients to your Bread Machine (except melted butter).
- Set the program to "Dough" cycle and let the cycle run.
- Remove the dough (using lightly floured hands) and carefully place it on a floured surface.
- Cover with a light film/cling paper and let the dough rise for 10 minutes.
- Take a large cookie sheet and grease with butter.
- Cut the risen dough into 15-20 pieces and shape them into balls.
- Place the balls onto the sheet (2 inches apart) and cover.
- Place in a warm place and let them rise for 30-40 minutes until the dough doubles.
- Preheat your oven at 375 degrees F, transfer the cookie sheet to your oven and bake for 12-15 minutes.
- Brush the top with a bit of butter, enjoy!

INGREDIENTS

- Melted Butter for grease
- 1 and 1/3 cups hot water
- tablespoons powdered milk
- tablespoons Crisco shortening
- 1 and ½ teaspoon salt
- 1 tablespoon lemon juice
- and ¼ cups bread flour
- ½ teaspoon nutmeg
- teaspoons grated lemon rind
- tablespoons poppy seeds
- 1 and ¼ teaspoons yeast
- teaspoons wheat gluten

Sweet Easter Bread

NUTRITION 150 calories, 11.6 g fat, 3.4 g total carb, 9.6 g protein

PREPARATION	COOKING TIME	SERVINGS
5 MINT	35 mins	20 slices

DIRECTION

- Add all ingredients to the Bread Machine.
- Select Dough setting and press Start. Mix the ingredients for about 4-5 minutes. After that press stop button.
- Smooth out the top of the loaf. Choose Bake mode and press Start. Let it bake for about 30 minutes.
- Remove bread from the bread machine and let it rest for 10 minutes. Enjoy!

INGREDIENTS

- teaspoons baking powder
- 1 cup water
- 1/2 cups almond flour
- 1/4 cup almond milk/ heavy cream
- cups whey isolate
- 1/2 cup sugar substitute
- 1/2 teaspoon salt
- 1/2 cup butter, melted
- teaspoons xanthan gum

Zucchini Apple Fritter Bread

NUTRITION 171 calories, 15 g fat, 6 g total carbs, 4 g protein

PREPARATION	COOKING TIME	SERVINGS
5 MINTS	1 hour	12 slices

DIRECTION

- Add all ingredients to the Bread Machine.
- Select Dough setting and press Start. Mix the ingredients for about 4-5 minutes. After that press stop button.
- Smooth out the top of the loaf. Choose Bake mode and press Start. Let it bake for about 50 minutes.
- For glaze, mix together 2-3 tablespoons heavy cream and 1/4 cup
- Remove bread from the bread machine, let it rest a little and drizzle glaze over zucchini apple fritter bread.

INGREDIENTS

- teaspoons apple extract
- 1 medium zucchini peeled, seeded and chopped
- 1/4 cup Sorkin Gold
- 1/2 cup unsweetened almond milk
- 1 teaspoon cinnamon
- 1/2 teaspoon xanthan gum (optional)
- 1/2 cup low carb sugar substitute
- teaspoons baking powder
- 1/2 cup butter, softened
- 1/2 cup coconut flour
- eggs
- 1 cup almond flour
- Glaze:
- 2-3 tablespoons heavy cream
- 1/4 cup SukrinMelis

Peanut Flour Bread

NUTRITION 152 calories, 13 g fat, 3 g total carbs, 7 g protein

PREPARATION	COOKING TIME	SERVINGS
5 MINT	1 *houe*	12

DIRECTION

- Add all ingredients to the Bread Machine.
- Select Dough setting and press Start. Mix the ingredients for about 4-5 minutes. After that press stop button.
- Smooth out the top of the loaf. Choose Bake mode and press Start. Let it bake for about 55 minutes.
- Remove bread from the bread machine and let it rest for 10 minutes. Enjoy!

INGREDIENTS

- eggs
- 1 teaspoon baking powder
- 1/2 cup butter
- tsp guar gum/xanthan gum (optional)
- oz. cream cheese
- 1 1/3 cups peanut flour
- 3/4 cup low carb sugar substitute
- 1 teaspoon vanilla extract

Summer Squash Bread

NUTRITION 154 calories, 14 g fat, 10 g total carbs, 5 g protein

PREPARATION	COOKING TIME	SERVINGS
15 MINTS	45 *mins*	8

DIRECTION

- Add all ingredients to the Bread Machine.
- Select Dough setting and press Start. Mix the ingredients for about 4-5 minutes. After that press stop button.
- Smooth out the top of the loaf. Choose Bake mode and press Start. Let it bake for about 50 minutes.
- Remove bread from the bread machine and let it rest for 10 minutes. Enjoy!

INGREDIENTS

- 1 teaspoon sugar-free vanilla extract
- 1 cup summer squash, shredded
- eggs, beaten
- 1/4 teaspoon ground nutmeg
- 1/2 cup Swerve or Sukrin
- 1 1/2 teaspoons ground cinnamon
- 1/4 cup butter, melted
- 1 1/2 teaspoons baking powder
- tablespoons vegetable oil
- 1 1/2 cups Carbquik

Fathead Dough Bagels

NUTRITION 360 calorie, 28 g fat, 8 g total carbs, 21 g protein

	PREPARATION	COOKING TIME	SERVINGS
DIRECTION	5	12 mins	6

- Line baking sheet with parchment paper.
- Add all ingredients to the Bread Machine.
- Select Dough setting. When the time is over, transfer the dough to the floured surface. Shape it into a ball and cut into about 6 even pieces.
- Form a long log with every part and join both ends, forming a bagel shape, then place on a baking sheet. Form all bagels in this way.
- Sprinkle bagels with sesame seeds and press them gently into dough, if needed.
- Bake in a preheated oven at 400 F until golden and firm, for about 10-14 minutes.

INGREDIENTS

- 1/2 cup mozzarella cheese, shredded
- sesame seeds (optional)
- 1 1/2 cup blanched almond flour
- large beaten eggs
- 1 tablespoon gluten-free baking powder
- oz. cream cheese, cubed

HealthyRecipesBlogs.com

Coconut Rolls

NUTRITION 102 calorie, 7 g fat, 5.8 g total carbs, 3 g protein

	PREPARATION	COOKING TIME	SERVINGS
DIRECTION	5 MINTS	25 mins	10 rolls

- Line baking sheet with parchment paper.
- Add all ingredients to the Bread Machine.
- Select Dough setting. When the time is over, transfer the dough to the floured surface. Shape it into a ball and cut into about 10 even pieces.
- Bake at temperature of 350 F for about 30-35 minutes.

INGREDIENTS

- 1/4 teaspoon pink Himalayan salt
- tablespoons butter
- 1/2 cup coconut flour
- large eggs
- tablespoons psyllium husk powder
- 3/4 cup water
- 1/2 teaspoon baking powder

Cauliflower Bread

NUTRITION *204 calories, 17 g fat, 6 g total carbs, 7 g protein*

	PREPARATION	COOKING TIME	SERVINGS
DIRECTION	5 MINT	50 mins	10 slices

DIRECTION

- Add all ingredients to the Bread Machine.
- Select Dough setting and press Start. Mix the ingredients for about 4-5 minutes. After that press stop button.
- Smooth out the top of the loaf. Choose Bake mode and press Start. Let it bake for about 45 minutes.
- Remove bread from the bread machine and let it rest for 10 minutes. Enjoy!

INGREDIENTS

- tablespoons canola oil
- 1 teaspoon salt
- cups cauliflower finely riced, microwaved for 3-4 minutes
- 1 tablespoon baking powder
- large eggs, separated
- 1 ¼ cups of superfine almond flour

Avocado Bread

NUTRITION *100 calories, 7.3 g fat, 5.7 g total carbs, 3.2 g protein*

	PREPARATION	COOKING TIME	SERVINGS
DIRECTION	5 MINS	45 mins	10 slices

DIRECTION

- Add all ingredients to the Bread Machine.
- Select Dough setting and press Start. Mix the ingredients for about 4-5 minutes. After that press stop button.
- Smooth out the top of the loaf. Choose Bake mode and press Start. Let it bake for about 40 minutes.
- Remove bread from the bread machine and let it rest for 10 minutes. Enjoy!

INGREDIENTS

- 1 tablespoon vanilla extract
- tablespoons cocoa powder unsweetened (optional)
- 1 1/2 cups avocado mashed, ripe
- 1/2 teaspoon salt
- tablespoons monk fruit/erythritol blend sweetener
- 3/4 teaspoon baking soda
- eggs large
- tablespoons coconut flour

Poppy-Seed Bread

NUTRITION 127 calories, 9 g fat, 2 g total carbs, 7 g protein

	PREPARATION	COOKING TIME	SERVINGS
DIRECTION	5 MINT	30 mins	8

DIRECTION

- Add all ingredients to the Bread Machine.
- Select Dough setting and press Start. Mix the ingredients for about 4-5 minutes. After that press stop button.
- Smooth out the top of the loaf. Choose Bake mode and press Start. Let it bake for about 25 minutes.
- Remove bread from the bread machine and let it rest for 10 minutes. Enjoy!

INGREDIENTS

- tablespoons sunflower seeds
- 1 tablespoon poppy seeds
- oz. cottage cheese
- 1 teaspoon sea salt
- eggs
- 1 teaspoon ground psyllium husk powder
- 1 tablespoon olive oil
- 1 teaspoon baking powder
- tablespoons chia seeds or flaxseed

Greek Olive Bread

NUTRITION Calories: 150 , Carbohydrates: 3g , Protein: 3g , Fat: 14g

	PREPARATION	COOKING TIME	SERVINGS
DIRECTION	5 MINTS	0 hour	20

DIRECTION

- Beat eggs in a mixing bowl for about 5 minutes. Add olive oil slowly while you continue to beat the eggs. Add in sour cream and apple cider vinegar and continue to beat for another 5 minutes.
- Combine all of the remaining ingredients together in a separate smaller bowl.
- Place all wet ingredients into bread machine pan.
- Put the remaining ingredients to the bread pan.
- Set bread machine to the French setting.
- When the bread is done, remove bread machine pan from the bread machine.
- Cool to some extent before moving to a cooling rack.
- The bread can be kept for up to 7 days on the counter.

INGREDIENTS

- eggs
- tbsps. ground flaxseed
- tsp psyllium powder
- tbsps. apple cider vinegar
- 1 tsp baking soda
- 1 tsp salt
- ½ cup sour cream
- ½ cup olive oil
- oz. black olives, chopped
- 1 tsp ground rosemary
- 1 ½ cups almond flour
- 1 tsp dried basil

Veggie Loaf

NUTRITION *Calories: 150, Carbohydrates: 3 , Protein: 3g, Fat: 14g*

PREPARATION	COOKING TIME	SERVINGS
20	0	20
	hour	

DIRECTION

- Grate carrots and zucchini, use a cheesecloth to drain excess water, set aside.
- Mix eggs and coconut oil into bread machine pan.
- Add the remaining ingredients to bread pan.
- Set bread machine to quick bread setting.
- When the bread is done, remove bread machine pan from the bread machine.
- Cool to some extent before transferring to a cooling rack.
- You can store your veggie loaf bread for up to 5 days in the refrigerator, or you can also be sliced and stored in the freezer for up to 3 months.

INGREDIENTS

- 1/3 cup coconut flour
- tablespoons chia Seed
- tbsps. psyllium husk powder
- ¼ cup sunflower seeds
- ¼ cup pumpkin seeds
- tbsp. flax seed
- 1 cup almond flour
- 1 cup zucchini, grated
- eggs
- ¼ cup coconut oil, melted
- 1 tbsp. paprika
- tsp cumin
- tsp baking powder
- tsp salt

Cajun Veggie Loaf

NUTRITION *Calories: 101 , Carbohydrates: 6g , Protein: 4g , Fat: 8g*

PREPARATION	COOKING TIME	SERVINGS
5	0	12
	hour	

DIRECTION

- Add water and ghee to bread machine pan.
- Add in the remaining ingredients.
- Set bread machine to basic setting.
- When done, remove from bread machine and allow to cool before slicing.
- Cool to some extent before transferring to a cooling rack.
- You can store your bread for up to 5 days in the refrigerator.

INGREDIENTS

- ½ cup water
- ¼ cup onion, chopped
- ½ cup green bell pepper, chopped
- tsp garlic, chopped finely
- tsp ghee
- cups almond flour
- 1 tbsp. inulin
- 1 tsp Cajun seasoning
- 1 tsp active dry yeast

Parmesan Italian Bread

NUTRITION Calories: 150 , Carbohydrates: 14g , Protein: 5g , Fat: 5g

	PREPARATION	COOKING TIME	SERVINGS
DIRECTION	16	0 hour	10

DIRECTION

- Dispense all wet ingredients into bread machine pan.
- Add all dry ingredients to pan.
- Set bread machine to French bread.
- When the bread is done, remove bread machine pan from the bread machine.
- Cool to some extent before transferring to a cooling rack.
- You can store your bread for up to 7 days.

INGREDIENTS

- 1 1/3 cup warm water
- tbsps. olive oil
- cloves of garlic, crushed
- 1 tbsp. basil
- 1 tbsp. oregano
- 1 tbsp. parsley
- cups almond flour
- 1 tbsp. inulin
- ½ cup parmesan cheese, grated
- 1 tsp active dry yeast

Bacon Jalapeño Cheesy Bread

NUTRITION Calories: 235 , Carbohydrates: 5g , Protein: 11g , Fat: 17g

	PREPARATION	COOKING TIME	SERVINGS
DIRECTION	22	0 hour	12

DIRECTION

- Cook the bacon in a larger frying pan, set aside to cool on paper towels. Save ¼ cup of bacon fat for the recipe, allow to cool slightly before using.
- Add wet ingredients to bread machine pan, including the cooled bacon grease.
- Add in the remaining ingredients.
- Set the bread machine to the quick bread setting.
- When the bread is done, remove bread machine pan from the bread machine.
- Cool to some extent before transferring to a cooling rack.
- Once on a cooling rack, top with the remaining cheddar cheese.
- You can store your bread for up to 7 days.

INGREDIENTS

- 1 cup golden flaxseed, ground
- ¾ cup coconut flour
- tsp baking powder
- ¼ tsp black pepper
- 1 tbsp. erythritol
- 1/3 cup pickled jalapeno
- oz. cream cheese, full fat
- eggs
- cups sharp cheddar cheese, shredded + ¼ cup extra for the topping
- tbsps. parmesan cheese, grated
- 1 ¼ cup almond milk
- Bacon Slices (cooked and crumbled)
- ¼ cup rendered bacon grease (from frying the bacon)

Raspberry Bread

NUTRITION *Calories: 300 , Carbohydrates: 14g , Protein: 5g , Fat: 30g*

	PREPARATION	COOKING TIME	SERVINGS
DIRECTION	20	0 *houe*	10

DIRECTION

- Lightly beat eggs before pouring into bread machine pan.
- Add in melted coconut oil, ghee, and lemon juice to pan.
- Add the remaining ingredients.
- Set bread machine to quick bread.
- When the bread is done, remove bread machine pan from the bread machine.
- Cool to some extent before transferring to a cooling rack.
- You can store your bread for up to 5 days.

INGREDIENTS

- cups almond flour
- ½ cup coconut flour
- ½ cup ghee
- ½ cup coconut oil, melted
- ½ cup erythritol
- eggs
- 1 tsp lemon juice
- ½ cup raspberries
- tsp baking powder

Whole-Wheat Sourdough Bread

NUTRITION *Calories: 155 , Fat: 2g , Carbohydrates: 2.9g , Fiber: 1g , Protein: 4g*

	PREPARATION	COOKING TIME	SERVINGS
DIRECTION	10	0 *hour*	8

DIRECTION

- Put all ingredients in the bread machine.
- Set the machine to Whole-Wheat/Whole-Grain bread, select light or medium crust, and press Start.
- When ready, remove the bread and allow about 5 minutes to cool the loaf.
- Put it on a rack to cool it completely

INGREDIENTS

- ⅔ cups hot water
- ⅔ cup No-Yeast Whole-Wheat Sourdough Starter, fed, active, and at room temperature
- teaspoons butter, melted
- teaspoons sugar
- 1 teaspoon salt
- 1¼ teaspoons instant yeast
- cups whole- almond flour

Blueberry Muffin Bread

NUTRITION Calories: 156 , Carbohydrates: 4g , Protein: 5g , Fat: 13g

PREPARATION	COOKING TIME	SERVINGS
15	0 hour	12

DIRECTION

- Using a small microwaveable bowl, combine your almond butter and coconut oil. Heat for about 10 seconds to melt (it may need an extra 5 or more seconds to melt depending on your microwave).
- Add the eggs into the bowl with the melted butter and oil and beat slightly.
- Add the egg mixture into your bread machine pan.
- Add the milk.
- Use a separate small mixing bowl to combine all of your dry ingredients.
- Pour dry ingredients on top of the wet mixture in your bread machine pan.
- Set the bread machine to its basic bread setting.
- Check the dough halfway through its kneading process to ensure it is smooth and tacky. If needed add a tablespoon more of flour if too wet, or a tablespoon of water if too dry.
- Let the dough continue to knead and bake in the bread machine.
- When the bread is done, remove bread machine pan from the bread machine.
- Cool to some extent before transferring to a cooling rack.
- You can store your bread for up to 4 days.

INGREDIENTS

- ½ cup almond butter
- 1/3 cup coconut oil
- ½ cup almond flour
- ½ cup erythritol
- ½ tsp salt
- tsp baking powder
- ½ cup almond milk, unsweetened
- eggs
- ½ cup blueberries

Lemon Blueberry Bread

NUTRITION Calories: 300 , Carbohydrates: 14g , Protein: 5g , Fat: 30g

PREPARATION	COOKING TIME	SERVINGS
10	0 hour	10

DIRECTION

- Lightly beat eggs before pouring into your bread machine pan.
- Add in melted coconut oil, ghee, and lemon juice to pan.
- Add the remaining dry ingredients including blueberries and lemon zest to the bread machine pan.
- Set bread machine to quick bread setting.
- When the bread is done, remove bread machine pan from the bread machine.
- Cool to some extent before transferring to a cooling rack.
- You can store your bread for up to 5 days.

INGREDIENTS

- cups almond flour
- ½ cup coconut flour
- ½ cup ghee
- ½ cup coconut oil, melted
- ½ cup erythritol
- eggs
- tbsps. lemon zest, about half a lemon
- 1 tsp lemon juice
- ½ cup blueberries
- tsp baking powder

Cheese Blend Bread

NUTRITION *Calories: 132 , Carbohydrates: 4g , Protein: 6g , Fat: 8 g*

PREPARATION	COOKING TIME	SERVINGS
25	0 houe	12

DIRECTION

- Place wet ingredients into bread machine pan.
- Add dry ingredients.
- Set the bread machine to the gluten free setting.
- When the bread is done, remove bread machine pan from the bread machine.
- Cool to some extent before transferring to a cooling rack.
- You can store your bread for up to 5 days.

INGREDIENTS

- oz. cream cheese
- ¼ cup ghee
- 2/3 cup almond flour
- ¼ cup coconut flour
- tbsps. whey protein, unflavored
- tsp baking powder
- ½ tsp Himalayan salt
- ½ cup parmesan cheese, shredded
- tbsps. water
- eggs
- ½ cup mozzarella cheese, shredded

Strawberries and Cream Bread

NUTRITION *Calories: 120 , Carbohydrates: 5g , Protein: 4g , Fat: 10g*

PREPARATION	COOKING TIME	SERVINGS
18	0 hour	10

DIRECTION

- Dispense all wet ingredients into bread machine pan.
- Add dry ingredients to pan.
- Set bread machine to the sweet bread setting.
- Check the dough while kneading to ensure more water does not need to be added. Otherwise just allow the bread machine to run its course.
- When the bread is done, remove bread machine pan from the bread machine.
- Cool to some extent before moving to a cooling rack.
- You can store your bread for up to 5 days.

INGREDIENTS

- ¾ cup whole milk
- ½ cup cream cheese
- ½ cup strawberries, sliced
- 1 tbsp. coconut oil, melted
- 1 tsp salt
- tbsps. inulin
- 1 tbsp. chia seeds
- cups almond Flour
- tsp instant yeast

3 Ingredient Breadticks

NUTRITION 2 Breadticks: , Total calories: 142 , Total fat: 9.2 grams , Fat (saturated): 4.9 grams , Cholesterol: 98.2 milligrams , Sodium: 297.1 milligrams , Carbohydrates: 3.1 grams , Fiber: 0.1 gram , Sugar: 0.9 grams, Protein: 11.4 grams

INGREDIENTS

- Dough:
- 1.5 cups of mozzarella cheese (shredded)
- eggs
- 1/8 tbsp. Italian seasoning
- Topping:
- Half cup of mozzarella cheese (shredded)
- tbsp. parmesan cheese (shredded, optional)
- 1/3 tbsp. parsley (finely chopped, optional)

DIRECTION

- Make the oven ready for baking by heating it to a temperature of 350 degrees Fahrenheit. Get a sheet of parchment paper and line one square, nine-by-nine inch baking pan.
- Put the cheese, seasoning and eggs in a food processor and blend until all the ingredients are mixed properly.
- Scoop out the batter into the lined baking pan. Spread out the mixture so that it forms an even layer. Put it in the oven. Bake for 20 minutes until the crust becomes fairly firm and the dough is not wet at any place. Take it out of the oven and allow it to cool.
- Heat the oven to a temperature of 425 degrees Fahrenheit.
- Remove the crust from the parchment paper. Put it in on a cooling rack (oven safe rack). This will help to make the bottom part to become crisp.
- Sprinkle the cheese meant for the topping. You can use either mozzarella or Parmesan cheese for this purpose.
- Put the cooling rack in the oven. Cook for five minutes until the cheese melts.

PREPARATION	COOKING TIME	SERVINGS
40	0	5
mins	hour	

Bread with Walnuts and Garlic

NUTRITION Calories: 100 , Fat: 4g , Carbohydrates 4.6 , Sugar 0g , Proteins: 2

INGREDIENTS

- cups almond flour
- teaspoons dry yeast
- 1 cup walnuts
- garlic cloves, chopped
- tablespoons Olive oil
- 1 cup garlic butter, melted
- cups water
- teaspoons sugar
- egg yolks
- Sea salt to taste

DIRECTION

- Preheat the oven to 290°-320°Fahrenheit and roast the walnuts in the oven for 10-15 minutes until lightly browned and crispy. Set aside to cool completely. Grind the walnuts using a food processor.
- Melt the unsalted butter by making it softer, by taking it out of the fridge and leaving for around 30 minutes or melt the butter using a frying pan. Meanwhile chop the garlic cloves.
- Lubricate the surface of the dough with the water or the egg yolk.
- Now close the lid and turn the bread machine on the basic/white bread program.
- After the breakfast wheat bread with garlic is ready, take it out and leave for 1 hour covered with the towel and then you can consume the bread, although we recommend eating your bread after 24 hours.

PREPARATION	COOKING TIME	SERVINGS
4	0	10
hours	mints	

American Cheese Beer Bread

NUTRITION *Calories: 94 , Fat: 6g , Carb: 4g , Protein: 1g*

INGREDIENTS

- ½ cups of fine almond flour
- 1 tsp. Of unsalted melted butter
- salt, one teaspoon
- an egg
- swerve sweetener, two teaspoons
- keto low-carb beer, one cup
- ¾ tsp. Of baking powder
- ½ cup of cheddar cheese, shredded
- ½ tsp. Of active dry yeast

DIRECTION

- Prepare a mixing container, where you will combine the almond flour, swerve sweetener, salt, shredded cheddar cheese, and baking powder.
- Prepare another mixing container, where you will combine the unsalted melted butter, egg, and low- carb keto beer.
- When the bread is ready, using oven mitts, remove the bread pan from the machine.

PREPARATION	COOKING TIME	SERVINGS
5	15	
mins	mins	10

Bread with Beef and Peanuts

NUTRITION *Carbohydrates 4 g , Fats 42 g , Protein 27 g, Calories 369*

INGREDIENTS

- oz. beef meat
- oz. herbs de Provence
- big onions
- cloves chopped garlic
- 1 cup of milk
- 20 oz. almond flour
- oz. rye flour
- teaspoons dry yeast
- 1 egg
- tablespoons sunflower oil
- 1 tablespoon sugar
- Sea salt
- Ground black pepper
- Red pepper

DIRECTION

- Sprinkle the beef meat with the herbs de Provence, salt, black, and red pepper and marinate in bear for overnight.
- Cube the beef and fry in a skillet or a wok on medium heat until soft (for around 20 minutes).
- Combine the beef pieces and the dough and mix in the bread machine.
- Cover the lid and turn the bread machine on the basic program.
- Bake the bread until the medium crust and after the bread is ready take it out and leave for 1 hour covered with the towel and only then you can slice the bread.

PREPARATION	COOKING TIME	SERVINGS
3	0	8
hours	mints	

Citus Bread

NUTRITION Carbohydrates 4 g , Fats 9.1 g , Protein 9.8 g , Calories 404

INGREDIENTS

- 1 egg
- tablespoons butter
- 1/3 cup sugar
- 1 tablespoon vanilla sugar
- ½ cup orange juice
- 2/3 cup milk
- 1 teaspoon salt
- cup almond flour
- 1 tablespoon instant yeast
- ¼ cup candied oranges
- ¼ cup candied lemon
- teaspoons lemon zest
- ¼ cup almond, chopped

DIRECTION

- Put all of the ingredients to your bread machine, carefully following the instructions of the manufacturer (except candied fruits, zest, and almond).
- Set the program of your bread machine to basic/sweet and set crust type to light or medium.
- Press starts.
- Once the machine beeps, add candied fruits, lemon zest, and chopped almonds.
- Wait until the cycle completes.
- Once the loaf is ready, take the bucket out and let the loaf cool for 5 minutes.
- Gently shake the bucket to remove loaf.
- Move it to a cooling rack, slice and serve.

PREPARATION	COOKING TIME	SERVINGS
3	0	8
mins	hour	

Chapter 30.
Famous Bread Recipes

Bread Machine Glazed Yeast Doughnuts

NUTRITION Calories: 130 calories; , Total Carbohydrate: 18 g , Total Fat: 7 g , Protein: 1 g

INGREDIENTS

- 1/2 cup evaporated milk
- 1/2 cup water
- 2 tbsp. butter
- One large egg, beaten
- 1/3 cup sugar
- 3 cups all-purpose flour
- 1 tsp. salt
- 2 tsp. active dry yeast
- Oil for deep-frying
- For the Chocolate Glaze
- 2 tbsp. butter
- 2 tbsp. cocoa
- 3 tbsp. hot water
- 1 1/2 cups powdered sugar
- 1/2 tsp. vanilla extract

DIRECTION

- Add all the ingredients to the bread machine.
- During the kneading cycle, you should cover the pan with plastic wrap and then transfer it to the refrigerator. (You may also transfer the mixture to a lightly greased bowl). Refrigerate overnight.
- Remove the dough to a lightly floured surface and roll to about 1/2-inch thick.
- Cut out into doughnut shapes or form strips into knots or cruller shapes. Do not forget to cover and let rise for about 1 hour.
- Fry in oil at 360 F until light and brown. Now, glaze with the use of chocolate icing or use your favorite icing.
- Chocolate or Vanilla Glaze
- Melt butter in a small saucepan over low heat; add cocoa and water. Stir constantly until the mixture is thick.
- Remove from heat, then gradually add powdered sugar and vanilla; beat with a whisk until smooth.
- Add additional hot water, 1/2 teaspoon at a time, until drizzling constancy.
- For the vanilla glaze, omit cocoa and add 1 1/2 teaspoons vanilla.

PREPARATION	COOKING TIME	SERVINGS
52 *mins*	20 *mins*	20

Bread Machine Kalamata Olive Bread

NUTRITION Calories: 130 calories, Total Carbohydrate: 18 g , Total Fat: 7 g , Protein: 1 g

INGREDIENTS

- 1/2 cup brine from olives
- 1 cup of warm water
- 2 tbsp. olive oil
- 3 cups bread flour
- 1 2/3 cups whole-wheat flour
- 1 1/2 tsp. salt
- 2 tsp. sugar
- 1 1/2 tsp. dried basil
- 2 tsp. active dry yeast
- 1/2 to 2/3 cup of finely chopped olives

DIRECTION

- Put the olive brine in a 2-cup measure; add warm water to make 1 1/2 cups volume.
- Place all ingredients, excluding the olives, in the bread machine according to your manufacturer's preferred order.
- Choose the basic or wheat setting on your bread machine.
- Add olives at the beep, indicating time to add mix-in ingredients.
- When your loaf is finished baking, slice it and enjoy it by itself, with butter or olive oil.

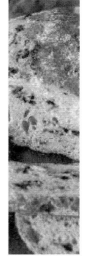

PREPARATION	COOKING TIME	SERVINGS
10 *mins*	2 *hours*	10

Dark Pumpernickel Bread

NUTRITION Calories: 130 calories, Total Carbohydrate: 18 g , Total Fat: 7 g , Protein: 1 g

INGREDIENTS

- 1 1/3 cups strong coffee
- 1/4 cup vegetable oil
- 1/4 cup molasses
- 1 cup whole wheat flour
- 1 cup rye flour
- 2 cups bread flour
- 2 1/2 tsp. caraway seeds
- 2 tbsp. unsweetened cocoa
- 1 1/2 tbsp. brown sugar
- 1 tsp. salt
- 2 1/2 tsp. active dry yeast

DIRECTION

- Fill bread machine and bake according to the bread machine manufacturer's recommendations.
- To make a free-form loaf, use the dough cycle. Remove the dough and shape on a parchment-paper-lined baking sheet.
- Cover the bread with a towel and allow it to rise for about 45 minutes to 1 hour in a draft-free place.
- Bake in a warmed oven for around 25 to 35 minutes. The loaf should sound hollow when tapped on the bottom.

PREPARATION	COOKING TIME	SERVINGS
10	2	16
mins	hour	

Bread Machine Hamburger Buns

NUTRITION Calories: 130 calories;, Total Carbohydrate: 18 g , Total Fat: 7 g , Protein: 3 g

INGREDIENTS

- 1 1/3 cups water
- 2 tbsp. nonfat milk powder
- 4 cups all-purpose flour
- 2 tbsp. shortening
- 3 tbsp. sugar
- 2 tsp. salt
- 2 1/2 tsp. active dry yeast
- Cornmeal
- One egg white (beaten with 1 tbsp. of water)
- Sesame seeds for topping

DIRECTION

- Add the water and nonfat milk powder to the bread machine, followed by the flour. Add the shortening followed by the sugar, salt, and yeast. Set to the dough cycle.
- When the bread machine finishes, turn the dough out onto a floured board and punch it down. Knead 4 or 5 times.
- Cover the dough with a clean towel besides rest for about 30 minutes in a warm, dry place.
- Lightly grease a large baking sheet; sprinkle with cornmeal. Alternatively, mark the baking sheet with parchment paper and sprinkle with cornmeal.
- Pat the dough into a circle and cut into eight even wedges. Form each wedge into a ball, and then flatten each one into a smooth and reasonably even circle, slightly bigger than a burger.
- Assemble the dough pieces on the baking sheet about 2 inches apart and rest for around 20 minutes.
- Preheat the oven.
- Brush the buns lightly utilizing the egg wash (a mixture of egg and water). If chosen, sprinkle with sesame seeds.
- Bake the buns for around 18 minutes or until the buns are nicely browned.
- Let cool before serving.

PREPARATION	COOKING TIME	SERVINGS
25	18	8
mins	mints	

Bread Machine Wheat Cornmeal Bread

NUTRITION Calories: 130 calories;, Total Carbohydrate: 18 g , Total Fat: 7 g , Protein: 3 g

INGREDIENTS

- 2 1/2 tsp. active dry yeast
- 1 1/3 cups water
- 2 tbsp. brown sugar
- One large egg, beaten
- 2 tbsp. butter, softened
- 1 1/2 tsp. salt
- 3/4 cup cornmeal
- 3/4 cup whole wheat flour
- 2 3/4 cups bread flour

DIRECTION

- Start by adding ingredients to the bread machine in the order suggested by your bread machine manufacturer. Set basic cycle, medium crust.
- Serve and enjoy!

PREPARATION	COOKING TIME	SERVINGS
10	2	12
mins	*hour*	

Bread Machine Sweet Potato Bread

NUTRITION Calories: 130 calories; , Total Carbohydrate: 18 g , Total Fat: 7 g , Protein: 1 g

INGREDIENTS

- 1/2 cup plus 2 tbsp. water
- 1 tsp. vanilla extract
- 1 cup plain mashed sweet potatoes
- 4 cups bread flour
- 1/4 tsp. of ground nutmeg and cinnamon
- 2 tbsp. butter
- 1/3 cup dark brown sugar
- 1 tsp. salt
- 2 tsp. active dry yeast
- 2 tbsp. dry milk powder
- Raisins or chopped pecans if desired

DIRECTION

- Add all the ingredients according to the manufacturer's suggested order.
- Set white bread setting, light crust.
- If desired, add raisins or pecans when your bread machine beeps for additional ingredients.
- Wait until baked, then slice and enjoy.

PREPARATION	COOKING TIME	SERVINGS
15	2	10
mins	*hours*	

Bread Machine Cocoa Bread

NUTRITION Calories: 130 calories;, Total Carbohydrate: 18 g , Total Fat: 7 g , Protein: 1 g

INGREDIENTS

- 1 cup milk
- One egg, plus one yolk
- 3 tsp. vegetable oil
- 1 tsp. vanilla extract
- 1 tsp. salt
- 3 cups bread flour
- 1/2 cup brown sugar
- 1/3 cup cocoa powder
- 1 tbsp. vital wheat gluten
- 2 1/2 tsp. bread machine yeast

DIRECTION

- Combine ingredients as instructed in your bread machine guide. Choose a basic or white bread setting and medium crust option.
- When the bread is done cooking, you may now remove the bread immediately from the pan and cool completely on a cooling rack before cutting.
- Serve and enjoy.

PREPARATION	COOKING TIME	SERVINGS
10 *mins*	3 *hour*	10

Bread Machine Pumpkin Yeast Bread

NUTRITION Calories: 130 calories, Total Carbohydrate: 18 g , Total Fat: 7 g , Protein: 1 g

INGREDIENTS

- 1/2 cup plus 2 tbsp. milk
-
- 1 cup mashed pumpkin
- 4 cups bread flour
- 2 tbsp. vegetable oil
- 2 tbsp. sugar
- 1 tsp. salt
- 2 1/4 tsp. active dry yeast

DIRECTION

- Add all of the fixings according to your bread machine manufacturer's suggestions
- Set white bread setting, light crust.
- Allow your machine to do its thing and enjoy the loaf when it is ready.
- Serve and enjoy!

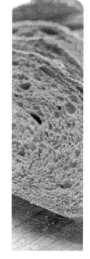

PREPARATION	COOKING TIME	SERVINGS
10 *mins*	3 *mins*	4

Bread Machine Bacon and Cheese Bread

NUTRITION Calories: 130 calories, Total Carbohydrate: 18 g , Total Fat: 7 g , Protein: 1 g

INGREDIENTS

- 1 1/3 cups water
- 2 tbsp. vegetable oil
- 1 tsp. salt
- 4 tbsp. sugar, divided
- 4 cups bread flour
- 3 tbsp. nonfat dry milk
- 2 tsp. dry active yeast
- 2 cups cheddar cheese, shredded
- Eight slices of bacon crumbled

DIRECTION

- Begin by placing ingredients in the bread pan in the order as listed or according to the manufacturer's recommendations. Press starts.
- The Cheddar cheese and bacon should be added to the fruit and nut signal. Depending on your machine, this could be anywhere from 30 to 40 minutes into the cycle.
- When baked, let's cool. Then slice and enjoy.

PREPARATION	COOKING TIME	SERVINGS
20	2.5	
mins	*hour*	*10*

Bread Machine Milk and Honey Bread

NUTRITION Calories: 130 calories, Total Carbohydrate: 18 g, Total Fat: 7 g, Protein: 1 g

INGREDIENTS

- 1 cup plus 1 tbsp. milk
- 3 tbsp. honey
- 3 tbsp. melted butter
- 3 cups bread flour
- 1 tsp. salt
- 2 tsp. active dry yeast

DIRECTION

- Initially, add the ingredients to the bread machine pan in the order recommended by your bread machine manufacturer.
- Next, choose the basic or white bread setting and the medium crust setting. Press Start Button.
- As soon as it is finished, remove the loaf. Place it on a wire rack for it to cool completely.
- Once cooled, slice the bread and serve.

PREPARATION	COOKING TIME	SERVINGS
15	2	
mins	*hours*	*15*

Texas Cheesy Bread

NUTRITION Calories 152 kcal, Fat 2 g , Carbohydrates , 27.3g , Protein 5.5 g , Cholesterol 4 mg , Sodium 220 mg

INGREDIENTS

- 1 C. warm water
- 1 tsp. salt
- 2 tbsp. white sugar
- 1/2 C. shredded Monterey Jack cheese
- 6 tbsp. fresh chopped jalapeño peppers
- 3 C. bread flour
- 1/2 tbsp. active dry yeast

DIRECTION

- In the bread machine pan, put all the ingredients in order as suggested by the manual.
- Select the Regular Basic Bread cycle and press the Start button.

PREPARATION	COOKING TIME	SERVINGS
5	3	12
mins	hour	

Cinnamon Pinwheels

NUTRITION Calories 162 kcal , Fat 5.5 g , Carbohydrates, 24.4g , Protein 4.1 g , Cholesterol 24 mg , Sodium 129 mg

INGREDIENTS

- 1 C. milk
- Two eggs
- 1/4 C. butter
- 4 C. bread flour
- 1/4 C. white sugar
- 1 tsp. salt
- 1 1/2 tsp. active dry yeast
- 1/2 C. chopped walnuts
- 1/2 C. packed brown sugar
- 2 tsp. ground cinnamon
- 2 tbsp. softened butter, divided
- 2 tsp. sifted confectioners' sugar, divided

DIRECTION

- Add the milk, eggs, 1/4 C. of the butter, bread flour, sugar, salt, and yeast in order as suggested by the manual into the bread machine.
- Select the Dough cycle and press the Start button.
- After the completion of the cycle, place the dough onto a floured surface.
- With your hands, thump down the dough and keep aside for about 10 minutes.
- In a small bowl, add the brown sugar, walnuts, and cinnamon.
- Place the dough onto a lightly floured surface and cut into two portions.
- Now, roll each dough portion into a 9x14-inch rectangle.
- Place 1 tbsp. of the softened butter over each dough rectangle evenly, followed by half of the walnut mixture.
- Roll each dough rectangle, and with your fingers, pinch seams to seal the filling.
- Place each loaf into a 9x5-inch greased loaf pan, seam side down
- With plastic wraps, cover the pans and keep aside in a warm place for about 30 minutes.
- Meanwhile, set your oven to 350 degrees F.
- Place the bread in the oven for about 30 minutes. (In the last 10 minutes of the cooking, cover each loaf pan with foil pieces slightly to avoid over-browning).
- Remove from the oven and keep onto a wire rack to cool for about 10 minutes.
- Remove the bread loaves from pans and place them onto wire racks to cool completely before slicing.
- Sprinkle top of each bread loaf with 1 tbsp. of the confectioners' sugar and cut into desired sized slices.

PREPARATION		COOKING TIME	SERVINGS
1	15	30	24
hour	mins	mints	

Garden Shed Bread

NUTRITION Calories 166 kcal , Fat 3.1 g , Carbohydrates 27.7g , Protein 6.6 g , Cholesterol 2 mg , Sodium 270 mg

INGREDIENTS

- 2/3 C. warm water
- 2/3 C. cottage cheese
- 2 tbsp. margarine
- 3 C. bread flour
- 1 tbsp. white sugar
- 1 tbsp. dry milk powder
- 1 tbsp. dried minced onion
- 1 tbsp. dill seed
- 1 tsp. salt
- 1 1/2 tbsp. active dry yeast

DIRECTION

- In a bread machine pan, place all the ingredients in order as suggested by the manual.
- Select the Basic Bread cycle and press the Start button

PREPARATION	COOKING TIME	SERVINGS
5	25	12
mins	mins	

Bahamas Oat Bread

NUTRITION Calories 106 kcal , Fat 1.8 g , Carbohydrates 18.9g , Protein 3.5 g , Cholesterol 3 mg , Sodium 126 mg

INGREDIENTS

- 3/4 C. hot water
- 1/2 C. rolled oats
- 1 1/2 tsp. molasses
- 1 tbsp. butter
- 1/2 tsp. salt
- 1 1/2 C. bread flour
- 1 tbsp. active dry yeast

DIRECTION

- In a container, add the hot water and oats and keep aside for about 2 minutes.
- Add the molasses and butter and stir until well combined.
- In a bread machine pan, add the oats mixture and remaining ingredients as suggested by the manual.
- Select the White Bread cycle with the Light Crust and press the Start button.

PREPARATION	COOKING TIME	SERVINGS
5	25	10
mins	mints	

Spiced Cranberry Rolls

NUTRITION Calories 242 kcal , Fat 1.8 g , Carbohydrates 53.5g , Protein 4.6 g , Cholesterol 0 mg , Sodium 199 mg

INGREDIENTS

- One large orange
- 1/3 C. honey
- 1 tbsp. vegetable oil
- 2 C. bread flour
- 1 C. whole wheat flour
- 1 tsp. salt
- 2 tsp. bread machine yeast
- 3/4 C. packed brown sugar
- 3/4 C. sweetened dried cranberries
- 1 tsp. ground cardamom

DIRECTION

- Grate the zest of orange finely into a small bowl and keep aside.
- Peel the orange and remove the seeds.
- Now, cut the orange into chunks.
- In a blender, add the orange zest and chunks and pulse until pureed.
- In a bread machine pan, place the orange puree, followed by the honey, oil, white flour, wheat flour, salt, and yeast in order as suggested by the manual.
- Select the Dough cycle and press the Start button.
- After the completion of the cycle, transfer the dough onto a floured surface.
- Cut the dough into 2-3 equal-sized portions and then roll each into 1/4-inch thickness.
- Spread the cranberries, brown sugar, and cardamom over each dough portion and roll to seal the filling.
- Then, cut each dough roll into 1-2-inch thick slices.
- At the bottommost of a greased baking dish, arrange the dough slices in a single layer.
- Keep aside in a warm area for about 1 hour.
- Meanwhile, set your oven to 375 degrees F.
- Place in the oven for about 20-25 minutes.
- Serve warm.

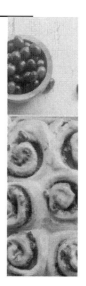

PREPARATION	COOKING TIME	SERVINGS
20	25	12
mins	mins	

PB & J Bread Machine

NUTRITION Calories 236 kcal , Fat 7.7 g , Carbohydrates 36.4g , Protein 7 g , Cholesterol 0 mg , Sodium 244 mg

INGREDIENTS

- 1 C. water
- 1 1/2 tbsp. vegetable oil
- 1/2 C. peanut butter
- 1/2 C. blackberry jelly
- 1 tbsp. white sugar
- 1 tsp. salt
- 1 C. whole wheat flour
- 2 C. bread flour
- 1 1/2 tsp. active dry yeast

DIRECTION

- In a bread machine pan, include all the ingredients in order as suggested by the manual.
- Select the Sweet, Raisin, or Basic cycle and press the Start button.

PREPARATION	COOKING TIME	SERVINGS
5	3	8
mins	hours	

Winter Night Hazelnut Bread with Sweet Frosting

NUTRITION Calories 195 kcal , Fat 7.2 g , Carbohydrates 28g , Protein 5.2 g , Cholesterol 39 mg , Sodium 103 mg

INGREDIENTS

- 1/2 C. hazelnuts
- C. eggnog
- 1 tbsp. eggnog
- tbsp. white sugar
- 1/2 tsp. salt
- tbsp. buller, softened
- One egg
- One egg yolk
- C. bread flour
- 1 1/2 tsp. instant yeast
- 2 tbsp. anise seed
- 1 tsp. ground cinnamon
- For the Glaze:
- 1/2 C. confectioners' sugar
- 1 tbsp. eggnog

DIRECTION

- Custom your oven to 350 degrees F before starting anything else.
- Place the hazelnuts onto a baking sheet in a single layer and cook in the oven for about 5-7 minutes.
- Remove from the oven and keep aside to cool completely.
- Next, in the pan of a bread machine, put 1 C. of the eggnog, sugar, salt, butter, egg, egg yolk, bread flour, yeast, anise seed, and cinnamon in order as suggested by the manual.
- Select the Basic cycle with the Medium Crust and press the Start button.
- After the completion of the first cycle, add the hazelnuts into the pan of the bread machine.
- After the completion of the cycle, transfer the bread onto a wire rack to cool.
- Meanwhile, in a bowl, add the remaining eggnog and confectioners' sugar and mix well for the glaze.
- Spread the glaze over the cooled bread and enjoy it.

PREPARATION	COOKING TIME	SERVINGS
25	45	16
mins	mins	

Maui Morning Bread

NUTRITION Calories 202 kcal , Fat 3.1 g , Carbohydrates 40.3g , Protein 4.7 g , Cholesterol 1 mg , Sodium 247 mg

INGREDIENTS

- 2 tbsp. vegetable oil
- 2 tbsp. honey
- 1 1/8 C. water
- 2 1/2 C. bread flour
- 1/2 C. whole wheat flour
- 1/2 tsp. ground cinnamon
- 1/2 tsp. ground mace
- 1 tbsp. dry milk powder
- 1 1/4 tsp. salt
- 1 C. dried cranberries
- Two dried pineapple rings, chopped
- 2 tsp. active dry yeast

DIRECTION

- Place it in a bread machine pan; add all the ingredients in order as suggested by the manual.
- Select the Basic Bread cycle and press the Start button.

PREPARATION	COOKING TIME	SERVINGS
5	3	12
mins	hours	

Margaret's Almond Bread

NUTRITION Calories 326 kcal , Fat 14.2 g , Carbohydrates 44.7g , Protein 6.2 g , Cholesterol 22 mg , Sodium 377 mg

INGREDIENTS

- 1 C. warm milk
- 1 1/2 tsp. salt
- 2 tbsp. margarine
- 3 C. bread flour
- 3 tbsp. white sugar
- 2 tsp. active dry yeast
- 1/2 C. semisweet chocolate chips
- 1/3 C. blanched slivered almonds
- 2 tbsp. unsweetened cocoa powder
- 1 tsp. almond extract
- 1/2 C. butter
- 1 C. confectioners' sugar
- 2 tsp. grated orange zest

DIRECTION

- In the bread machine pan, pour the milk, salt, and 2 tbsp. of the margarine, flour, sugar, and yeast in order as suggested by the manual.
- Select the Basic or Rapid cycle and press the Start button.
- Just before the start of second kneading, press the Stop.
- Transfer the dough into a bowl.
- Add the almonds, chocolate chips, cocoa powder, and almond extract and mix well.
- Place the dough into the pan of the bread machine and press Start to start the cycle.
- Meanwhile, for the orange butter: in a food processor, add 1 C. of the confectioners' sugar, 1/2 C. of the butter, and orange zest and pulse until smooth.
- Spread the orange butter over warm bread and enjoy it.

PREPARATION	COOKING TIME	SERVINGS
10	3	12
mins	hour	

Lena's Raisin Bread

NUTRITION Calories 256 kcal , Fat 5.2 g , Carbohydrates 44.8g , Protein 7.3 g , Cholesterol 30 mg , Sodium 278 mg

INGREDIENTS

- 1 C. milk
- 3 tbsp. butter
- 1 tbsp. brown sugar
- One egg
- 1 tsp. salt
- 1 tbsp. ground cinnamon
- 1 1/2 tsp. bread machine yeast
- 3 C. bread flour
- 1/2 C. raisins
- 1/2 C. dried cherries

DIRECTION

- In the bread machine pan, add all the fixings except the cherries and raisins.
- Select the White Bread cycle and press the Start button.
- Just 5 minutes before the completion of the cycle, add the cherries and raisins.

PREPARATION	COOKING TIME	SERVINGS
5	2	10
mins	hours	

Carolina Cantaloupe Bread

NUTRITION Calories 166 kcal , Fat 3.2 g , Carbohydrates 28.1g , Protein 6 g , Cholesterol 19 mg , Sodium 195 mg

INGREDIENTS

- 2 1/4 C. cubed cantaloupe
- 1 (.25 oz.) package instant yeast
- 3 1/4 C. bread flour
- 2 tbsp. vital wheat gluten
- 1/3 C. milk powder
- 3 tbsp. white sugar
- 1 tsp. salt
- 1/2 tsp. paprika
- One egg
- 3 tbsp. butter, softened
- 1 tbsp. orange zest

DIRECTION

- In a food processor, add 1 1/2 C. of the cantaloupe and pulse until pureed.
- In a bread machine pan, add the yeast, flour, gluten, milk powder, sugar, salt, paprika, egg, butter, orange zest, remaining cantaloupe cubes, and cantaloupe puree in order as suggested by the manual.
- Select the White Bread cycle and press the Start button.
- Next is to place the bread onto a wire rack to cool before slicing.
- Cut into desired sized slices and enjoy.

PREPARATION	COOKING TIME	SERVINGS
20	3	15
mins	hour	

Collagen Bread

NUTRITION Calories: 77 , Total fat: 5 grams , Fat (saturated): 2 grams , Carbohydrates: 1 gram , Fiber: 1 gram , Protein: 7 grams , Cholesterol: 77 grams , Sodium: 86 milligrams , Potassium: 51 milligrams (Culver, n.d.)

INGREDIENTS

- oz. almond flour
- eggs (pastured)
- 1 tbsp. coconut oil (unflavored)
- 1 tsp. of baking powder (aluminum free)
- 1 tsp. xanthan gum
- 1 pinch salt
- 1 pinch Stevia (optional)
-

DIRECTION

- Heat the oven at temperature 325 degrees Fahrenheit.
- Apply coconut oil generously on the bottom portion of a one and a half quart ceramic or glass loaf dish. If you like, you can use parchment paper for this purpose. Do not oil or line the sides so that the bread can get attached to the four sides and remain lifted while cooling.
- Place the whites of the eggs in a large bowl and whisk them until peaks start forming. Keep it aside.
- Whisk all the dry items in one small bowl. Add Stevia if you are using it. If you don't like eggs, add Stevia. This will help to counteract the flavor without making the loaf sweet.
- Take another small bowl and mix the coconut oil and egg yolks.
- Mix the dry mixture, oil mixture, and the whites of eggs to form a batter. It should be thick and gooey.
- Pour it into the loaf dish you have prepared.
- Bake for 40 minutes until the bread rises significantly.
- Move it out and cool it down completely. This may take about one or two hours. It is alright if the bread sinks a bit during this time.
- Run a sharp knife along the edges of the loaf and release it from the dish.

PREPARATION	COOKING TIME	SERVINGS
1 50	0	12 slices
hour mins	mints	

Simple Keto Bread

NUTRITION Calories: 90 , Fat: 7 grams , Carbohydrates: 2 grams , Fiber: 0.75 grams , Protein: 3 grams (Gaedke, n.d.)

INGREDIENTS

- 16 oz. almond flour
- oz. butter
- eggs
- 1 tbsp. of baking powder
- drops Stevia (optional)
- 1 pinch salt

DIRECTION

- Preheat the oven at 375 degrees Fahrenheit.
- Separate the whites of the eggs. Whisk them until peaks start forming.
- Put the yolks of the eggs, one third portion of whisked egg whites, butter, baking powder, salt, and almond flour in one food processor and blend them. If you are using Stevia to balance the taste of eggs you can add that too. After blending, a thick lumpy dough will be formed.
- Put the rest of the whisked egg whites. Blend once again. But do not over mix.
- Pour the batter into one buttered eight-by-four loaf pan.
- Keep it in the oven and bake for 30 minutes.
- After it cools cut into 20 slices.

PREPARATION	COOKING TIME	SERVINGS
35	0	20 slices
mins	hour	

Paleo Bread

NUTRITION Fat: 24 grams , Carbohydrates: 3 grams , Protein: 9 grams (Ashley, n.d.)

INGREDIENTS

- 1 lb. almond flour
- eggs
- oz. ghee
- 1/8 tsp. salt
- 1 tsp. of baking powder

DIRECTION

- Prepare the oven for baking by heating it to a temperature of 350 degrees Fahrenheit. Take some parchment paper and line one loaf pan.
- Whisk the eggs for one minute at a high speed with a hand mixer. Add the ghee and whisk again.
- Decrease the speed and mix the rest of the ingredients gradually to form a thick batter.
- Put the batter in the baking pan. Spread it with one spatula.
- Then bake for forty to 45 minutes until the top part becomes golden brown.
- Place it on a cooling rack and allow it to cool for ten minutes. After that cut it into slices.

PREPARATION	COOKING TIME	SERVINGS
55	0	12
mins	mints	

Coconut Bread

NUTRITION Calories: 108 , Fats: 8.7 grams , Carbohydrates: 3.4 grams , Fibers: 2.1 grams , Protein: 4.2 grams , Sugar: 0.5 grams , Sodium: 86 milligrams (Jess, n.d.)

INGREDIENTS

- oz. coconut flour
- eggs
- oz. coconut oil
- oz. almond milk (unsweetened)
- 1/8 tbsp. salt
- 1/8 tbsp. of baking soda

DIRECTION

- Preheat the oven at 350 degrees Fahrenheit.
- Use parchment paper to line one eight-by-four inch loaf pan.
- Combine salt, coconut flour and baking soda in one bowl.
- Mix the oil, milk and eggs in a separate bowl.
- Slowly mix the wet items with the dry items. Mix well to form a batter.
- Dispense it into the loaf pan and bake for 40 to 50 minutes.

PREPARATION	COOKING TIME	SERVINGS
50 mins	0 hour	10 slices

Bread With Macadamia Nuts

NUTRITION 1 Slice: , Calories: 151 , Fat: 14 grams , Total carbohydrates: 4 grams , Net carbohydrates: 1 gram , Fiber: 3 grams , Protein: 5 grams (Deanna, 2018)

INGREDIENTS

- 1/2 cup macadamia nuts
- eggs
- oz. coconut flour
- 1/2 tsp. vinegar (apple cider)
- 1/2 tsp. of baking soda

DIRECTION

- Heat the oven beforehand to a temperature of 350 degrees Fahrenheit.
- Place the nuts in a food processor. Pulse them until they form into nut butter. In case it is difficult to blend without liquid you can add the eggs, one by one, until the right consistency is reached.
- Add the coconut flour, vinegar, and baking soda to it. Pulse until everything is combined properly.
- Grease one baking pan and put the batter in it. Smoothen the surface of the batter with a spatula.
- Move the pan on the oven's bottom rack and bake for 30 to forty minutes. By then the top part should become golden brown.
- Move the pan out and let the bread cool in it for 15 to 20 minutes.

PREPARATION	COOKING TIME	SERVINGS
40 mins	0 mints	10 slices

Low Carb Bread with Blueberries

NUTRITION Calories 156 , Total fat 13 grams , Fat (saturated) 3 grams , Carbohydrates 4 grams , Fiber 1 gram , Sugar 1 gram , Protein 5 grams , Cholesterol 78 milligrams , Sodium 171 milligrams , Potassium 192 milligrams , Vitamin A 215IU , Calcium 106 milligrams , Iron 1 milligram

PREPARATION	COOKING TIME	SERVINGS
55	0 hour	12 slices

DIRECTION

- Heat the oven at 350 degrees Fahrenheit.
- Melt butter and almond butter in the microwave for 30 seconds. Stir to combine them.
- Take a large bowl and whisk the almond flour, baking powder, and salt. Pour the melted butter and stir the mixture.
- In one separate bowl, whisk the eggs and almond milk. Pour them into the almond flour mixture.
- Add the blueberries to the batter.
- Place a parchment paper on one loaf pan. Grease the paper lightly.
- Put the batter in the pan. Bake for 45 minutes.
- Before moving out from the pan, cool it for 30 minutes.
- Cut the loaf and toast the slices before serving.

INGREDIENTS

- oz. almond butter
- oz. butter
- oz. almond flour
- oz. almond milk (without sugar)
- 1/8 tbsp. salt
- 2/3 tbsp. of baking powder
- eggs
- oz. blueberries

Cinnamon Flavored Bread

NUTRITION Calories: 221 , Total fats: 15.4 grams , Fat (saturated): 4.3 grams , Carbohydrates: 10.7 grams , Fiber: 3.1 grams , Sugar: 3.7 grams , Protein: 9.3 grams , Cholesterol: 103.3 milligrams , Sodium: 315.2 milligrams , Iron: 1.5 milligrams (Cotter, 2019)

PREPARATION	COOKING TIME	SERVINGS
40	0 hour	8 slices

DIRECTION

- Heat the oven beforehand to a temperature of 350 degrees Fahrenheit. Lay a piece of parchment paper on the bottom part of an eight-by-four bread pan and oil the sides of the pan.
- Take a large bowl and mix coconut flour, almond flour, baking soda, ground flaxseeds, salt, and one and a half teaspoon cinnamon in it.
- Whisk the eggs in another bowl. Then add honey, vinegar, and two tablespoons butter in it.
- Mix the wet items into the dry ones and prepare the batter. Make sure that there are no bulges in the coconut or almond flours.
- Dispense the batter into the greased pan and bake for 30 to 35 minutes. Take it out of the oven.
- Whisk one tablespoon of butter and mix one and a half teaspoon of cinnamon in it. Brush this mixture on the bread.
- Allow it to cool and then serve.

INGREDIENTS

- 1 lb. almond flour
- 1 oz. coconut flour
- oz. flaxseeds (ground)
- eggs
- 1/2 tbsp. vinegar (apple cider)
- 1/8 tbsp. salt
- 1/3 tbsp. of baking soda
- tbsp. honey
- tbsp. butter
- tsp. cinnamon
- 1/2 tsp. chia seeds

Best Keto Bread

NUTRITION Calories: 90, Fat: 7g, Carb: 2g, Protein: 3g

	PREPARATION	COOKING TIME	SERVINGS	
DIRECTION	10 MINT	30 mins	20	*INGREDIENTS*

DIRECTION
- Preheat the oven to 375F.
- To the egg whites, add cream of tartar and beat until soft peaks are formed.
- Using a food processor, combine stevia, salt, baking powder, almond flour, melted butter, 1/3 of the beaten egg whites, and egg yolks. Mix well.
- Then add the remaining 2/3 of the egg whites and gently process until fully mixed. Don't over mix.
- Lubricate a (8 x 4) loaf pan and pour the mixture in it.
- Bake for 30 minutes.
- Enjoy.

INGREDIENTS
- 1 ½ cup almond flour
- drops liquid stevia
- 1 pinch Pink Himalayan salt
- ¼ tsp. cream of tartar
- tsp. baking powder
- ¼ cup butter, melted
- large eggs, separated

Bread De Soul

NUTRITION Calories: 200, Fat: 15.2g, Carb: 1.8g, Protein: 10g

	PREPARATION	COOKING TIME	SERVINGS	
DIRECTION	10 MINTS	45 mins	16	*INGREDIENTS*

DIRECTION
- Preheat the oven to 325F.
- Using a bowl, microwave cream cheese and butter for 1 minute.
- Remove and blend well with a hand mixer.
- Add olive oil, eggs, heavy cream, and few drops of sweetener and blend well.
- Blend the dry ingredients in another bowl.
- Mix the wet ingredients with the dry ones and mix using a spoon. Don't use a hand blender to avoid whipping it too much.
- Lubricate a bread pan and pour the mixture into the pan.
- Bake in the oven until golden brown, about 45 minutes.
- Cool and serve.

INGREDIENTS
- ¼ tsp. cream of tartar
- ½ tsp. baking powder
- 1 tsp. xanthan gum
- 1/3 tsp. baking soda
- ½ tsp. salt
- 2/3 cup unflavored whey protein
- ¼ cup olive oil
- ¼ cup heavy whipping cream
- drops of sweet leaf stevia
- eggs
- ¼ cup butter
- oz. softened cream cheese

Chia Seed Bread

NUTRITION Calories: 405, Fat: 37g, Carb: 4g, Protein: 14g

	PREPARATION	COOKING TIME	SERVINGS	
DIRECTION	10 MINT	40 mins	16 slices	INGREDIENTS

DIRECTION

- Preheat the oven to 350F.
- Using a bowl, beat eggs on high for 1 to 2 minutes.
- Beat in the xanthan gum and combine coconut oil and melted butter into eggs, beating continuously.
- Set aside the sesame seeds, but add the rest of the ingredients.
- Line a loaf pan with baking paper and place the mixture in it. Top the mixture with sesame seeds.
- Bake for 35 to 40 minutes until a toothpick inserted comes out clean.

INGREDIENTS

- ½ tsp. xanthan gum
- ½ cup butter
- 2Tbsp. coconut oil
- 1Tbsp. baking powder
- 3Tbsp. sesame seeds
- 2Tbsp. chia seeds
- ½ tsp. salt
- ¼ cup sunflower seeds
- cups almond flour
- 7eggs

Special Keto Bread

NUTRITION Calories: 227, Fat: 21g, Carb: 4g, Protein: 7g

	PREPARATION	COOKING TIME	SERVINGS	
DIRECTION	15 MINTS	40 mins	14	INGREDIENTS

DIRECTION

- Preheat the oven to 400F.
- Using a bowl, combine salt, almond meal, and baking powder.
- Drip in oil while mixing, until it forms a crumbly dough.
- Make a little round hole in the middle of the dough and pour eggs into the middle of the dough.
- Pour water and whisk eggs together with the mixer in the small circle until it is frothy.
- Start making larger circles to combine the almond meal mixture with the dough until you have a smooth and thick batter.
- Line your loaf pan with parchment paper.
- Dispense batter into the prepared loaf pan and sprinkle poppy seeds on top.
- Bake in the oven for 40 minutes in the center rack until firm and golden brown.
- Cool in the oven for 30 minutes.
- Slice and serve.

INGREDIENTS

- 2tsp. baking powder
- ½ cup water
- 1Tbsp. poppy seeds
- 2cups fine ground almond meal
- 5large eggs
- ½ cup olive oil
- ½ tsp. fine Himalayan salt

Keto Fluffy Cloud Bread

NUTRITION Calories: 185, Fat: 16.4g, Carb: 3.9g, Protein: 6.6

PREPARATION	COOKING TIME	SERVINGS
25	25 mins	3

DIRECTION

- Preheat the oven at 300F and line a baking tray with parchment paper.
- Whisk egg whites using a bowl.
- Mix egg yolks with cream cheese, salt, cream of tartar, psyllium husk powder, and baking powder in a bowl.
- Fold in the egg whites carefully and transfer to the baking tray.
- Place in the oven and bake for 25 minutes.
- Remove from the oven and serve.

INGREDIENTS

- 1 pinch salt
- ½ Tbsp. ground psyllium husk powder
- ½ Tbsp. baking powder
- ¼ tsp. cream of tarter
- 2 eggs, separated
- ½ cup, cream cheese

Splendid Low-Carb Bread

NUTRITION Calories: 97, Fat: 5.7g, Carb: 7.5g,. Protein: 4.1g

PREPARATION	COOKING TIME	SERVINGS
15 MINTS	70 mins	12

DIRECTION

- Lubricate a loaf pan and preheat the oven at 350F.
- Using a bowl, whisk the salt, psyllium husk powder, onion or garlic powder, coconut flour, almond flour, and baking powder.
- Stir in egg whites, oil, and apple cider vinegar. Bit by bit add the hot water, stirring until dough increase in size. Do not add too much water.
- Mold the dough into a rectangle and transfer to grease loaf pan.
- Bake in the oven for 60 to 70 minutes, or until crust feels firm and brown on top.
- Cool and serve.

INGREDIENTS

- ½ tsp. herbs, such as basil, rosemary, or oregano
- ½ tsp. garlic or onion powder
- 1 Tbsp. baking powder
- 5 Tbsp. psyllium husk powder
- ½ cup almond flour
- ½ cup coconut flour
- ¼ tsp. salt
- 1½ cup egg whites
- 3 Tbsp. oil or melted butter
- 2 Tbsp. apple cider vinegar
- 1/3 to ¾ cup hot

Coconut Flour Almond Bread

NUTRITION *Calories: 475, Fat: 38g, Carb: 7g, Protein: 19g*

	PREPARATION	COOKING TIME	SERVINGS
DIRECTION	10 MINT	30 mins	4

INGREDIENTS

- Preheat the oven to 400F.
- Mix the eggs in a bowl for a few minutes.
- Add in the butter and coconut oil and mix once more for 1 minute.
- Add the almond flour, coconut flour, baking soda, psyllium husk, and ground flaxseed to the mixture. Let sit for 15 minutes.
- Lightly lubricate the loaf pan with coconut oil. Pour the mixture in the pan.
- Place in the oven and bake until a toothpick inserted in it comes out dry, about 25 minutes.

- 1Tbsp. butter, melted
- 1Tbsp. coconut oil, melted
- 6eggs
- 1tsp. baking soda
- 2Tbsp. ground flaxseed
- 1½ Tbsp. psyllium husk powder
- 5Tbsp. coconut flour
- 1½ cup almond flour

Quick Low-Carb Bread Loaf

NUTRITION *Calories: 174, Fat: 15g,, Carb: 5g, Protein: 5g*

	PREPARATION	COOKING TIME	SERVINGS
DIRECTION	45	45 mins	16

INGREDIENTS

- Preheat the oven to 350F. Cover the bread loaf pan with baking paper.
- Beat the eggs until creamy.
- Add in the coconut flour and almond flour, mixing them for 1 minute. Next, add the xanthan gum, coconut oil, baking powder, butter, and salt and mix them until the dough turns thick.
- Put the completed dough into the prepared line of the bread loaf pan.
- Set in the oven and bake for 40 to 45 minutes. Check with a knife.
- Slice and serve.

- 2/3 cup coconut flour
- ½ cup butter, melted
- 3Tbsp. coconut oil, melted
- 11/3 cup almond flour
- ½ tsp. xanthan gum
- 1tsp. baking powder
- 6large eggs
- ½ tsp. salt

Keto Bakers Bread

NUTRITION Calories: 41, Fat: 3.2g, Carb: 1g, Protein: 2.4g

PREPARATION	COOKING TIME	SERVINGS
10	20 mins	12

DIRECTION

- Heat 2 racks in the middle of the oven at 350F.
- Line 2 baking pan with parchment paper, then grease with cooking spray.
- Isolate egg whites from the egg yolks and place them in separate mixing bowls.
- Beat the egg whites and cream of tartar with a hand mixer until stiff, about 3 to 5 minutes. Do not over-beat.
- Whisk the cream cheese, salt, and egg yolks until smooth.
- Slowly fold the cheese mix into the whites until fluffy.
- Spoon ¼ cup measure of the batter onto the baking sheets, 6 mounds on each sheet.
- Bake for 20 to 22 minutes, alternating racks halfway through.
- Cool and serve.

INGREDIENTS

- Pinch of salt
- 4Tbsp. light cream cheese softened
- ½ tsp. cream of tartar
- 4eggs, yolks, and whites separated

Almond Flour Lemon Bread

NUTRITION Calories: 115, Fat: 9.9g, Carb: 3.3g, Protein: 5.2g

PREPARATION	COOKING TIME	SERVINGS
15	45 mins	16

DIRECTION

- Preheat the oven to 350F.
- Whip the cream of tartar and whites until soft peaks form.
- Using a bowl, combine salt, egg yolks, melted butter, and lemon juice. Mix well.
- Add coconut flour, almond flour, herbs, and baking powder. Mix well.
- To the dough, add 1/3 the egg whites and mix until well-combined.
- Add the remaining egg whites mixture and slowly mix to incorporate everything. Do not over mix.
- Lubricate a loaf pan with butter or coconut oil.
- Pour mixture into the loaf pan and bake for 30 minutes.

INGREDIENTS

- 1tsp. French herbs
- 1tsp. lemon juice
- 1tsp. salt
- 1tsp. cream of tartar
- 2tsp. baking powder
- ¼ cup melted butter
- 5large eggs, divided
- ¼ cup coconut flour
- 1½ cup almond flour

Seed and Nut Bread

NUTRITION Calories: 131, Fat: 12g, Carb: 4g, Protein: 5g

PREPARATION	COOKING TIME	SERVINGS
10 MINT	40 mins	24

DIRECTION

- Preheat the oven to 325F. Line a loaf pan with parchment paper.
- In a giant bowl, whisk together the oil, eggs, psyllium husk powder, vinegar, salt, and liquid stevia.
- Stir in the pepitas, almonds, sunflower seeds, and flaxseeds until well combined.
- Dispense the batter into the prepared loaf pan, smooth it out and let it rest for 2 minutes.
- Bake for 40 minutes.
- Cool, slice, and serve.

INGREDIENTS

- 3 eggs
- ¼ cup avocado oil
- 1 tsp. psyllium husk powder
- 1 tsp. apple cider vinegar
- ¾ tsp. salt
- 5 drops liquid stevia
- 1½ cups raw unsalted almonds
- ½ cup raw unsalted pepitas
- ½ cup raw unsalted sunflower seeds
- ½ cup flaxseeds

Blueberry Bread Loaf

NUTRITION Calories: 155, Fat: 13g, Carb: 4g, Protein: 3g

PREPARATION	COOKING TIME	SERVINGS
20	65 mins	12

DIRECTION

- Preheat the oven at 350F and line a loaf pan with baking paper.
- Using a bowl, mix granulated swerve, heavy whipping cream, eggs, and baking powder.
- Once combined, add the butter, vanilla extract, salt, cinnamon, and sour cream. Then add the coconut flour to the batter.
- Pour a layer about ½ inch of dough into the bread pan. Place ¼ cup blueberries on top of the dough. Keep repeating until the dough and blueberry layers are complete.
- Bake for 65 to 75 minutes.
- Meanwhile, in a bowl, beat the vanilla extract, butter, heavy whipping cream, lemon zest, and confectioner swerve. Mix until creamy.
- Cool the bread once baked. Then drizzle the icing topping on the bread.
- Slice and serve.

INGREDIENTS

- For the bread dough:
- 10 Tbsp. coconut flour
- 9 Tbsp. melted butter
- 2/3 cup granulates swerve sweetener
- 1½ tsp. baking powder
- 2 Tbsp. heavy whipping cream
- 1½ tsp. vanilla extract
- ½ tsp. cinnamon
- 2 Tbsp. sour cream
- 6 large eggs
- ½ tsp. salt
- ¾ cup blueberries
- For the topping:
- 1 Tbsp. heavy whipping cream
- 2 Tbsp. confectioner swerve sweetener
- 1 tsp. melted butter
- 1/8 tsp. vanilla extract
- ¼ tsp. lemon zest

Cloud Bread Loaf

NUTRITION *84 calories, 4.5 g fat, 0.8 g total carb, 7.5 g protein*

PREPARATION	COOKING TIME	SERVINGS
5	50 mins	12

DIRECTION

- Add all ingredients to the Bread Machine.
- Select Dough setting and press Start. Mix the ingredients for about 4-5 minutes. After that press stop button.
- Smooth out the top of the loaf. Choose Bake mode and press Start. Let it bake for about 45 minutes.
- Remove bread from the bread machine and let it rest for 10 minutes. Enjoy!

INGREDIENTS

- 1/2 teaspoon baking powder
- 1/2 cup whey protein powder
- eggs separated
- 1/4 teaspoon salt
- 1/2 teaspoon cream of tartar
- 1/4 teaspoon onion powder
- ounces 170g sour cream
- 1/4 teaspoon garlic powder

Conclusion

This book has presented you with some of the easiest and delicious bread recipes you can find.

These loaves of bread are made using the everydayingredients you can find locally, so there's no need to order anything or go to any specialty stores for any of them. With these pieces of bread, you can enjoy the same meals you used to enjoy but stay on track with your diet as much as you want.

Moreover, we have learned that the bread machine is a vital tool to have in our kitchen. It is not that hard to put into use. All you need to learn is how it functions and what its features are. You also need to use it more often to learn the dos and don'ts of using the machine.

The bread machine comes with instructions that you must learn from the manual to use it the right way. There is a certain way of loading the ingredients that must be followed, and the instructions vary according to the make and the model. So, when you first get a machine, sit down and learn the manual from start to finish; this allows you to put it to good use and get better results. The manual will tell you exactly what to put in it, as well as the correct settings to use, according to the different ingredients and the type of bread you want to make.

Having a bread machine in your kitchen makes life easy. Whether you are a professional baker or a home cook, this appliance will help you get the best bread texture and flavors with minimum effort. Bread making is an art, and it takes extra care and special technique to deal with a specific type of flour and bread machine that enables you to do so even when you are not a professional. In this book, we have discussed all bread machines and how we can put them to good use. Basic information about flour and yeast is also discussed to give all the beginners an idea of how to deal with the major ingredients of bread and what variety to use to get a particular type of bread. And finally, some delicious bread recipes were shared so that you can try them at home!

Conversion Tables

3 teaspoons	1 tablespoon
2 tablespoons	1 ounce
4 tablespoons	¼ cup
8 tablespoons	½ cup
16 tablespoons	1 cup
2 cups	1 pint
4 cups	1 quart
4 quarts	1 gallon

Type	Imperial	Imperial	Metric
Weight	1 dry ounce	28g	
	1 pound	16 dry ounces	0.45 kg
Volume	1 teaspoon	5 ml	
	1 dessert spoon	2 teaspoons	10 ml
	1 tablespoon	3 teaspoons	15 ml
	1 Australian tablespoon	4 teaspoons	20 ml
	1 fluid ounce	2 tablespoons	30 ml
	1 cup	16 tablespoons	240 ml
	1 cup	8 fluid ounces	240 ml
	1 pint	2 cups	470 ml
	1 quart	2 pints	0.95 l
	1 gallon	4 quarts	3.8 l
Length	1 inch	2.54 cm	

Numbers are rounded to the closest equivalent

Gluten-Free – Conversion Tables

All-Purpose Flour	Rice Flour	Potato Starch	Tapioca	Xanthan Gum
½ cup	1/3 cup	2 tablespoons	1 tablespoon	¼ teaspoon
1 cup	½ cup	3 tablespoons	1 tablespoon	½ teaspoon
¼ cup	¾ cup	1/3 cup	3 tablespoons	2/3 teaspoon
1 ½ cup	1 cup	5 tablespoons	3 tablespoons	2/3 teaspoon
1 ¾ cup	1 ¼ cup	5 tablespoons	3 tablespoons	1 teaspoon
2 cups	1 ½ cup	1/3 cup	1/3 cup	1 teaspoon
2 ½ cups	1 ½ cup	½ cup	¼ cup	1 1/8 teaspoon
2 2/3 cups	2 cups	½ cup	¼ cup	1 ¼ teaspoon
3 cups	2 cups	2/3 cup	1/3 cup	1 ½ cup

Flour: Quantity and Weight

Flour Amount
1 cup = 140 grams
3/4 cup = 105 grams
1/2 cup = 70 grams
1/4 cup = 35 grams

Sugar: Quantity and Weight

Sugar
1 cup = 200 grams
3/4 cup = 150 grams
2/3 cup = 135 grams
1/2 cup = 100 grams
1/3 cup = 70 grams
1/4 cup = 50 grams

Powdered Sugar
1 cup = 160 grams
3/4 cup = 120 grams
1/2 cup = 80 grams
1/4 cup = 40 grams

Cream: Quantity and Weight

Cream Amount

1 cup = 250 ml = 235 grams
3/4 cup = 188 ml = 175 grams
1/2 cup = 125 ml = 115 grams
1/4 cup = 63 ml = 60 grams
1 tablespoon = 15 ml = 15 grams

Butter: Quantity and Weight

Butter Amount
1 cup = 8 ounces = 2 sticks = 16
tablespoons =230 grams
1/2 cup = 4 ounces = 1 stick = 8
tablespoons = 115 grams
¼ cup = 2 ounces = ½ stick = 4 table-
spoons= 58 grams

Oven Temperature Equivalent Chart

Fahrenheit (°F)	Celsius	
(°C)	Gas Mark	
220	100	
225	110	1/4
250	120	1/2
275	140	1
300	150	2
325	160	3
350	180	4
375	190	5
400	200	6
425	220	7
450	230	8
475	250	9
500	260	

* Celsius (°C) = T (°F)-32] * 5/9

** Fahrenheit (°F) = T (°C) * 9/5 + 32

*** Numbers are rounded to the closest equivalent

Made in the USA
Middletown, DE
25 January 2021

32341570R00163